ANTHROPOLOGY

by Sir Edward B. Tylor

ABRIDGED AND WITH A FOREWORD
BY LESLIE A. WHITE

ANN ARBOR PAPERBACKS
The University of Michigan Press

Third printing 1970
First edition as an Ann Arbor Paperback 1960
Copyright © by The University of Michigan 1960
All rights reserved
ISBN 0-472-06044-9
Published in the United States of America by
The University of Michigan Press and
in Don Mills, Canada, by Longmans Canada Limited
Manufactured in the United States of America

FOREWORD *by Leslie A. White*

TYLOR'S *Anthropology,* first published in 1881, is still one of the best general introductions to the subject in the English language. To be sure, there have been great additions to our factual knowledge since 1881, and there has been some progress along theoretical lines, especially in particular techniques of interpretation. But so far as fundamental propositions, philosophic outlook, and literary style are concerned, Tylor's work has not been surpassed and has seldom been equaled.

It was Tylor who introduced the term culture into anthropological literature as a definite, technical term. And to him, culture consisted of real things and events in the external world, not "abstractions that have no ontological reality," as is the fashion among so many American anthropologists today. Man is an animal species, and he makes life secure and continuous by exercising control over his environment. Man's first need, says Tylor, "is to get his daily food"; his "next great need is to defend himself." The cultivation of cereals has been "the mainstay of human life and the great moving power of civilization." Tylor remarks upon the importance of energy harnessed in nonhuman forms, such as water power and coal, in the development of culture.

All aspects of culture are treated in *Anthropology:* technological, social, ceremonial, ideological, and esthetic. And everywhere the present is linked with the past. Tylor views the culture of mankind as a whole, as one piece; he does not leave the reader with the impression that there are two quite separate cultural worlds, ours and that of the primitives, as many anthropologists of recent years have done. It is significant to note that in some controversial issues of his day, and even in recent times, Tylor has proved to be right. He held, in opposition to Darwin, that man's mind differs in kind, not merely in degree, from that of other species: a "mental gulf . . . divides the lowest savage from the highest ape." In a day when theories of primordial promiscuity were widely held, Tylor staunchly defended the theory that "mankind can never have lived as a mere struggling crowd, each for himself. Society is always made up of families or households bound together by kindly ties . . . . the whole framework of society is founded" upon the family. He sees a fundamental difference between the societies of preliterate peoples and those of modern times, in contrast with some of the students of Franz Boas who have maintained that the difference is merely one of degree, not one of kind. And his discussion of the transition from primitive to civil society is illuminating and sound. With the increase of property, war comes to be carried on "as a business." Two of "the greatest facts in history [are] the organized army, where the several forces are led by their own captains under a general, and the confederation of tribes . . . Out of such alliances . . . . there arise nations. . . ."

To turn to some points upon which the anthropologist of today might wish to take issue with Tylor, or at least question his position, we note that he speaks of "higher" and "lower" races. "There seems to be in mankind inbred temperament and inbred capacity of mind," he says. This view has, of course, been challenged, but nothing definite has been proved one way or another. His belief that environment, particularly climate, has been a significant determinant of racial differences may be challenged, also. But both of these matters are biological, and Tylor was not a biologist; he merely accepted views that he thought were most reasonable in the light of the facts then known. Perhaps the greatest difference between Tylor and anthropologists of today is to be found in the field of religion. But even here it is not so much that Tylor was "wrong," as that his interpretations were not sufficiently comprehensive. Incidentally, Tylor did not deny the existence of a belief in a supreme being among preliterate peoples as some of our modern textbooks assert.

This edition of *Anthropology* omits Chapters II, "Man and Other Animals," and III, "Races of Mankind" with Figures 5–46— first because these chapters deal with the biological rather than the cultural component of anthropology, and second, because they are the least consonant with modern knowledge and views. Tylor was not a biologist. Otherwise, the text remains as it appeared in the original edition.

We may well conclude this brief note by pointing to one of the most fundamental characteristics of *Anthropology:* it is a treatise on cultural evolution. Culture has developed by stages; each has grown out of the previous one. "This is the great principle," says

Tylor, "which every scholar must lay firm hold of, if he intends to understand either the world he lives in or the history of the past." In view of the vehement attacks upon cultural evolutionism by such anthropologists as Father Wilhelm Schmidt and Franz Boas and their respective followers, one of whom declared that "the theory of cultural evolution (is) to my mind the most inane, sterile and pernicious theory in the whole history of science," Tylor's words come to us again as a breath of fresh air. If we may judge by the number of anthropologists who have flocked to the banner of evolutionism during the recent Darwin Centennial celebrations, Tylor is as modern in his outlook today as he was when *Anthropology* was first published.

Ann Arbor, Michigan

AUTHOR'S PREFACE

In times when subjects of education have multiplied, it may seem at first sight a hardship to lay on the already heavily-pressed student a new science. But it will be found that the real effect of Anthropology is rather to lighten than increase the strain of learning. In the mountains we see the bearers of heavy burdens contentedly shoulder a carrying-frame besides, because they find its weight more than compensated by the convenience of holding together and balancing their load. So it is with the science of Man and Civilization, which connects into a more manageable whole the scattered subjects of an ordinary education. Much of the difficulty of learning and teaching lies in the scholar's not seeing clearly what each science or art is for, what its place is among the purposes of life. If he knows something of its early history, and how it arose from the simpler wants and circumstances of mankind, he finds himself better able to lay hold of it than when, as too often happens, he is called on to take up an abstruse subject not at the beginning but in the middle. When he has learnt something of man's rudest means of conversing by gestures and cries, and thence has been led to see how the higher devices of articulate speech are improvements on such lower methods, he makes a fairer start in the science of language than if he had fallen unprepared among the subtleties of grammar, which unexplained look like arbitrary rules framed to perplex rather than to inform. The dislike of so many beginners to geometry as expounded by Euklid, the fact that not one out of three ever really understands what he is doing, is of all things due to the scholar not being shown first the practical common-sense starting-point, where the old carpenters and builders began to make out the relations of distances and spaces in their work. So the law-student plunges at once into the intricacies of legal systems which have grown up through the struggles, the reforms, and even the blunders of thousands of years; yet he might have made his way clearer by seeing how laws begin in their simplest forms, framed to meet the needs of savage and barbaric tribes. It is needless to make a list of all the branches of education in knowledge and art; there is not one which may not be the easier and better learnt for knowing its history and place in the general science of Man.

With this aim in view, the present volume is an introduction to Anthropology, rather than a summary of all it teaches. It does not deal with strictly technical matter, out of the reach of readers who have received, or are receiving, the ordinary higher English education. Thus, except to students trained in anatomy, the minute modern researches as to distinction of races by skull measurements and the like would be useless. Much care has been taken to make the chapters on the various branches of the science sound as far as they go, but the more advanced work must be left to special students.

While the various departments of the science of Man are extremely multifarious, ranging from body to mind, from language to music, from fire-making to morals, they are all matters to whose nature and history every well-informed person ought to give some thought. It is much, however, for any single writer to venture to deal even in the most elementary way with so immense a variety of subjects. In such a task I have the right to ask that errors and imperfections should be lightly judged. I could not have attempted it at all but for the help of friends eminent in various branches of the science, whom I have been able to consult on doubtful and difficult points. My acknowledgments are especially due to Professor Huxley and Dr. E. A. Freeman, Sir Henry Maine, Dr. Birch, Mr. Franks, Professor Flower, Major-General Pitt-Rivers, Professor Sayce, Dr. Beddoe, Dr. D. H. Tuke, Professor W. K. Douglas, Mr. Russell Martineau, Mr. R. Garnett, Mr. Henry Sweet, Mr. Rudler, and many other friends whom I can only thank unnamed. The illustrations of races are engraved from photographic portraits, many of them taken by the permission of Messrs. Dammann of Huddersfield from their valuable Albums of Ethnological Photographs.

E. B. T.

February, 1881.

CONTENTS

ANTHROPOLOGY

CHAPTER I

MAN, ANCIENT AND MODERN

THE student who seeks to understand how mankind came to be as they are, and to live as they do, ought first to know clearly whether men are new-comers on the earth, or old inhabitants. Did they appear with their various races and ways of life ready-made, or were these shaped by the long, slow growth of ages? In order to answer this question, our first business will be to take a rapid survey of the varieties of men, their languages, their civilization, and their ancient relics, to see what proofs may thus be had of man's age in the world. The outline sketch thus drawn will also be useful as an introduction to the fuller examination of man and his ways of life in the chapters which follow.

First, as to the varieties of mankind. Let us suppose ourselves standing at the docks in Liverpool or London, looking at groups of men of races most different from our own. There is the familiar figure of the African negro, with skin so dark-brown as to be popularly called black, and black hair so naturally frizzed as to be called woolly. Nor are these the only points in which he is unlike us. Indeed, the white men who blacken their faces and friz their hair to look like negroes make a very poor imitation, for the negro features are quite distinct; we well know the flat nose, wide nostrils, thick protruding lips, and, when the face is seen in profile, the remarkable projecting jaws. A hatter would at once notice that the negro's head is narrower in proportion than the usual oval of the hats made for Englishmen. It would be possible to tell a negro from a white man even in the dark by the peculiar satiny feel of his skin, and the yet more peculiar smell which no one who has noticed it is ever likely to mistake. In the same docks, among the crews of Eastern steamers, we observe other well-marked types of man. Indigenous peoples of Southern India are represented by men unlike the lighter-complexioned high-caste Hindus, dark-brown of skin, with black, silky, wavy hair, and a face wide-nosed, heavy-jawed, fleshy-lipped. More familiar is the Chinese, whom the observer marks down by his less than European stature, his jaundice-yellow skin, and coarse, straight black hair; the special character of his features is neatly touched off on his native china-plates and paper-screens which show the snub nose, high cheek-bones, and that curious slant-ing set of the eyes which we can imitate by putting a finger near the outer corners of our own eyes and pushing upward. By comparing such a set of races with our own countrymen, we are able to make out the utmost differ-ences of complexion and feature among mankind. While doing so, it is plain that white men, as we agree to call ourselves, show at least two main race-types. Going on board a merchant-ship from Copenhagen, we find the crew mostly blue-eyed men of fair complexion and hair, a remarkable contrast to the Genoese vessel moored alongside, whose sailors show almost to a man swarthy complexions and lustrous black eyes and hair. These two types of man have been well described as the fair-whites and the dark-whites.

It is only within modern times that the distinctions among races have been worked out by scientific methods. Yet since early ages, race has attracted notice from its connexion with the political questions of countryman or foreigner, conqueror or conquered, freeman or slave, and in consequence its marks have been watched with jealous accuracy. ' In the Southern United States, till slavery was done away a few years ago, the traces of negro descent were noted with the utmost nicety. Not only were the mixed breeds regularly classed as mulattos, quadroons, and down to octaroons, but even where the mixture was so slight that the untrained eye noticed nothing beyond a brunette complexion, the intruder who had ventured to sit down at a public dinner-table was called upon to show his hands, and the African taint detected by the dark tinge at the root of the finger-nails.

Seeing how striking the broad distinctions of race are, it was to be expected that ancient inscriptions and figures should give some view of the races of man as they were at the beginning of historical times. It is so in Egypt, where the oldest writings of the world appear. More than 4000 years ago we begin to find figures of the Egyptians themselves, in features much the same as in later times. In the sixth dynasty, beyond 3000 B.C., the celebrated inscription of Prince Una makes mention of the *Nahsi*, or negroes, who were levied and drilled by ten thousands for the Egyptian army. Under the twelfth dynasty, on the walls of the tomb of Knumhetp, there is represented a procession of *Amu*, who are seen by their features to be of the race to which Syrians and Hebrews belonged. Especially the wall-paintings of the tomb of Rekh-ma-ra at Thebes, of the eighteenth dynasty, have preserved coloured portraits of the four great races distinguished by the Egyptians. These are the red-brown Egyptians themselves, the people of Palestine with their aquiline profile and brownish complexion, the flat-nosed, thick-lipped African negroes, and the fair-skinned Libyans. Thus mankind was already divided into well-marked races, distinguished by colour and features. It is surprising to notice how these old-world types of man are still to be recognized. The Ethiopian of the ancient monuments can at this day be closely matched. Notwithstanding the many foreign invasions of Egypt, the mass of the village population is true-bred enough for men to be easily picked out as representatives of the times of the Pharaohs. Their portraits have only to be drawn in the stiff style of the monuments, with the eye conventionally shown full-front in the profile face, and we have before us the very Egyptians as they depicted themselves in the old days when they held the Israelites in bondage. In the same way, the ancient Assyrian portraits of the tribute-bearers of Jehu, King of Israel, show the strongly-marked Israelite type of features to be seen at this day in every city of Europe. Altogether, the evidence of ancient monuments, geography, and history, goes to prove that the great race-divisions of mankind are of no recent growth, but were already settled before the beginning of the historical period. Since then their changes seem to have been comparatively slight, except in the forming of mixed races by intermarriage.

Hence it follows that the historic ages are to be looked

on as but the modern period of man's life on earth.
Behind them lies the prehistoric period, when the chief
work was done of forming and spreading over the world
the races of mankind. Though there is no scale to
measure the length of this period by, there are sub-
stantial reasons for taking it as a long stretch of time.
Looking at an ethnological map, coloured to show what
race of men inhabits each region, it is plain at a glance
that the world was not peopled by mere chance scattering
of nations, a white tribe here and a brown tribe there,
with perhaps a black tribe in between. Far from this,
whole races are spread over vast regions as though they
grew there, and the peculiar type of the race seems more
or less connected with the climate it lives in. Especially
it is seen that the mass of black races belong to the
equatorial regions in Africa and the Eastern Archipelago,
the yellow race to Central and Southern Asia, the white
race to temperate Asia and Europe. Some guess may
even be made from the map which district was the
primitive centre where each of these races took shape,
and whence it spread far and wide. Now if, as some
have thought, the Negroes, Mongolians, Whites, and other
races, were distinct species, each sprung from a separate
origin in its own region, then the peopling of the globe
might require only a moderate time, the races having
only to spread each from its own birthplace. But the
opinion of modern zoologists, whose study of the species
and breeds of animals makes them the best judges, is
against this view of several origins of man, for two
principal reasons. First, that all tribes of men, from
the blackest to the whitest, the most savage to the most
cultured, have such general likeness in the structure of
their bodies and the working of their minds, as is easiest
and best accounted for by their being descended from a
common ancestry, however distant. Second, that all
the human races, notwithstanding their form and colour,
appear capable of freely intermarrying and forming
crossed races of every combination, such as the millions
of mulattos and mestizos sprung in the New World from
the mixture of Europeans, Africans, and native Americans; this again points to a common ancestry of all the
races of man. We may accept the theory of the unity
of mankind as best agreeing with ordinary experience
and scientific research. As yet, however, the means are
very imperfect of judging what man's progenitors were
like in body and mind, in times before the forefathers of

the present Negroes, and Tatars, and Australians, had become separated into distinct stocks. Nor is it yet clear by what causes these stocks or races passed into their different types of skull and limbs, of complexion and hair. It cannot be at present made out how far the peculiarities of single ancestors were inherited by their descendants and became stronger by in-breeding; how far, when the weak and dull-witted tribes failed in the struggle for land and life, the stronger, braver, and abler tribes survived to leave their types stamped on the nations sprung from them; how far whole migrating tribes underwent bodily alteration through change of climate, food, and habits, so that the peopling of the earth went on together with the growth of fresh races fitted for life in its various regions. Whatever share these causes and others yet more obscure may have had in varying the races of man, it must not be supposed that such differences as between an Englishman and a Gold Coast negro are due to slight variations of breed. On the contrary, they are of such zoological importance as to have been compared with the differences between animals which naturalists reckon distinct species, as between the brown bear with its rounded forehead, and the polar bear with its whitish fur and long flattened skull. If then we are to go back in thought to a time when the ancestors of the African, the Australian, the Mongol, and the Scandinavian, were as yet one undivided stock, the theory of their common descent must be so framed as to allow causes strong enough and time long enough to bring about changes far beyond any known to have taken place during historical ages. Looked at in this way, the black, brown, yellow, and white men whom we have supposed ourselves examining on the quays, are living records of the remote past, every Chinese and Negro bearing in his face evidence of the antiquity of man.

Next, what has language to tell of man's age on the earth? It appears that the distinct languages known number about a thousand. It is clear, however, at the first glance that these did not all spring up separately. There are groups of languages which show such close likeness in their grammars and dictionaries as proves each group to be descended from one ancestral tongue. Such a group is called a family of languages, and one of the best known of such families may be taken as an example of their way of growth. In ancient times Latin (using the word in a rather wide sense) was the language of Rome and other Italian districts, and with the spread of the Roman empire it was carried far and wide so as to oust the early languages of whole provinces. Undergoing in each land a different course of change, Latin gave rise to the Romance family of languages, of which Italian, Spanish, and French are well-known members. How these languages have come to differ after ages of separate life we judge by seeing that sailors from Dieppe cannot make themselves understood in Malaga, nor does a knowledge of French enable us to read Dante. Yet the Romance languages keep the traces of their Roman origin plainly enough for Italian, Spanish, and French sentences to be taken and every word referred to something near it in classical Latin, which may be roughly treated as the original form. Familiar proverbs are here given as illustrations, with the warning to the reader that the Latin words do not form sentences, but merely show the sources of the modern words which do.

ITALIAN.

E meglio un uovo oggi che una gallina domani.
est melius unum ovum hodie quid una gallina de mane.
  i.e. Better is an egg to-day than a hen to-morrow.

Chi va piano va sano, chi va sano va lontano.
qui vadit planum vadit sanum, qui vadit sanum vadit longum.
  i.e. He who goes gently goes safe, he who goes safe goes far.

SPANISH.

Quien canta sus males espanta.
quem cantat suos malos expav(ere).
  i.e. He who sings frightens away his ills.

Por la calle de despues se va á la casa de nunca.
per illam callem de de-ex-post se vadit ad illam casam de nunquam.
  i.e. By the street of by and by one goes to the house of never.

FRENCH.

Un tiens vaut mieux que deux tu l' auras.
unum tene valet melius quod duos tu illum habere-habes.
  i.e. One take-it is worth more than two thou-shalt-have-its.

Parler de la corde dans la maison d' un pendu.
parabola de illam chordam de intus illam mansionem de unum pend(o).
  i.e. (Never to) talk of a rope in the house of a hanged man.

It is plain on the face of such sentences as these that Italian, Spanish, and French are in fact transformed Latin, their words having been gradually altered as they descended, generation after generation, from the parent tongue. Now even if Latin were lost, philologists would still be able, by comparing the set of Romance languages, to infer that such a language must have existed to give rise to them all, though no doubt such a reconstruction of Latin would give but a meagre notion, either of its stock of words or its grammatical inflexions. This kind of argument by which a lost parent-language is discovered from the likeness among its descendants, may be well seen in another set of European tongues. Let us suppose ourselves listening to a group of Dutch sailors; at first their talk may seem unintelligible, but after a while a sharp ear will catch the sound of well-known words, and perhaps at last whole sentences like these :—*Kom hier ! Ga aan boord ! Is de maan op ? Hoe is het weder ? Niet goed. Het is een hevige storm, en bitter koud nu.* The spelling of these words, different from our mode, disguises their resemblance, but as spoken they come very near corresponding sentences in English, somewhat thus :—*Come here ! Go on board ! Is the moon up ? How is the weather ? Not good. It is a heavy storm, and bitter cold now.* Now it stands to reason that no two languages could have come to be so like, unless both were descended from one parent tongue. The argument is really much like that as to the origin of the people themselves. As we say, these Dutch and English are beings so nearly alike that they must have descended from a common stock, so we say, these languages are so alike that they must have been derived from a common language. Dutch and English are accordingly said to be closely related to one another, and the language of Friesland proves on examination to be another near relative. Thence it is inferred that a parent language or group of dialects, which may be called the original Low-Dutch, or Low-German, must once have been spoken, though it is not actually to be found, not happening to have been written down and so preserved.

Now it is easy to see that as ages go on, and the languages of a family each take their separate course of change, it must become less and less possible to show their relationship by comparing whole sentences. Philologists have to depend on less perfect resemblances, but such are sufficient when not only words from the dictionary correspond in the two languages, but also these are worked up into actual speech by corresponding forms of grammar. Thus when Sanskrit, the ancient language of the Brahmans in India, is compared with Greek and Latin, it appears that the Sanskrit verb *dâ* expresses the idea to give, and makes its present tense by reduplicating and adding a person-affix, so becoming *dadâmi*, nearly as Greek makes *didōmi*; from the same root Sanskrit makes a future participle *dâsyamânas*, corresponding to Greek *dōsomenos*, while Sanskrit *dâtâr* matches Greek *dotēr* = giver. So where Latin has *vox*, *vocis, vocem, voces, vocum, vocibus*, Sanskrit has *vâk, vâcas, vâcam, vâcas, vâcâm, vâgbhyas*. When such thorough-going analogy as this is found to run through several languages, as Sanskrit, Greek, and Latin, no other explanation is possible but that an ancient parent language gave rise to them all, they having only varied off from it in different directions. In this way it is shown that not only are these particular languages related by descent, but that groups of ancient and modern languages in Asia and Europe, the Indian group, the Persian group, the Hellenic or Greek group, the Italic or Latin group, the Slavonic group to which Russian belongs, the Teutonic group which English is a member of, the Keltic group which Welsh is a member of, are all descendants of one common ancestral language, which is now theoretically called the Aryan, though practically its nature can be made out only in a vague way by comparing its descendant languages. Some of these have come down to us in forms which are extremely ancient, as antiquity goes in our limited chronology. The sacred books of India and Persia have preserved the Sanskrit and Zend languages, which by their structure show to the eye of the philologist an antiquity beyond that of the earliest Greek and Latin inscriptions and the old Persian cuneiform rock-writing of Darius. But the Aryan languages, even in their oldest known states, had already become so different that it was the greatest feat of modern philology to demonstrate that they had a common origin at all. The faint likeness by which Welsh still shows its relationship to Greek and German may give some idea of the time that may have elapsed since all three were developed off from the original Aryan tongue, which itself probably ceased to exist long before the historical period began.

Among the languages of ancient nations, another great group holds a high place in the world's history. This is the Semitic family, which includes the Hebrew and

Phœnician, and the Assyrian deciphered from the wedge-characters of Nineveh. Arabic, the language of the *Koran*, is the great modern representative of the family, and the closeness with which it matches Hebrew may be shown in familiar phrases. The Arab still salutes the stranger with *salâm alaikum*, " peace upon you," nearly as the ancient Hebrew would have said *shâlôm lâchem*, that is, " peace to you," and the often-heard Arabic exclamation *bismillah* may be turned into Hebrew, as *be-shêm hâ-Elohim*, " in the name of God." So the Hebrew names of persons mentioned in the Bible give the interpretation of many Arabic proper names, as where *Ebed-melech*, " servant of the king," who took Jeremiah out of the dungeon, bore a name nearly like that of the khalif *Abd-el-Melik*, in Mohammedan history. But no one of these Semitic languages has any claim to be the original of the family, standing to the others as Latin does to Italian and French. All of them, Assyrian, Phœnician, Hebrew, Arabic, are sister-languages, pointing back to an earlier parent language which has long disappeared. The ancient Egyptian language of the hieroglyphics cannot be classed as a member of the Semitic family, though it shows points of resemblance which may indicate some remote connexion. There are also known to have existed before 2000 B.C. two important languages not belonging to either the Aryan or Semitic family; these were the ancient Babylonian and the ancient Chinese. As for the languages of more outlying regions of the world, such as America, when they come into view they are found likewise to consist of many separate groups or families.

This slight glimpse of the earliest known state of language in the world is enough to teach the interesting lesson that the main work of language-making was done in the ages before history. Going back as far as philology can take us, we find already existing a number of language-groups, differing in words and structure, and if they ever had any relationship with one another no longer showing it by signs clear enough for our skill to make out. Of an original primitive language of mankind, the most patient research has found no traces. The oldest types of language we can reach by working back from known languages show no signs of being primitive tongues of mankind. Indeed, it may be positively asserted that they are not such, but that ages of growth and decay have mostly obliterated the traces how each particular sound came to express its particular sense. Man, since the historical period, has done little in the way of absolute new creation of language, for the good reason that his wants were already supplied by the words he learnt from his fathers, and all he had to do when a new idea came to him was to work up old words into some new shape. Thus the study of languages gives much the same view of man's antiquity as has been already gained from the study of races. The philologist, asked how long he thinks mankind to have existed, answers that it must have been long enough for human speech to have grown from its earliest beginnings into elaborate languages, and for these in their turn to have developed into families spread far and wide over the world. This immense work had been already accomplished in ages before the earliest inscriptions of Egypt, Babylon, Assyria, Phœnicia, Persia, Greece, for these show the great families of human speech already in full existence.

Next, we have to look at culture or civilization, to see whether this also shows signs of man having lived and laboured in ages earlier than the earliest which historical records can tell of. For this purpose it is needful to understand what has been the general course of arts, knowledge, and institutions. It is a good old rule to work from the known to the unknown, and all intelligent people have much to tell from their own experience as to how civilization develops. The account which an old man can give of England as he remembers it in his schoolboy days, and of the inventions and improvements he has seen come in since, is in itself a valuable lesson. Thus, when starting from London by express train to reach Edinburgh by dinner-time, he thinks of when it used to be fair coach-travelling to get through in two days and nights. Catching sight of a signal-post on the line, he remembers how such semaphores (that is, sign-bearers) were then the best means of telegraphing, and stood waving their arms on the hills between London and Plymouth, signalling the Admiralty messages. Thinking of the electric telegraph which has superseded them reminds him that this invention arose out of a discovery made in his youth as to the connexion between electricity and magnetism. This again suggests other modern scientific discoveries that have opened to us the secrets of the universe, such as the spectrum-analysis which now makes out with such precision the materials

of the stars which is just what our fathers were quite
certain no man on earth ever could know. Our inform-
ant can tell us, too, how knowledge has not only increased,
but is far more widely spread than formerly, when the
thriving farmer's son could hardly get schooling practically so good as the labourer's son is now entitled to of
right. He may then go on to explain to his hearers how,
since his time, the laws of the land have been improved
and better carried out, so that men are no longer hanged
for stealing, that more is done to reform the criminal
classes instead of merely punishing them, that life and
property are safer than in old times. Last, but not least,
he can show from his own recollection that people are
morally a shade better than they were, that public
opinion demands a somewhat higher standard of conduct
than in past generations, as may be seen in the sharper
disapproval that now falls on cheats and drunkards.
From such examples of the progress in civilization that
has come in a single country and a single lifetime, it is
clear that the world has not been standing still with us,
but new arts, new thoughts, new institutions, new rules
of life, have arisen or been developed out of the older
state of things.

Now this growth or development in civilization, so
rapid in our own time, appears to have been going on
more or less actively since the early ages of man. Proof of
this comes to us in several different ways. History, so far
as it reaches back, shows arts, sciences, and political institutions beginning in ruder states, and becoming in the
course of ages more intelligent, more systematic, more
perfectly arranged or organized to answer their purposes. Not to give many instances of a fact so familiar,
the history of parliamentary government begins with the
old-world councils of the chiefs and tumultuous assemblies of the whole people. The history of medicine goes
back to the times when *epilepsy* or " seizure " (Greek,
epilēpsis) was thought to be really the act of a demon
seizing and convulsing the patient. But our object here
is to get beyond such ordinary information of the history
books, and to judge what stages civilization passed
through in times yet earlier. Here one valuable aid is
archæology, which for instance shows us the stone
hatchets and other rude instruments which belonged to
early tribes of men, thus proving how low their state of
arts was ; of this more will be said presently. Another
useful guide is to be had from survivals in culture.

Looking closely into the thoughts, arts, and habits of
any nation, the student finds everywhere the remains
of older states of things out of which they arose. To
take a trivial example, if we want to know why so
quaintly cut a garment as the evening dress-coat is worn,
the explanation may be found thus. The cutting away
at the waist had once the reasonable purpose of pre-
venting the coat skirts from getting in the way in riding,
while the pair of useless buttons behind the waist are
also relics from the times when such buttons really
served the purpose of fastening these skirts behind; the
curiously cut collar keeps the now misplaced notches
made to allow of its being worn turned up or down, the
smart facings represent the old ordinary lining, and the
sham cuffs now made with a seam round the wrist are
survivals from real cuffs when the sleeve used to be
turned back. Thus it is seen that the present ceremonial
dress-coat owes its peculiarities to being descended from
the old-fashioned practical coat in which a man rode
and worked. Or again, if one looks in modern English
life for proof of the Norman Conquest eight centuries
ago, one may find it in the " *Oh yes ! Oh yes !* " of the
town-crier, who all unknowingly keeps up the old French
form of proclamation, " *Oyez ! Oyez !* " that is, " Hear
ye ! Hear ye ! " To what yet more distant periods of
civilization such survivals may reach is well seen in
an example from India. There, though people have for
ages kindled fire for practical use with the flint and steel,
yet the Brahmans, to make the sacred fire for the daily
sacrifice, still use the barbaric art of violently boring a
pointed stick into another piece of wood till a spark
comes. Asked why they thus waste their labour when
they know better, they answer that they do it to get
pure and holy fire. But to us it is plain that they are
really keeping up by unchanging custom a remnant of
the ruder life once led by their remote ancestors. On
the whole, these various ways of examining arts and
sciences all prove that they never spring forth perfect,
like Athene out of the split head of Zeus. They come on
by successive steps, and, where other information fails,
the observer may often trust himself to judge from the
mere look of an invention how it probably arose. Thus
no one can look at a cross-bow and a common long-bow
without being convinced that the long-bow was the
earlier, and that the cross-bow was made afterwards by
fitting a common bow on a stock, and arranging a trigger

to let go the string after taking aim. Though history
fails to tell us who did this and when, we feel almost as
sure of it as of the known historical facts that the match-
lock led up to the wheel-lock, and that again to the flint-
lock musket, and that again to the percussion musket,
and that again to the breech-loading rifle.

Putting these various means of information together,
it often becomes possible to picture the whole course of
an art or an institution, tracing it back from its highest
state in the civilized world till we reach its beginnings in
the life of the rudest tribes of men. For instance, let us
look at a course of modern mathematics, as represented
in the books taken for university honours. A student
living in Queen Elizabeth's time would have had no
infinitesimal calculus to study, hardly even algebraic
geometry, for what is now called the higher mathematics
was invented since then. Going back into the Middle
Ages, we come to the time when algebra had been just
brought in, a novelty due to the Hindu mathematicians
and their scholars, the Arabs; and next we find the
numeral ciphers, 0, 1, 2, 3, &c., beginning to be known as
an improvement on the old calculating board and the
Roman I, II, III. In the classic ages yet earlier, we
reach the time when the methods of Euklid and the other
Greek geometers first appeared. So we get back to what
was known to the mathematicians of the earliest historical period in Babylonia and Egypt, an arithmetic
clumsily doing what children in the lower standards are
taught with us to do far more neatly, and a rough
geometry consisting of a few rules of practical mensuration. This is as far as history can go toward the beginnings of mathematics, but there are other means of
discovering through what lower stages the science arose.
The very names still used to denote lengths, such as
cubit, hand, foot, span, nail, show how the art of mensuration had its origin in times when standard measures
had not yet been invented, but men put their hands and
feet alongside objects of which they wished to estimate
the size. So there is abundant evidence that arithmetic
came up from counting on the fingers and toes, such as
may still be seen among savages. Words still used for
numbers in many languages were evidently made during
the period when such reckoning on the hands and feet
was usual, and they have lasted on ever since. Thus a
Malay expresses five by the word *lima*, which (though he
does not know it) once meant " hand," so that it is seen

to be a survival from ages when his ancestors, wanting
a word for five, held up one hand and said " hand."
Indeed, the reason of our own decimal notation, why we
reckon by tens instead of the more convenient twelves,
appears to be that our forefathers got from their own
fingers the habit of counting by tens which has been
since kept up, an unchanged relic of primitive man.
The following chapters contain many other cases of such
growth of arts from the simplest origins. Thus, in
examining tools, it will be seen how the rudely chipped
stone grasped in the hand to hack with, led up to the
more artificially shaped stone chisel fitted as a hatchet
in a wooden handle, how afterwards when metal came
in here was substituted for the stone a bronze or iron
blade, till at last was reached the most perfect modern
foresters' axe, with its steel blade socketed to take the
well-balanced handle. Specimens such as those in
Chapter VIII show these great moves in the development of the axe, which began before chronology and
history, and has been from the first one of man's chief
aids in civilizing himself.

It does not follow from such arguments as these that
civilization is always on the move, or that its movement
is always progress. On the contrary, history teaches
that it remains stationary for long periods, and often
falls back. To understand such decline of culture, it
must be borne in mind that the highest arts and the
most elaborate arrangements of society do not always
prevail, in fact they may be too perfect to hold their
ground, for people must have what fits with their circumstances. There is an instructive lesson to be learnt
from a remark made by an Englishman at Singapore,
who noticed with surprise two curious trades flourishing
there. One was to buy old English-built ships, cut them
down and rig them as junks; the other was to buy
English percussion muskets and turn them into old-
fashioned flintlocks. At first sight this looks like mere
stupidity, but on consideration it is seen to be reasonable
enough. It was so difficult to get Eastern sailors to
work ships of European rig that it answered better to
provide them with the clumsier craft they were used to;
and as for the guns, the hunters far away in the hot,
damp forests were better off with gunflints than if they
had to carry and keep dry a stock of caps. In both
cases, what they wanted was not the highest product of
civilization, but something suited to the situation and

easiest to be had. Now the same rule applies both to
taking in new civilization and keeping up old. When
the life of a people is altered by emigration into a new
country, or by war and distress at home, or mixture with
a lower race, the culture of their forefathers may be no
longer needed or possible, and so dwindles away. Such
degeneration is to be seen among the descendants of
Portuguese in the East Indies, who have intermarried
with the natives and fallen out of the march of civilization, so that newly-arrived Europeans go to look at them
lounging about their mean hovels in the midst of
luxuriant tropical fruits and flowers, as if they had been
set there to teach by example how man falls in culture
where the need of effort is wanting. Another frequent
cause of loss of civilization is when people once more
prosperous are ruined or driven from their homes, like
those Shoshonee Indians who have taken refuge from
their enemies, the Blackfeet, in the wilds of the Rocky
Mountains, where they now roam, called Digger Indians
from the wild roots they dig for as part of their miserable
subsistence. Not only the degraded state of such
outcasts, but the loss of particular arts by other peoples,
may often be explained by loss of culture under unfavourable conditions. For instance, the South Sea Islanders,
though not a very rude people, when visited by Captain
Cook used only stone hatchets and knives, being indeed
so ignorant of metal that they planted the first iron nails
they got from the English sailors, in the hope of raising
a new crop. Possibly their ancestors never had metals,
but it seems as likely that these ancestors were an Asiatic
people to whom metal was known, but who, through
emigration to ocean islands and separation from their
kinsfolk, lost the use of it and fell back into the stone
age. It is necessary for the student to be alive to the
importance of decline in civilization, but it is here more
particularly mentioned in order to point out that it in
no way contradicts the theory that civilization itself is
developed from low to high stages. One cannot lose a
thing without having had it first, and wherever tribes
are fallen from the higher civilization of their ancestors,
this only leaves it to be accounted for how that higher
civilization grew up.

On the whole it appears that wherever there are found
elaborate arts, abstruse knowledge, complex institutions,
these are results of gradual development from an earlier,
simpler, and ruder state of life. No stage of civilization

comes into existence spontaneously, but grows or is developed out of the stage before it. This is the great principle which every scholar must lay firm hold of, if he intends to understand either the world he lives in or the history of the past. Let us now see how this bears on the antiquity and early condition of mankind. The monuments of Egypt and Babylonia show that toward 6000 years ago certain nations had already come to an advanced state of culture. No doubt the greater part of the earth was then peopled by barbarians and savages, as it remained afterwards. But in the regions of the Nile and the Euphrates there was civilization. The ancient Egyptians had that greatest mark of a civilized nation, the art of writing; indeed the hieroglyphic characters of their inscriptions appear to have been the origin of our alphabet. They were a nation skilled in agriculture, raising from their fields fertilized by the yearly inundation those rich crops of grain that provided subsistence for the dense population. How numerous and how skilled in constructive art the ancient Egyptians were is seen by every traveller who looks on the pyramids which have made their name famous through all history. The great pyramid of Gizeh still ranks among the wonders of the world, a mountain of hewn limestone and syenite, whose size Londoners describe by saying that it stands on a square the size of Lincoln's-Inn-Fields, and rises above the height of St. Paul's. The perfection of its huge blocks and the beautiful masonry of the inner chambers and passages show the skill not only of the stonecutter but of the practical geometer. The setting of the sides to the cardinal points is so exact as to prove that the Egyptians were excellent observers of the elementary facts of astronomy; the day of the equinox can be taken by observing the sunset across the face of the pyramid, and the neighbouring Arabs still adjust their astronomical dates by its shadow. As far back as anything is known of them, the Egyptians appear to have worked in copper and iron, as well as gold and silver. So their arts and habits, their sculpture and carpentry, their reckoning and measuring, their system of official life with its governors and scribes, their religion with its orders of priesthood and its continual ceremonies, all appear the results of long and gradual growth. What, perhaps, gives the highest idea of antiquity is to look at very early monuments, such as the tomb of prince Teta of the 4th dynasty in the British

Museum, and notice how Egyptian culture had even then begun to grow stiff and traditional. Art was already reaching the stage when it seemed to men that no more progress was possible, for their ancestors had laid down the perfect rule of life, which it was sin to alter by way of reform. Of the early Babylonians or Chaldæans less is known, yet their monuments and inscriptions show how ancient and how high was their civilization. Their writing was in cuneiform or wedge-shaped characters, of which they seem to have been the inventors, and which their successors, the Assyrians, learnt from them. They were great builders of cities, and the bricks inscribed with their kings' names remain as records of their great temples, such, for instance, as that dedicated to the god of Ur, at the city known to Biblical history as Ur of the Chaldees. Written copies of their laws exist, so advanced as to have provisions as to the property of married women, the imprisonment of a father or mother for denying their son, the daily fine of a half-measure of corn levied on the master who killed or ill-used his slaves. Their astrology, which made the names of Chaldæan and Babylonian famous ever since, led them to make those regular observations of the heavenly bodies which gave rise to the science of astronomy. The nation which wrote its name thus largely in the book of civilization dates back into the same period of high antiquity as the Egyptian. These, then, are the two nations whose culture is earliest vouched for by inscriptions done at the very time of their ancient grandeur, and therefore it is safer to appeal to them than to other nations which can only show as proofs of their antiquity writings drawn up in far later ages. Looking at their ancient civilization, it seems to have been formed by men whose minds worked much like our own. No superhuman powers were required for the work, but just human nature groping on by roundabout ways, reaching great results, yet not half knowing how to profit by them when reached; solving the great problem of writing, yet not seeing how to simplify the clumsy hieroglyphics into letters; devoting earnest thought to religion and yet keeping up a dog and cat worship which was a jest even to the ancients; cultivating astronomy and yet remaining mazed in the follies of astrology. In the midst of their most striking efforts of civilization, the traces may be discerned of the barbaric condition which prevailed before; the Egyptian pyramids are burial-mounds like those of præhistoric England, but huge in size and built of hewn stone or brick; the Egyptian hieroglyphics, with their pictures of men and beasts and miscellaneous things, tell the story of their own invention, how they began as a mere picture-writing like that of the rude hunters of America. Thus it appears that civilization, at the earliest dates where history brings it into view, had already reached a level which can only be accounted for by growth during a long præhistoric period. This result agrees with the conclusions already arrived at by the study of races and language.

Without attempting here to draw a picture of life as it may have been among men at their first appearance on the earth, it is important to go back as far as such evidence of the progress of civilization may fairly lead us. In judging how mankind may have once lived, it is also a great help to observe how they are actually found living. Human life may be roughly classed into three great stages, Savage, Barbaric, Civilized, which may be defined as follows. The lowest or *savage* state is that in which man subsists on wild plants and animals, neither tilling the soil nor domesticating creatures for his food. Savages may dwell in tropical forests where the abundant fruit and game may allow small clans to live in one spot and find a living all the year round, while in barer and colder regions they have to lead a wandering life in quest of the wild food which they soon exhaust in any place. In making their rude implements, the materials used by savages are what they find ready to hand, such as wood, stone, and bone, but they cannot extract metal from ore, and therefore belong to the Stone Age. Men may be considered to have risen into the next or *barbaric* state when they take to agriculture. With the certain supply of food which can be stored till next harvest, settled village and town life is established, with immense results in the improvement of arts, knowledge, manners, and government. Pastoral tribes are to be reckoned in the barbaric stage, for though their life of shifting camp from pasture to pasture may prevent settled habitation and agriculture, they have from their herds a constant supply of milk and meat. Some barbaric nations have not come beyond using stone implements, but most have risen into the Metal Age. Lastly, *civilized* life may be taken as beginning with the art of writing, which, by recording history, law, knowledge, and religion for the service of ages to come, binds together the past and the future in an unbroken chain of intellectual and moral progress. This classification of three great stages of culture is practically convenient, and has the advantage of not describing imaginary states of society, but such as are actually known to exist. So far as the evidence goes, it seems that civilization has actually grown up in the world through these three stages, so that to look at a savage of the Brazilian forests, a barbarous New Zealander or Dahoman, and a civilized European, may be the student's best guide to understanding the progress of civilization, only he must be cautioned that the comparison is but a guide, not a full explanation.

In this way it is reasonably inferred that even in countries now civilized, savage and low barbaric tribes must have once lived. Fortunately it is not left altogether to the imagination to picture the live of these rude and ancient men, for many relics of them are found which may be seen and handled in museums. It has now to be considered what sort of evidence of man's age is thus to be had from archæology and geology, and what it proves.

When an antiquary examines the objects dug up in any place, he can generally judge in what state of civilization its inhabitants have been. Thus if there are found weapons of bronze or iron, bits of fine pottery, bones of domestic cattle, charred corn and scraps of cloth, this would be proof that people lived there in a civilized, or at least a high barbaric condition. If there are only rude implements of stone and bone, but no metal, no earthenware, no remains to show that the land was tilled or cattle kept, this would be evidence that the country had been inhabited by some savage tribe. One of the chief questions to be asked about the condition of any people is whether they have metal in use for their tools and weapons. If so, they may be said to be in the metal age. If they have no copper or iron, but make their hatchets, knives, spear-heads, and other cutting and piercing instruments of stone, they are said to be in the stone age. Wherever such stone implements are picked up, as they often are in our own ploughed fields, they prove that stone-age men have once dwelt in the land. It is an important fact that in every region of the inhabited world ancient stone implements are thus found in the ground, showing that at some time the inhabitants were in this respect like the modern savages. In countries where the people have long been metal-workers, they have often lost all memory of what these stone things are, and tell fanciful stories to account for their being met with in ploughing or digging. One favourite notion, in England and elsewhere, is that the stone hatchets are " thunderbolts " fallen from the sky with the lightning flash. It has been imagined that in the East, the seat of the most ancient civilizations, some district might be found without any traces of man having lived there in a state of early rudeness, so that in this part of the world he might have been civilized from the first. But it is not so. In Assyria, Palestine, Egypt, as in other lands, one may find sharp-chipped flints which show that here also tribes in the stone age once lived, before the use of metal brought in higher civilization.

Whether it may be considered or not that Europe was a quarter of the globe inhabited by the earliest tribes of men, it so happens that remains found in Europe furnish at present the best proofs of man's antiquity. To understand these, it must be explained that the stone age had an earlier and a later period, as may be plainly seen in looking at a good collection of stone implements. Fig. 1 is intended to give some idea of those in use in the later stone age. The hatchet is neatly shaped and edged by rubbing on a grinding-stone, as is also the hammer-head. The spear and arrows, scraper, and flake-knife it would have been waste of labour to grind, but they are chipped out with much skill. On the whole, these stone implements are much like those which the North American Indians have been using to our own day. The question is how long ago tribes who made such stone implements were living in Europe. As to this, we may fairly judge from the position in which they are found in Denmark. The forests of that country are mainly of beeches, but in the peat-mosses lie innumerable trunks of oaks, which show that at an earlier period oak-forests prevailed, and deeper still there lie trunks of pine trees, which show that there were pine-forests still older than the oak-forests. Thus there have been three successive forest-periods, the beech, the oak, and the pine, and the depth of the peat-mosses, which in places is as much as thirty feet, shows that the period of the pine trees was thousands of years ago. While the forests have been changing, the condition of the people living among them has changed also. The modern woodman cuts down the beech-trees with his iron axe, but among the oak-trunks in the peat are found bronze swords and shield-bosses, which show that the inhabitants of the country were then in the bronze age, and lastly, a flint hatchet taken out from where it lay still lower in the peat beneath the pine-trunks, proves that stone-age men in Denmark lived in the pine-forest period, which carries them back to high antiquity. In England, the tribes who have left such stone implements were in the land before the invasion of that Keltic race whom we call the ancient Britons, and who no doubt came armed with weapons of metal. The stone hatchet-blades and arrow-heads of the older population lie scat-

FIG. 1.—Later Stone Age (neolithic) implements. *a*, stone celt or hatchet; *b*, flint spear-head; *c*, scraper; *d*, arrow-heads; *e*, flint flake-knives; *f*, core from which flint-flakes taken off; *g*, flint-awl; *h*, flint saw; *i*, stone hammer-head.

tered over our country, hill and dale, moor and fen, near the surface of the ground, or deeper underground in peat-mosses, or beds of mud and silt. Such bogs or mud-flats began at a date which chronologists would call ancient. But they are what geologists, accustomed to vaster periods of time, consider modern. They belong to the newer alluvial deposits, that is, they were formed within the times when the lie of the land and the flow of the streams were much as they are now. To get an idea of this, one has only to look down from a hillside into a wide valley below, and notice how its flat flooring of mud and sand, stretching right across, must have been laid down by flood-waters following very much their present course along the main stream and down the side slopes. The people of the newer stone age, whose implements are seen in Fig. 1, lived within this historic-

ally ancient, but geologically modern, period, and relics
of them are found only in places where man or nature
could then have placed them.

But there had been a still earlier period of the stone
age, when yet ruder tribes of men lived in our parts of
the world, when the climate and the face of the country
were strangely different from the present state of things.
On the slopes of river valleys such as that of the Ouse,
in England, and the Somme, in France, 50 or 100 feet
above the present river-banks, and thus altogether out
of the reach of any flood now, there are beds of so-called
drift gravel.   Out of these beds have been dug numerous
rude implements of flint, chipped into shape by the hands

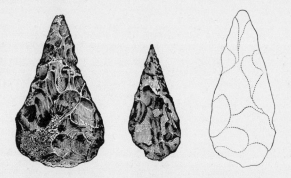

FIG. 2.—Earlier Stone Age (palæolithic) flint picks or hatchets.

of men who had gained no mean dexterity in the art, as
any one will find who will try his hand at making one,
with any tools he thinks fit. The most remarkable
implements of this earlier stone age are the picks or
hatchets shown in Fig. 2.   The coarseness of their finish,
and the absence of any signs of grinding, even at the
edges of hacking or cutting instruments, show that the
makers had not come nearly to the skill of the later
stone age.   It is usual to distinguish the two kinds of
implements, and the periods they belong to, by the terms
introduced by Sir J. Lubbock, palæolithic and neolithic,
that is " old-stone " and " new-stone." Looking now
at the high gravel-beds in which palæolithic implements
such as those shown in Fig. 2 occur, it is evident from
their position that they had nothing to do with the

water-action which is now laying down and shifting sand-banks and mud-flats at the bottom of the valleys, nor with the present rain-wash which scours the surface of the hillsides. They must have been deposited in a former period when the condition of land and water was different from what it is now. How far this state of things was due to the valleys not being yet cut out to near their present depth, to the whole country lying lower above the sea-level, or to the rivers being vastly larger than at present from the heavier rainfall of a pluvial period, it would be raising too intricate geological questions to discuss here. Geology shows the old drift-gravels to belong to times when the glacial or icy period with its arctic climate was passing, or had passed away, in Europe. From the bones and teeth found with the flint implements in the gravel-beds, it is known what animals inhabited the land at the same time with the men of the old stone age. The mammoth, or huge woolly elephant, and several kinds of rhinoceros, also extinct, browsed on the branches of the forest trees, and a species of hippopotamus much like that at present living frequented the rivers. The musk-ox and the grizzly bear, which England harboured in this remote period, may still be hunted in the Rocky Mountains, but the ancient cave-bear, which was one of the dangerous wild beasts of our land, is no longer on the face of the earth. The British lion was of a larger breed than those now in Asia and Africa, and perhaps than those which Herodotus mentions as prowling in Macedonia in the fifth century B.C., and falling on the camels of Xerxes' army. To judge by such signs as the presence of the reindeer, and the mammoth with its hairy coat, the climate of Europe was severer than now, perhaps like that of Siberia. How long man had been in the land there is no clear evidence. For all we know, he may have lasted on from an earlier and more genial period, or he may have only lately migrated into Europe from some warmer region. Implements like his are not unknown in Asia, as where in Southern India, above Madras, there lies at the foot of the Eastern Ghâts a terrace of irony clay or laterite, containing stone implements of very similar make to those of the drift-men in Europe.

These European savages of the mammoth-period resorted much to shelter at the foot of overhanging cliffs, and to caverns such as Kent's Hole near Torquay, where the implements of the men and the bones of the beasts are found together in abundance. In Central France especially, the examination of such bone-caves has brought to light evidence of the whole way of life of a group of ancient tribes. The reindeer, which have now retreated to high northern latitudes, were then plentiful in France, as appears from their bones and antlers imbedded with remains of the mammoth under the stalagmite floors of the caves of Perigord. With them are found rude stone hatchets and scrapers, pounding-stones, bone spear-heads, awls, arrow-straighteners, and other objects belonging to a life like that of the modern Esquimaux who hunt the reindeer on the coasts of Hudson's Bay. Like the Esquimaux also, these early French and Swiss savages spent their leisure time in

Fig. 3.—Sketch of mammoth from cave of La Madeleine (Lartet and Christy

carving figures of animals. Among many such figures found in the French caves is a mammoth, Fig. 3, scratched on a piece of its own ivory, so as to touch off neatly the shaggy hair and huge curved tusks which distinguish the mammoth from other species of elephant. There has been also found a rude representation of a man, Fig. 4, grouped with two horses' heads and a snake or eel; this is interesting as being the most ancient human portrait known.

Thus it appears that man of the older stone age was already living when such a river as the Thames flowed at a height approaching a hundred feet above the level of its present bed, and when the climate was of that Lapland kind suited to the woolly mammoth and the reindeer, and the rest of the un-English looking group of animals now perished out of this region, or extinct altogether. From all that is known of the slowness

with which such alterations take place anywhere in the
lie of the land, the climate, and the wild animals, we
cannot suppose changes so vast to have happened
without a long lapse of time before the newer stone age
came in, when the streams had settled down to near
their present levels, and the climate and the wild
creatures had become much as they were within the
historical period. It is also plain from the actual remains
found that these most ancient known tribes were wild
hunters and fishers, such as we should now class as
savages. It is best, however, not to apply to them the
term primitive men, as this might be understood to mean
that they were the first men who appeared on earth, or
at least like them. The life the men of the mammoth-
period must have led at Abbeville or Torquay shows on
the face of it reasons against its being man's primitive

FIG. 4.—Sketch of man and horses from cave (Lartet and Christy).

life. These old stone-age men are more likely to have
been tribes whose ancestors while living under a milder
climate gained some rude skill in the arts of procuring
food and defending themselves, so that afterwards they
were able by a hard struggle to hold their own against
the harsh weather and fierce beasts of the quaternary
period.

How long ago this period was, no certain knowledge is
yet to be had. Some geologists have suggested twenty
thousand years, while others say a hundred thousand or
more, but these are guesses made where there is no scale
to reckon time by. It is safest to be content at present
to regard it as a geological period lying back out of the
range of chronology. It is thought by several eminent
geologists that stones shaped by man, and therefore
proving his presence, occur in England and France in
beds deposited before the last glacial period, when much
of the continent lay submerged under an icy sea, where
drifting icebergs dropped on what is now dry land their

huge boulders of rock transported from distant mountains. This cannot be taken as proved, but if true it
would immensely increase our estimate of man's age.
At any rate the conclusive proofs of man's existence
during the quaternary or mammoth period do not even
bring us into view of the remoter time when human life
first began on earth. Thus geology establishes a principle which lies at the very foundation of the science of
anthropology. Until of late, while it used to be reckoned
by chronologists that the earth and man were less than
6000 years old, the science of geology could hardly exist,
there being no room for its long processes of building up
the strata containing the remains of its vast successions
of plants and animals. These are now accounted for on
the theory that geological time extends over millions of
years. It is true that man reaches back comparatively
little way into this immense lapse of time. Yet his first
appearance on earth goes back to an age compared with
which the ancients, as we call them, are but moderns.
The few thousand years of recorded history only take us
back to a præhistoric period of untold length, during
which took place the primary distribution of mankind
over the earth and the development of the great races,
the formation of speech and the settlement of the great
families of language, and the growth of culture up to the
levels of the old world nations of the East, the forerunners
and founders of modern civilized life.

Having now sketched what history, archæology, and
geology teach as to man's age and course on the earth,
we shall proceed in the following chapters to describe
more fully Man and his varieties as they appear in
natural history, next examining the nature and growth
of Language, and afterwards the development of the
knowledge, arts, and institutions, which make up
Civilization.

CHAPTER IV

LANGUAGE

THERE are various ways in which men can communicate with one another. They can make *gestures*, utter *cries*, speak *words*, draw *pictures*, write *characters* or *letters*. These are signs of various sorts, and to understand how they do their work let us begin by looking at such signs as are most simple and natural.

When for any reason people cannot talk together by word of mouth, they take to conversing by gestures, in what is called dumb show or pantomime. Every reader of this has been able from childhood to carry on conversation in this way, more or less cleverly. Imagine a simple case. A boy opens the parlour door, his brother sitting there beckons to him to be quiet for his father is asleep; the boy now intimates by signs that he has come for the key of the box, to which his brother answers by other signs that it is in the pocket of his coat hanging in the hall, concluding with a significant gesture to be off and shut the door quietly after him. This is the *gesture-language* as we all know how to use it. But to see what a full and exact means of communication it may be worked up to, it should be watched in use among the deaf-and-dumb, who have to depend so much upon it. To give an idea how far gestures can be made to do the work of spoken words, the signs may be described in which a deaf-and-dumb man once told a child's story in presence of the writer of this account. He began by moving his hand, palm down, about a yard from the ground, as we do to show the height of a child—this meant that it was a child he was thinking of. Then he tied an imaginary pair of bonnet-strings under his chin (his usual sign for female), to make it understood that the child was a little girl. The child's mother was then brought on the scene in a similar way. She beckons to the child and gives her twopence, these being indicated by pretending to drop two coins from one hand into the other; if there had been any doubt as to whether they were copper or silver coins, this would have been settled by pointing to something brown, or even by one's contemptuous way of handling coppers which at once distinguishes them from silver. The mother also gives the child a jar, shown by sketching its shape with the forefingers in the air, and going through the act of handing it over. Then by imitating the unmistakable kind of twist with which one turns a treacle-spoon, it is made known that it is treacle the child has to buy. Next, a wave of the hand shows the child being sent off on her errand, the usual sign of walking being added, which is made by two fingers walking on the table. The turning of an imaginary door-handle now takes us into the shop, where the counter is shown by passing the flat hands as it were over it. Behind this counter a figure is pointed out; he is shown to be a man by the usual sign of putting one's hand to one's chin and drawing it down where the beard is or would be; then the sign of tying an apron round one's waist adds the information that the man is the shopman. To him the child gives her jar, dropping the money into his hand, and moving her forefinger as if taking up treacle, to show what she wants. Then we see the jar put into an imaginary pair of scales which go up and down; the great treacle-jar is brought from the shelf and the little one filled, with the proper twist to take up the last trickling thread; the grocer puts the two coins in the till, and the little girl sets off with the jar. The deaf-and-dumb story-teller went on to show in pantomime how the child, looking down at the jar, saw a drop of treacle on the rim, wiped it off with her finger and put the finger in her mouth, how she was tempted to take more, how her mother found her out by the spot of treacle on her pinafore, and so forth.

The student anxious to master the principles of language will find this gesture-talk so instructive that it will be well to explain its working more closely. The signs used are of two kinds. In the first kind things actually present are shown. Thus if the deaf-mute wants to mention " hand " or " shoe," he touches his own hand or shoe. Where a speaking man would say " I," " thou," " he," the deaf-mute simply points to

himself and the other persons. To express " red " or
" blue " he touches the inside of his own lip or points to
the sky. In the second kind of signs ideas are conveyed
by imitation. Thus pretending to drink may mean
" water," or " to drink," or " thirsty." Laying the cheek
on the hand expresses " sleep " or " bedtime." A significant jerk of the whip-hand suggests either " whip,"
or " coachman," or " to drive," as the case may be. A
" lucifer " is indicated by pretending to strike a match,
and " candle " by the act of holding up the forefinger
like a candle and pretending to blow it out. Also in the
gesture-language the symptoms of the temper one is in
may be imitated, and so become signs of the same temper
in others. Thus the act of shivering becomes an expressive sign for " cold "; smiles show " joy,"
" approval," " goodness," while frowns show " anger,"
" disapproval," " badness." It might seem that such
various meanings to one sign would be confusing, but
there is a way of correcting this, for when a single sign
does not make the meaning clear others are brought in
to supplement it. Thus if one wants to express " a
pen," it may not be sufficient to pretend to write with
one, as that might be intended for " writing " or " letter,"
but if one then pretends to wipe and hold up a pen, this
will make it plain that the pen itself is meant.

The signs hitherto described are self-expressive, that is,
their meaning is evident on the face of them, or at any
rate may be made out by a stranger who watches their
use. Of such self-expressive or natural signs, the
gesture-language mostly consists. But where deaf-
mutes live together, there come into use among them
signs which a stranger can hardly make out until it is
explained to him how they arose. They will, for instance, mention one another by nickname-signs, as when
a boy may be referred to by the sign of sewing, which on
inquiry proves to have been given him because his father
was a tailor. Such signs may be very far-fetched; for
instance, at the Berlin Deaf-and-dumb Institution, the
sign of chopping off a head means a Frenchman, and on
inquiry it appears that the children, struck by reading
of the death of Louis XVI. in the history-book, had fixed
on this as a sign-name for the whole nation. But to
any new child who learnt these signs without knowing
why they were chosen, they would seem artificial.

Next to studying the gesture-language among the
deaf-and-dumb, the most perfect way of making out its

principles is in its use by people who can talk but do not understand one another's language. Thus the celebrated sign-languages of the American prairies, in which conversation is carried on between hunting-parties of whites and natives, and even between Indians of different tribes, are only dialects (so to speak) of the gesture-language. Thus " water " is expressed by pretending to scoop up water in one's hand and drink it, " stag " by putting one's thumbs to one's temples and spreading out the fingers. There is a great deal of variety in the signs among particular tribes, but such a way of communication is so natural all the world over that, when outlandish people, such as Laplanders, have been brought to be exhibited in our great cities, they have been comforted in their loneliness by meeting with deaf-and-dumb children, with whom they at once fell to conversing with delight in the universal language of signs. Signs to be understood in this way must be of the natural self-expressive sort. Yet here also there are some which a stranger might suppose to be artificial, till he learnt that they are old signs which have lost their once plain intention. Thus a North American sign for " dog " is to draw one's two first fingers along like poles being trailed on the ground. This seemingly senseless sign really belongs to the days when the Indians had few horses, and used to fasten the tent-poles on the dogs to be dragged from place to place; though the dogs no longer have to do this, custom keeps up the sign.

It has to be noticed that the gesture-language by no means matches, sign for word, with our spoken language. One reason is that it has so little power of expressing abstract ideas. The deaf-mute can show particular ways of making things, such as building a wall or cutting out a coat, but it is quite beyond him to make one sign include what is common to all these, as we use the abstract term to " make." Even " in " and " out " must be expressed in some such clumsy way as by pretending to put the thing talked of in, and take it out. Next let us compare an English sentence with the signs by which the same meaning would be expressed among the deaf-and-dumb. It will at once be seen that many words we use have no signs at all corresponding to them. Thus when we should say in words, " *The* hat *which* I left on *the* table *is* black," this statement can be practically conveyed in gestures, and there will be signs for what we may call the " real " words, such as *hat, leave, black*.

But for what may be called the " grammatical " words, *the*, *which*, *is*, there will be no signs, for the gesture-language has none. Again, grammars lay down distinctions between substantives, adjectives, and verbs. But these distinctions are not to be found in the gesture-language, where pointing to a grass-plot may mean " grass " or " green," and pretending to warm one's hands may suggest " warm " or " to warm oneself," or even " fireplace." Nor (unless where artificial signs have been brought in by teachers) is there anything in the gesture-language to correspond with the inflexions of words, such as distinguish *goest* from *go*, *him* from *he*, *domum* from *domus*. What is done is to call up a picture in the minds of the spectators by first setting up something to be thought about, and then adding to or acting on it till the whole story is told. If the signs do not follow in such order as to carry meaning as they go, the looker-on will be perplexed. Thus in conveying to a deaf-and-dumb child the thought of a green box, one must make a sign for " box " first, and then show, as by pointing to the grass outside, that its colour is " green." The proper gesture-syntax is " box green," and if this order were reversed as it is in the English language, the child might fail to see what grass had to do with a box. Such a sentence as English " cats kill mice " does not agree with the order of the deaf-mute's signs, which would begin by showing the tiny mouse running, then the cat with her smooth fur and whiskers, and lastly the cat's pouncing on the mouse—as it were " mouse cat kill."

This account of the gesture-language will have made it clear to the reader by what easy and reasonable means man can express his thoughts in visible signs. The next step will be to show the working of another sort of signs, namely, the sounds of the human voice in language. Sounds of voice may be spoken as signs to express our feelings and thoughts on much the same principles as gestures are made, except that they are heard instead of being seen.

One kind of sounds used by men as signs consists of emotional cries or tones. Men show pain by uttering groans as well as by distortion of face; joy is expressed by shouts as well as by jumping; when we laugh aloud, the voice and the features go perfectly together. Such sounds are gestures made with the voice, sound-gestures, and the greater number of what are called interjections are of this class. By means of such cries and tones, even the complicated tempers of sympathy, or pity, or vexation, can be shown with wonderful exactness. Let any one put on a laughing, sneering, or cross face, and then talk, he may notice how his tone of voice follows; the attitude of features belonging to each particular temper acts directly on the voice, especially in affecting the musical quality of the vowels. Thus the speaker's tones become signs of the emotion he feels, or pretends to feel. That this mode of expression is in fact musical, is shown by its being imitated on the violin, which by altering its quality of tone can change from pain to joy. The human voice uses other means of expression belonging to music, such as the contrast of low and loud, slow and quick, gentle and violent, and the changes of pitch, now rising in the scale and now falling. A speaker, by skilfully managing these various means, can carry his hearer's mind through moods of mild languor and sudden surprise, the lively movement of cheerfulness rising to eager joy, the burst of impetuous fury gradually subsiding to calm. We can all do this, and what is more, we do it without reference to the meaning of the words used, for emotion can be expressed and even delicately shaded off in pronouncing mere nonsense-syllables. For instance, the words of an Italian opera in England are to a great part of the audience mere nonsense-syllables serving as a means of musical and emotional expression. Clearly this kind of utterance ought to be understood by all mankind, whatever be the language they may happen to speak. It is so, for the most savage and outlandish tribes know how to make such interjections as *ah! oh!* express by their tone such feelings as surprise, pain, entreaty, threatening, disdain, and they understand as well as we do the growling *ur-r-r!* of anger, or the *puh!* of contempt.

The next class of sounds used as expressive signs are imitative. As a deaf-and-dumb child expresses the idea of a cat by imitating the creature's act of washing its face, so a speaking child will indicate it by imitating its *miaou.* If the two children wish to show that they are thinking of a clock, the dumb one will show with his hand the swinging of the pendulum, while the speaking one will say " *tick-tack.*" Here again the sounds are gestures made with the voice, or sound-gestures. In this way an endless variety of objects and actions can be brought to mind by imitating their proper sounds. Not only do children delight in such vocal imitations, but they have come into ordinary language, as when people speak of the *coo* of the pigeon, the *hee-haw* of the donkey, the *ding-dong* of the bell, and the *rat-tat* of the knocker. It need hardly be said that these ways of expression are understood by mankind all the world over.

Now joining gesture-actions and gesture-sounds, they will form together what may be called a Natural Language. This natural language really exists, and in wild regions even has some practical value, as when a European traveller makes shift to converse in it with a party of Australians round their camp-fire, or with a Mongol family in their felt tent. What he has to do is to act his most expressive mimic gestures, with a running accompaniment of exclamations and imitative noises. Here then is found a natural means of intercourse, much fuller than mere pantomime of gestures only. It is a common language of all mankind, springing so directly from the human mind that it must have belonged to our race from the most remote ages and most primitive conditions in which man existed.

Here a very interesting question arises, on which every student has the means of experimenting for himself. How far are the communications of the lower animals, by their actions and sounds, like this natural language of mankind? Every one who attends to the ways of beasts and birds is sure that many of their movements and cries are not made as messages to one another, but are merely symptoms of the creature's own state of mind; for instance, when lambs frisk in the meadow, or eager horses paw in the stable, or beasts moan when suffering severe pain. Animals do thus when not aware that any other creature is present, just as when a man in a room by himself will clench his fist in anger, or groan in pain, or laugh aloud. When gestures and cries serve as signals to other creatures, they come nearer to real signs. The lower animals as well as man do make gestures and cries which act as communications, being perceived by others, as when horses will gently bite one another to invite rubbing, or rabbits stamp on the ground and other rabbits answer, and birds and beasts plainly call one another, especially males and females at pairing-time. So distinct are the gestures and cries of animals under different circumstances that by experience we know their meaning almost certainly. Human language does not answer its purpose more perfectly than the hen's cluck to call her chickens, or the bellow of rage with which the bull, tossing his head, warns off a dog near his paddock. As yet, however, no observer has been able to follow the workings of mind even in the dog that jumps up for food and barks for the door to be opened. It is hard to say how far the dog's mind merely associates jumping up with being fed, and barking with being let in, or how far it forms a conception like ours of what it is doing and why it does it. Anyhow, it is clear that the beasts and birds go so far in the natural language as to make and perceive gestures and cries as signals. But a dog's mind seems not to go beyond this point, that a good imitation of a mew leads it to look for a cat in the room; whereas a child can soon make out from the nurse saying *miaou* that she means something about some cat, which need not even be near by. That is, a young child can understand what is not proved to have entered into the mind of the cleverest dog, elephant, or ape, that a sound may be used as the sign of a thought or idea. Thus, while the lower animals share with man the beginnings of the natural language, they hardly get beyond its rudiments, while the human mind easily goes on to higher stages.

In describing the natural language of gestures and exclamations, we have as yet only looked at it as used alone where more perfect language is not to be had. It has now to be noticed that fragments of it are found in the midst of ordinary language. A people may speak English, or Chinese, or Choctaw, as their mother-tongue, but nevertheless they will keep up the use of the expressive gestures and interjections and imitations which belong to natural language. Mothers and nurses use these in teaching little children to think and speak. It is needless to print examples of this nursery talk, for unless our readers' minds have already been struck by it they are not likely to study philology to much purpose. In the conversation of grown people, the self-expressive or natural sounds become more scanty, yet they are real and unmistakable, as the following examples will serve to show.

As for gestures, many in constant use among our own and other nations must have come down from generation to generation since primitive ages of mankind, as when the orator bows his head, or holds up a threatening hand, or thrusts from him an imaginary intruder, or points to the sky, or counts his friends or enemies on his fingers.

Next, as to emotional sounds, a variety of these is actually used in every language. For instances, a few may be cited from among the interjections set down in grammars :

English—*ah! oh! ugh! foh! ha! ha! tut!* (t-t) *sh!*
Sanskrit—*aho!* (surprise), *âha!* (reproach), *um!* (vexation).
Malay—*eh!* (triumph), *weh!* (compassion), *chih!* (dislike).
Galla—*o! wayo!* (sorrow), *mê!* (entreaty).
Australian—*náh!* (surprise), *pooh!* (contempt).

As for imitative words, all languages of mankind, ancient and modern, savage and civilized, contain more or less of them, and any English child can see how the following set of animals and instruments are named by appropriate sound :—

Ass = *eō* (Egyptian).
Crow = *kâka* (Sanskrit).
Cat = *mau* (Chinese).
Nightingale = *bulbul* (Persian).
Hoopoe = *upupa* (Latin).
Rattlesnake = *shi-shi-gwa* (Algonquin).
Fly = *bumberoo* (Australian).

Drum = *dundu* (Sanskrit).
Flute = *ulule* (Galla).
Whistle = *pipit* (Malay).
Bell = *kwa-lal-kwa-lal* (Yakama).
Blow-tube = *pub* (Quiché).
Gun = *pung* (Botokudo).

Such words are always springing up afresh in dialect or slang; for instance, English *pop,* meaning ginger-beer; German *gaggele,* an egg, from the cackle of the hen as she laid it; French " maître *fifi,*" a scavenger (as it were " master *fie-fie* "). In the same way many actions are expressed by appropriate sounds. Thus in the Tecuna language of Brazil the verb to sneeze is *haitschu,* while the Welsh for a sneeze is *tis.* In the Chinuk jargon the expressive sound *humm* means to stink, and the drover's *kish-kish* becomes a verb meaning to drive horses or cattle. It is even possible to find a whole sentence made with imitative words, for the Galla of Abyssinia, to express " the smith blows the bellows," says, *tumtun bufa bufti,* much as an English child might say " the *tumtum puffs* the *puffer.*" Such words being taken direct from nature, it is to be expected that people of quite different language should sometimes hit on nearly the same imitations. Thus the Ibo language of West

Africa has the word *okoko* for the bird we call a *cock*. The English verbs to *pat* and to *bang* seem to come from imitations of sound, much the same being found elsewhere; as when the Japanese say *pata-pata* to express the sound of flapping or clapping, and the Yoruba negroes have the verb *gbang*, to beat.

Students whose attention is once directed to this class of self-expressive words will notice them at a glance in each fresh language they master. It takes more careful observation to trace them when the sound has been transferred by the process of metaphor (*i.e.* carrying over) to some new meaning not close to the original sense, but there are plenty of clear cases to choose illustrations from. In the Chinuk jargon of the West Coast of America, a tavern is called a " *heehee*-house," a term which puzzles a foreigner till he understands that among the people who speak this curious dialect the imitative word *heehee* signifies not only laughter but the amusement which causes it, so that the term in fact means " amusement-house." It might seem difficult to hit upon an imitative word to denote a courtier, but the Basuto of South Africa do this perfectly; they have a word *ntsi-ntsi*, which means a fly, being, indeed, an imitation of its buzz, and they simply transfer this word to mean also the flattering parasite who buzzes round the chief like a fly round meat. These instances from uncivilized languages are like those which appear among the most polished nations, as when we English take the imitative verb to *puff* from its proper sense of blowing, to express the idea of inflated, hollow praise. Now if the pronunciation of such words becomes changed, their origin may be only recognized by old records happening to preserve their first sound. Thus when English *woe* is traced back to Anglo-Saxon *wá*, it is found to be an actual groan turned (like German *weh*) into a substantive expressing sorrow or distress. So an Englishman would hardly guess from the present pronunciation and meaning of the word *pipe*, what its origin was; yet when he compares it with the Low Latin *pipa*, French *pipe*, pronounced more like our word *peep*, to chirp, and meaning such a reed-pipe as shepherds played on, he then sees how cleverly the very sound of the musical pipe has been made into a word for all kinds of tubes, such as tobacco-pipes and water-pipes. Words like this travel like Indians on the war-path, wiping out their footmarks as they go. For all we know, multitudes of our ordinary words may have thus been made from real sounds, but have now lost beyond recovery the traces of their first expressiveness.

We have not yet come to the end of the intelligible ways in which sound can be made to express sense. When people want to show alteration in the meaning of a word, it is enough to make some change in its pronunciation. It is not difficult to see how, in the Wolof language of West Africa, where *dagou* means to walk, *dâgou* signifies to walk proudly; *dagana* means to ask humbly, but *dagâna* to demand. In the Mpongwe language the meaning can be actually reversed by changing the pronunciation : as " mi *tonda*," I love, but " mi *tonda*," I love not. The English reader can manage to do much the same tricks by varying the tones of his own verbs *walk, ask, love*. This process of expressing difference of sense by difference of sound may be carried much farther. An instructive instance of clear symbolism by sound is to be found in a word coined by the chemist Guyton de Morveau. In his names for chemical compounds he had already the term *sulfate* (made on a Latin pattern like *sulphuratus*), but afterwards he wanted a word to denote a sulphur-salt of different proportions, and thereupon, to express the fact that there was an alteration, he changed a vowel and made the term *sulfite*. He perhaps did not know that he was here resorting to a device found in many rude languages. Thus in Manchu, contrast of sound serves to indicate difference of sex, *chacha* meaning " male," and *cheche* " female," *ama* " father " and *eme* " mother." So distances are often expressed by altering the vowel, as in Malagasy *ao* means a little way off, *eo* still nearer, *io* close at hand. In this way it is easy to make sets of expressive personal pronouns; as in the Tumal language *ngi* " I," *ngo* " thou," *ngu* " he." Another well-known process is reduplication or doubling, which serves a number of different purposes. It shows repetition or strengthening of meaning, as where the Polynesian *aka* " to laugh," becomes *akaaka* " to laugh much," while *loa* " long," becomes *lololoa* " very long." Our words *haw-haw* and *bonbon* are like these. It is also easy to form plurals by reduplication, as Malay *orang* " man," *orang-orang* " men"; Japanese *fito* " man," *fito-bito* " men." Among the kinds of reduplication best known to us is that which marks tenses in verbs, like *didōmi* and *tetupha* in Greek, *momordi* in Latin.

These clever but intelligible devices for making the

sound follow the sense show how easily man gets beyond mere imitation. Language is one branch of the great art of sign-making or sign-choosing, and its business is to hit upon some sound as a suitable sign or symbol for each thought. Whenever a sound has been thus chosen there was no doubt a reason for the choice. But it did not follow that each language should choose the same sound. This is well shown by the peculiar class of words belonging to children's language or baby-language, of which the word *baby* itself is one. These words are made up all over the world from the few simple syllables which children first utter, chosen almost anyhow to express the nursery ideas of mother, father, nurse, toy, sleep, &c. Thus while we have our way of using *papa* and *mama*, the Chilians say *papa* for " mother," and the Georgians *mama* for " father," while in various languages *dada* may mean " father," " cousin," " nurse "; *tata* " father," " son," " good-bye ! " Such children's words often find their way into the language of grown people, and any slight change makes them look like ordinary words. Thus in English one might hardly suspect *pope* and *abbot* of having their origin in baby-words, yet this is evident when they are traced back to Latin *papa* and Syriac *abba*, both meaning " father."

These nursery words have already come beyond the " natural language " of self-expressive gestures and sounds. From its simple and clear facts we thus pass to the more difficult and obscure principles of " articulate language." On examining English, or any other of the thousand tongues spoken in the world, it is found that most of the words used show no such connexion between sound and sense as is so plain in the natural or self-expressive words. To illustrate the difference, when a child calls a pocket timepiece a *tick-tick*, this is plainly self-expressive. But when we call it a *watch*, this word does not show why it is used. It is known that the instrument had its name from telling the hours like a *watch*-man, whose name denotes his duty to *watch*, Anglo-Saxon *wæccan*, from *wacan*, to move, *wake*; but here explanation comes to a stop, for no philologist has succeeded in showing why the syllable *wac* came to denote this particular idea. Or if the same child call a locomotive engine a *puff-puff*, this is self-expressive. Grown people call it an *engine*, a term which came through French from Latin *ingenium*, which meant that which is " in-born," thence natural ability or genius, thence an effort of genius, invention or contrivance, and

thence a machine. By going farther back and taking
the Latin word to pieces, it is seen that the syllables *in*
and *gen* convey the ideas of " in " and " birth "; but
here again etymology breaks down, for why these sounds
were chosen for these meanings no one knows. Thus it
is with at least nine-tenths of the words in dictionaries;
there is no apparent reason why the word *go* should
not have signified the idea of coming, and the word *come*
the idea of going; nor can the closest examination show
cause why in Hebrew *chay* means live, and *mêth* dead,
or why in Maori *pai* means good and *kino* bad. It is
maintained by some philologists that emotional and
imitative sounds such as have been described in this
chapter are the very source of all language, and that
although most words now show no trace of such origin,
this is because they have quite lost it in the long change
of pronunciation and meaning they have gone through,
so that they are now become mere symbols, which children
have to learn the meaning of from their teachers. Now
all this certainly has taken place, but it would be unscientific to accept it as a complete explanation of the
origin of language. Besides the emotional and imitative
ways, several other devices have here been shown in
which man chooses sounds to express thoughts, and who
knows what other causes may have helped ? All we have
a right to say is that, from what is known of man's ways
of choosing signs, it is likely that there was always some
kind of fitness or connexion which led to each particular
sound being taken to express a particular thought. This
seems to be the most reasonable opinion to be held as to
the famous problem of the Origin of Language.

At the same time, what little is known of man's ways
of making new words out of suitable sounds, is of great
importance in the study of human nature. It proves that,
so far as language can be traced to its actual source, that
source does not lie in some lost gifts or powers of man,
but in a state of mind still acting, and not above the level
of children and savages. The origin of language was not
an event which took place long ago once for all, and then
ceased entirely. On the contrary, man still possesses,
and uses when he wants it, the faculty of making new
original words by choosing fit and proper sounds. But
he now seldom puts this faculty to serious use, for this
good reason, that whatever language he speaks has its
stock of words ready to furnish an expression for almost
every fresh thought that crosses his mind.

CHAPTER V

LANGUAGE—*(continued)*

A SENTENCE being made up of its connected sounds as a limb is made up of its joints, we call language *articulate* or " jointed," to distinguish it from the *inarticulate* or " unjointed " sounds uttered by the lower animals. Such conversation by gestures and exclamations as was shown in the last chapter to be a natural language common to mankind is half-way between the communications of animals and full human speech. Every people, even the smallest and most savage tribe, has an articulate language, carried on by a whole system of sounds and meanings, which serves the speaker as a sort of catalogue of the contents of the world he lives in, taking in every subject he thinks about, and enabling him to say what he thinks about it. What a complicated and ingenious apparatus a language may be, the Greek and Latin grammars sufficiently show. Yet the more carefully such difficult languages are looked into, the more plainly it is seen that they grew up out of earlier and simpler kinds of speech. It is not our business here to make a systematic survey of the structure of languages, such as will be found in the treatises of Max Müller, Sayce, Whitney, and Peile. What we have to attend to is that many of the processes by which languages have been built up are still to be found at work among men, and that grammer is not a set of arbitrary rules framed by grammarians, but the result of man's efforts to get easier, fuller, and exacter expression for his thoughts. It may be noticed that our examples are oftener taken from English than from any other tongue. The reason of this is not merely the convenience of using the most familiar words as instances, but that English is of all existing languages perhaps the best for explaining the development of language in general. While its words may in great part be traced to high antiquity, its structure has passed through extreme changes in coming down to modern times, and in its present state the language at once keeps up relics of ancient formations and has the freest growth actually going on. Thus, in one way or another, English has something to show in illustration of three out of four of the processes known to have helped in the making of language, at any time and anywhere.

As in the course of ages man's knowledge became wider and his civilization more complex, his language had to keep up with them. Comparatively few and plain expressions had sufficed for his early rude condition, but now more and more terms had to be added for the new notions, implements, arts, offices, and relations of more highly organized society. Etymology shows how such new words are made by altering and combining old ones, carrying on old words from the old state of things to do duty in the new, shifting their meanings, and finding in any new thought some resemblance to an old one that would serve to give it a name. English is full of traces of these ways of word-making and word-shifting. For instance, that spacious stone building is still called, as its rough predecessors were, a *barrack* (that is, hut); in it a *regiment* (that is, a ruling or command) of *soldiers* (that is, paid men) of the *infantry* (that is, lads, who fought on foot) are being *inspected* (that is, looked into); each *company* (that is, those who have bread together) being under a *captain* (that is, head-man) and his *lieutenants* (that is, place-holders). On the front of the building is a *clock*, a machine which keeps on its old name, meaning a bell, from the ages when its predecessor was only a bell on which a watchman struck the hours; in later times were added the *weights*, lumps of metal so called from the weights of the balance, the *pendulum* (or hanger), and what are metaphorically called the *face* and *hands*, for showing on a *scale* (or ladder) the *hours* (or times), divided into *minutes* (or smalls), and then again into *seconds* (or followings). These instances are intentionally not drawn from the depths of etymology, but are taken to show the ordinary ways in which language finds means to supply the new terms of advancing society. It will be worth while to give a few cases showing that the languages of less civilized races do their duty in much the same ways. The Aztecs called a boat a " water-house " (*acalli*), and thence the censer in which they burnt copal as incense came to be called a " little copal-boat " (*copalacaltontli*). The Vancouver Islanders, when they saw how a screw-steamer went, named it at once *yetseh-yetsokleh*, that is, the " kick-kicker." The Hidatsas of the Missouri till lately had only hard stone for their arrows and hatchets; so when they became acquainted with iron and copper they made names for these metals—*uetsasipisa* and *uetsahisisi*, that is to say, " stone black " and " stone red." The horse, when brought by the white men among peoples who had never seen it, had to be named, and accordingly the Tahitians called it " pig-carry-man," while the Sioux Indians said it was a " magic-dog."

As a help to understand how words have come to express still more difficult thoughts, it is well to remember the contrast between the gesture-language and spoken English (p. 30). It was seen how the deaf-and-dumb fall short of our power of expressing general and abstract ideas. Not that they cannot conceive such ideas at all. They use signs as general terms when they can lay hold of some quality or action as the mark of a whole class. Thus flapping one's arms like wings means any bird, or birds in general, and the sign of legs-four, means beasts, or quadrupeds in general. The pretence of pouring something out of a jug expresses the notion of fluid, which they understand, as we do, to comprise water, tea, quicksilver; and they probably have, though more dimly than we, such other abstract notions as the whiteness common to all white things, and the length, breadth, and thickness which all solid objects have. But while the deaf-mute's sign must always make us think of the very thing it imitates, the spoken word can shift its meaning so as to follow thought wherever it goes. It is instructive to look at words in this light, to see how, starting from thoughts as plain as those shown by the signs of the American savage, they can come on to the most difficult terms of the lawyer, the mathematician and the philosopher. To us words have become, as Lord Bacon said, counters for notions. By means of words we are enabled to deal with abstract ideas, got by comparing a number of thoughts, but so as only to attend to what they have in common. The reader of this no doubt uses easily, and perhaps correctly, such words as *sort, kind, thing, cause,* to *make, be, do, suffer.* If he will try to get clear to his mind what is actually meant by

these words, that is, what sense they carry with them
wherever used, he may teach himself the best lesson
he ever learnt, either in language or philosophy.   To
Englishmen who know no language but their own, these
words are indeed, as it were, counters, chosen at random
to express thoughts.   Having learnt by practice how and
where to apply them, they are seldom even conscious of
their highly abstract nature.   The philologist cannot
trace the complete history of them all, but he knows
enough to satisfy him that they came out of words easier
to understand.   As in the Bornu language of Africa,
tando, to " weave," has become a general verb to " make,"
and in Hebrew *bârâ*, to " cut " or " hew," has come to
be used for the making of the heavens and earth;   so
our word to *make* may have meant originally to fit, or
join.   The English word *sort* comes from Latin *sors*, a
" lot," through such a set of meanings as allotment,
oracle, fate, condition, chance, portion;   *kind* meant of
one kindred or descent;   to *be* may have meant to grow;
to *suffer* meant to bear as a burden.   It belongs to high
metaphysics to talk of the *apprehension* of *ideas*;   but
these now abstruse words originally meant " catching
hold " of " sights."   One use of etymology is that it
teaches how men thus contrived, from words which
expressed plain and easy thoughts, to make terms for
more complex and abstruse thoughts.   This is the high
road along which the human mind has travelled from
ignorance to knowledge.

The next contrivance of language to be noticed is the
use of " grammatical " words, which serve to connect the
" real " words and show what they have to do with one
another.   This again is well seen by looking at the gesture
language (p. 30).   If a deaf-and-dumb man wants to
convey in gestures " John is come, he has brought the
harness of the pony and put it on a bench," he can communicate the sense of this well enough, but he does it by
merely giving the real parts, as " John, harness, pony,
carry, bench, put."   But the articles " a " and " the,"
the preposition " of," the conjunction " and," the substantive verb " is," and the pronouns " he," " it," are
grammatical devices which have not signs in his natural
system, and which he does not even learn the meaning
of till he is taught to read.   Nevertheless, the deaf-mute,
if obliged to be very exact in his account, can actually
give us a good idea of the way in which we speaking-people
have come to use grammatical words.   Though he cannot

intimate that it is *a* bench, he can hold up one finger to show that it is *one* bench; though he has no sign for *the* pony, he can as it were point it out so as to show it is *that* pony; instead of expressing *of* the pony as we do, he can go farther by pretending to take the harness *off* the pony. Now English etymology often shows that our grammatical words were made in very much this way out of real words; *an* or *a* was originally the numeral "one," still Scotch *ane*; *the* is of the same family of words with *that* and *there*; *of* is derived from the same source with *off*; the conjunction *and* may be traced back to the more real meaning of "further" or "thereto"; the verb to *have* has become a mere auxiliary in "I *have* come," yet it keeps its old full sense of to hold or grasp, when one man seizing another cries "I *have* him!" When an Englishman says he "*stands* corrected," this does not mean that he is on his legs, but the verb has sunk into a grammatical auxiliary, now conveying little more than the passive sense he "is corrected." It is curious to notice pronouns being thus formed from more real words. As the deaf-mute simply points with his finger to express "I" and "thou," so the Greenlander's *uvanga* = "I," *ivdlit* = "thou," are plainly derived from *uv* = "here," *iv* = "there." Quite a different device appears in Malay, where *âmba* = "slave" is used as a pronoun "I," and *tuwan* = "lord" as a pronoun "thou." How this came to pass is plainly shown by Hebrew, in such phrases as are translated in the English Bible, "*thy servant* saith," "*my lord* knoweth"; these terms are on the road to become mere personal pronouns meaning "I" and "thou," as in the Malay they actually have done. An exact line cannot be drawn between real and grammatical words in English or any other language, for the good reason that words pass so gradually from the real into the grammatical stage, that the same word may be used in both ways. But though the distinction is not an exact one, it should be noticed attentively. Any one who will try to tell an intelligible story in English real words only, without the help of the grammatical particles which are the links and hinges of the sentence, will see how the use of grammatical words was one of the greatest moves made by man in the formation of articulate speech.

Philology goes still further in explaining how the complicated devices of grammar arose from simple beginnings. The distinction of "parts of speech," familiar to us in a highly-developed state from the Greek and Latin grammars, is a useful means of showing the relations among the several thoughts talked of in the sentence. But it is possible to do without parts of speech, and it is not to be supposed that they existed in the earliest forms of language. In the gesture language it has been already noticed that there is no such distinction even between noun and verb. In classical Chinese, *thwan* means round, a ball, to make round, to sit round, and so on; *ngan* means quiet, quietly, to quiet, to be quiet, &c. We English can quite enter into this, for our language has so far dropped the ancient inflexions as to break up distinctions between parts of speech in almost Chinese fashion, using a word either as substantive, adjective, or verb, as the people's *quiet*, a *quiet* people, to *quiet* the people, and without scruple turning a verb into a substantive, as a workmen's *strike*, or a substantive into a verb, as to *horse* a coach. The very formation of new parts of speech may be seen going on, as where Chinese shows how prepositions may be made out of nouns or verbs. Thus " kuo *chung*," that is " kingdom *middle*," is used to mean " in the kingdom," and " sha jin *i* thing," that is, " kill man *use* stick," expresses " to kill a man *with* a stick." So an African language, the Mandingo, may be caught in the act of making prepositions out of the nouns *kang*, " neck," and *kono*, " belly," when they say " put table *neck* " for " *on* the table," and " house *belly* " for " *in* the house."

We have next to look at the way in which language grows by combining its words to form new ones. To see this, words have to be noticed not as they stand by themselves, but as they come together in actual speaking. Language consists of sentences, and a sentence is made up of words, each word being a distinct spoken sound carrying a distinct meaning. The simplest notion of a sentence may be had from such a language as Chinese, where it can be taken apart into words which are each a single syllable. Thus *kou chi shi jin sse*, that is " dog sow eat man food " means that dogs and sows eat the food of men. The class of languages which can be taken to pieces in this perfect way are called *analytic* or isolating. In most languages of the world, however, which are more or less *synthetic* or compounding, the tendency is not so strong to keep words separate, and they are apt to attach themselves together. To bring clearly before our minds how the joining or compounding of words takes place, let us notice rather more closely than usual one of our English sentences. On listening, it will appear that the spoken words have not really breaks between them as in writing, but the syllables run on continuously till the speaker pauses, and what marks a word is, not its being really separated, but its having an emphasis, or stress (as it is called by Mr. Sweet). Now, from time to time, certain words may be noticed becoming actually fixed together. How this joining gradually takes place we sometimes try to show by writing them differently, as *hard ware, hard-ware, hardware*; or *steam ship, steam-ship, steamship*. On listening to such joined words, it is found that one of the two has lost its stress, the whole compound having now but one stress. This is how in talking English our minds give a sign by our voices that two words have become one. The next step is when the sound of one of the part-words becomes slurred or broken down, as in the end-words of *waterman, wrongful*. Or both the simple words may have broken down, as in *boatswain* and *coxswain*, where writing keeps up the original meaning of the *swain* in charge of the *boat* or *cock*-boat, but in actual speaking the words have shrunk to what may be spelt *bōsun, coxun*. Now this process of forming a new word by (so to speak) welding together two or more old ones, is one of the chief acts by which word-makers, ancient and modern, have furnished themselves with more manageable terms, which again as the meanings of the separate parts were less cared for, were cut shorter in speaking. When this has not gone too far, philologists can still get back to the original elements of such words, discerning the *fourteen night* in *fortnight*; the *unus* and *decem* in *undecim*, shrunk still farther in French *onze*; the *jus, dico*, in Latin *judex*, which in English comes down to *judge*.

As examples how word-compounding goes on in unfamiliar tongues, may be taken the Malay term for " arrow," which is *anak-panah*, or " child-(of-the)-bow "; and the native Australian term for " unanimous," which is *gurdugynyul*, or " heart-one-come." To show how such compound words become shortened, take the Mandingo word for " sister," *mbadingmuso*, which is made up of *mi bado dingo muso*, meaning " my-mother-child-female." The natives of Vancouver's Island gave to a certain long-bearded Englishman the name *Yakpus*; this appears to have come from *yakhpekukselkous*, made

up of words signifying " long-face-hair-man," which in
speaking had been cut down to *yakpus*. No one who
did not happen to be told the history of this word could
ever have guessed it. This is an important lesson in
the science of language, for it is likely that tens of
thousands of words in the languages of the world may
have come into the state in which we find them by the
shortening of long compound words, and when this has
been done recklessly as in the last example, and the
history lost, all reasonable hope is gone of ever getting
back to the original form and meaning. Nor does this
process of contraction affect only compound words, but
it may act on a whole sentence, fusing it as it were into
one word. Here the synthetic or compounding principle
reaches its height. As a contrast to the analytic Chinese
sentence given at page 45 , to show the perfect distinctness of their words, we may take a sentence of an African
language to show how utterly that distinctness may be
lost. When a Grebo negro wishes to express that he is
very angry, he says in his metaphorical way " it has
raised a bone in my breast." His full words for expressing this would be *e ya mu kra wudi*, but in speaking he
runs them together so that what he actually utters is
yamukroure. Where such breaking down has gone
on unchecked, it is easy to see how the language of a
barbaric tribe may alter so much in a few generations
as hardly to be recognized. Indeed, any one who will
attend to how English words run together in talking may
satisfy himself that his own language would undergo
rapid changes like those of barbaric tongues, were it
not for the schoolmaster and the printer, who insist on
keeping our words fixed and separate.

The few examples here given of new words made by
compounding old ones may serve to illustrate the great
principle that such combination, far from being a mere
source of confusion, has been one of the great means
of building up language. Especially, one of the great
discoveries in modern philology is how grammatical
formation and inflexion has partly come about by a kind
of word-compounding. It must have seemed to the old
scholars a mysterious and arbitrary proceeding that
Latin should have fixed upon a set of meaningless
affixes to inflect and make into different parts of speech
*ago, agis, agit, agere, agens, actum, actor, actio, activus,
activè*, &c. But the mystery to some extent disappeared
when it was noticed how in modern languages the run-

ning together of words produced something of the kind. Thus the *hood* of *womanhood*, *priesthood*, which is now a mere grammatical suffix, was in old English a word of itself, *hâd*, meaning form, order, state; and the suffix *-ly* was once the distinct word " like," as is seen by Anglo-Saxon saying cwên-*lic*, " queen-*like*," where modern English says queen*ly*. In Chaucer's English it is seen how the pronoun *thou* had dwindled into a mere verb-ending,

> " He pokyd Johan, and seyde, Slepist*ow* ?
> Herdist*ow* ever slik a sang er now ? "

In English the future tense of the verb to give is " I will give," or, colloquially, " I'll give." Here writing separates what speaking joins, but the modern French future tense *donnerai*, *donneras*, is the verb *donner* with the auxiliary verb *ai*, *as*, both spoken and written on to it, so that " je donnerai " is a phrase like " I have to give." The plural *donnerons*, *donnerez*, can no longer be thus taken to pieces, for the remains of the auxiliary verb have passed into meaningless grammatical affixes *ons*, *ez*. There is reason to suppose that many of the affixes of Greek and Latin grammar arose in this way by distinct words combining together and then shrinking. Not that it would be safe to assert that all affixes came into existence in this particular way. As was pointed out in the last chapter, men wanting to utter a thought are clever enough to catch up in very far-fetched ways a sound to express it. Thus the prefix *ge*, which German uses to make past participles with, seems to have originally signified " with " or " together," which sense it still retains in such words as *gespiele*, " playfellow "; but by a curious shifting of purpose it came to serve as a means of forming participles, as *spielen*, to play, *gespielt*, played. It was so used also in Anglo-Saxon, as *clypian*, to call, *geclypod*, called, which word in its later form *yclept* still keeps up among us a trace of the old grammatical device. Philologists have to keep their eyes open to this power which language-makers have of using sounds for some new purpose they were not intended for. Thus, in English, the change of vowels in *foot*, *feet*, and in *find*, *found*, now serves as a means of declining the noun and conjugating the verb. But history happens to show that the vowel change was not originally made with this intention at all. The Anglo-Saxon declension proves that the vowel was not then a sign of number in the noun; it

was singular *fôt, fôtes, fêt,* plural *fêt, fôta, fôtum.* Nor was
it a sign of tense in the Anglo-Saxon verb, where the
perfect of *findan,* to find, had different vowels in its
singular, *ic fand,* I found, and its plural, *we fundon,* we
found. It was the later Englishmen who, knowing
nothing of the real reasons which brought about the
variation of the vowels, took to using them to mark
singular from plural, and present from perfect.

It is the work of grammarians in examining any
language to take all its combined words to pieces as far
as possible. Greek and Latin grammars now teach
how to analyse words by stripping off their affixes, so
as to get down to the real part or root, which is generally
a simple sound expressing a simple notion. A root is
best understood by considering it to have been once a
separate word, as it would be in such a language as
English. Even in languages where the roots seldom
appear without some affix attached, they may stand by
themselves as imperative, like Latin *dic !* say ! Turkish,
sev ! love ! But in many languages roots can only be
found as imaginary forms, by comparing a group of words
and getting at the common part belonging to them all.
Thus in Latin it appears from *gnosco, gnotus,* &c., that
there must be a root *gno* which carries the thought of
knowing. Going on to Greek, there is found in *gignōskō,
gnōsis, gnōmē,* &c., the same root *gno* with the same
meaning. Turning next to Sanskrit, a similar sound,
jnâ, appears as the root-form for knowing. In this
way, by comparing the whole set of Aryan or Indo-
European languages, it appears that there must have
been in ancient times a word something like *gna,* meaning
to know, which is to be traced not only in Sanskrit,
Greek, and Latin, but in many other languages of the
family, as Russian *znat,* English *know.* A few more such
Aryan roots, which the reader recognizes at once in well-
known languages, are *sta,* to stand, *sad,* to sit, *ga,* to go,
i, to go, *ma,* to measure, *da,* to give, *vid,* to see, *rag,* to
rule, *mar,* to die. These simple sounds seem to have
already become fixed to carry their meanings in the
remote ages when the ancestors of the Aryan peoples
wandered with their herds on the highlands of Central
Asia. It is not needful to tell the student of anthropology how interesting it is to arrive thus at the earliest
known root-words of any family. But it should at the
same time be noticed that, even in the earliest of these sets
of roots, we seldom come to anything like an actual origin

or beginning. Some few may indeed have been taken direct from the natural language, for instance *ru*, to roar, and if this was so here is a real origin. But most roots, to whatever languages of the world they may belong, are like the group given above, where it is impossible to say confidently how their sound came to express their meaning. Unless this can be done, it is safest not to take such roots as really primitive formations, for they may have a long lost history of the utmost change. How this may happen, our own language has a useful lesson to teach. Imagine one who knows no language but English trying to get at its roots. To him the verb to *roll* might seem a root-word, a primitive element of language; indeed it actually has been fancied a natural sound imitating the act of rolling. Yet any philologist would tell him that English *roll* is a comparatively modern form, which came through a long series of earlier stages; it was borrowed from French *rolle*, *roller*, now *rôle*, *rouler*, all from Latin *rotulus*, diminutive of *rota*, a wheel, even this coming from a more ancient verb and signifying a runner or goer. Still more adventurous is the history of another English word which has now all the parts of a verb, to *check*, *checking*, *checked*, besides such forms as a *check* in one's course, the *check*-string to stop the coachman, the *check*-valve to stop the water in a pipe. This word *check* has all the simplicity of sound and sense which might belong to an original root-word. Yet, strange to say, it is really the Persian word *shah*, meaning "king," which came to Europe with the game of chess as the word of challenge to the king, and thence by a curious metaphor passed into a general word for stopping anybody or anything. For all that is known, many root-words among the Greeks or Jews, or even the simple-looking monosyllables of the Chinese, may during prehistoric ages have travelled as far from their real origin as these English verbs. Thus the roots from which language grows may often be themselves sprung as it were from yet earlier seeds or cuttings, grown at home or imported from abroad, and, though in our time words mostly come from the ancient roots, the power of striking new roots is not yet dead.

Having now, in such a broad way as suits the present purpose, looked at the formation of words, something may be said as to how language contrives to show the relations among the words of a sentence. This is done by what grammarians call syntax, concord, and govern-

ment.   It has been seen (p. 95) that the gesture-language,
though wanting in grammatical forms, has a strongly
marked syntax.   The deaf-mute's signs must follow one
another in proper order, otherwise they may convey a
wrong meaning or seem nonsense.   So, in spoken
languages which do not inflect their words, such as the
Chinese, syntax is the main part of grammar; thus *li
ping* = sharp weapons, *ping li* = weapons (are) sharp;
chi kuo = to govern the kingdom, but *kuo chi* = the
kingdom is governed.   This seems quite natural to us,
for modern English has come far towards the Chinese
plan of making the sense of the sentence depend on the
order of the words, thus marking the difference between
rank of families and *families of rank*, or between *men
kill lions* and *lions kill men*.   In Latin it is very different,
where words can be put about with such freedom that
the English reader may be hardly able to make sense of
one of Tacitus' sentences without fresh sorting the words
into some order he can think them in.   Especially in
Latin verses there is often hardly more syntax than if
the words were nonsense-syllables arranged only to scan.
The sense has to be made out from the grammatical
inflections, as where it is seen that in " vile potabis
modicis Sabinum cantharis," the cheapness has to do
with the wine and the smallness with the mugs.   It is
because so many of the inflections have disappeared
from English, that the English translation has to obtain
a proper understanding by stricter order of words.
Where the meaning of sentences depends on order or
syntax, that order must be followed, but it must be borne
in mind that this order differs in different languages.
For a single instance, in Malay, where *orang* = man and
utan = forest, savages and apes are called *orang utan*,
which is just opposite to the English construction
" forest man."

Every one who can construe Greek and Latin sees what
real service is done by government and agreement in
showing how the words of a sentence hang together, what
quality is stated of what thing, or who is asserted to act
on what.   But even Greek and Latin have changed so
much from their earlier state, that they often fail to show
the scholar clearly what they mean to do, and why.
It is useful to make acquaintance with the languages
of ruder nations, which show government and agreement in earlier and plainer stages of growth.   One
great object of grammatical construction is to make it

quite clear which of two nouns concerned is subject and which object: for instance, whether it was a chief who killed a bear, or a bear who killed a chief. A particle properly attached will do this, as when the Algonquin Indians put on the syllable *un* both to noun and verb, in a way which we may try to translate by the pronoun *him*, thus :—

Ogimau	ogi	nissa*un*	mukw*un*.
chief	he-did	kill-*him*	bear-*him*.
Mukwah	ogi	nissa*un*	ogima*un*.
bear	he-did	kill-*him*	chief-*him*.

This gives a notion of the natural manner in which grammatical government may have come into use to mark the parts of the sentence. At the same time, it shows that different languages may go different ways to work, for here the verb and object agree together, and the subject (so to speak) governs both, which is quite unlike our familiar rule of the verb agreeing with the nominative or subject. To see the working of concord or agreement in a far clearer and completer form than Latin can show it, we may look at the Hottentot language, where a sentence may run somewhat thus, " That woman-*she*, our tribe's-*she*, rich-being-*she*, another village-in-dwelling-*she*, praise-we-do cattle-of-*she*, *she*-does present-us two calves-of-*she*-form." Here the pronoun running through the whole sentence makes it clear to the dullest hearer that it is the woman who is rich, who dwells in another village, whose cattle are praised, and who gives two of her calves. The terminations in a Greek or Latin sentence, which show the agreement of substantive and adjective with their proper verb, are remains of affixes which may have once carried their signification as plainly as they still do in the language of the Hottentots. A different plan of concord, but even more instructive to the classical scholar, appears in the Zulu language, which divides things into classes, and then carries the marking syllables of the class right through the sentence, so as to connect all the words it is attached to. Thus " u-*bu*-kosi *b*-etu o-*bu*-kulu *bu*-ya-bonakala si-*bu*-tanda," means " our great kingdom appears, we love it." Here *bu*, the mark of the class to which kingdom belongs, is repeated through every word referring to it. To give an idea how this acts in holding the sentence together, Dr. Bleek translates it by repeating the *dom* of king*dom* in a similar way; " the king-*dom*, our *dom*, which *dom* is the great *dom*, the *dom* appears,

we love the *dom*." This is clumsy, but it answers the
great purpose of speech, that of making one's meaning
certain beyond mistake. So, by using different class-
syllables for singular and plural, and carrying them
on through the whole sentence, the Zulu shows the
agreement in number more plainly than Greek or Latin
can do. But the Zulu language does not recognize by
its class-syllables what we call gender. It is in fact one
of the puzzles of philology, what can have led the speaker
of Aryan languages like Greek, or Semitic languages like
Hebrew, to classify things and thoughts by sex so un-
reasonably as they do. For Latin examples, take the
following groups : *pes* (masc.), *manus* (fem.), *brachium*
(neut.) ; *amor* (masc.), *virtus* (fem.), *delictum* (neut.).
German shows gender in as practically absurd a state, as
witness *der* Hund, *die* Ratte; *das* Their, *die* Pflanze. In
Anglo-Saxon, *wíf* (English *wife*) was neuter, while
wíf-man (i.e. " wife-man," English *woman*) was mascu-
line. Modern English, in discarding an old system of
grammatical gender that had come to be worse than
useless, has set an example which French and German
might do well to follow. Yet it must be borne in mind
that the devices of language, though they may decay
into absurdity, were never originally absurd. No
doubt the gender-system of the classic languages is the
remains of an older and more consistent plan. There
are languages outside our classical education which
show that *gender* (that is *genus*, kind, class) is by no
means necessarily according to sex. Thus in the
Algonquin languages of North America, and the Dravidian
languages of South India, things are divided not as male
or female, but as alive or dead, rational or irrational,
and put accordingly in the animate or major gender, or
in the inanimate or minor gender. Having noticed how
the Zulu concord does its work by regularly repeating
the class-sign, we seem to understand how in the Aryan
languages the signs of number and gender may have
come to be used as a simular means of carrying through
the sentence the information that this substantive
belongs to that adjective and that verb. Yet even in
Sanskrit, Greek, Latin, and Gothic, such concord falls
short of the fullness and clearness it has among the
barbarians of Africa, while in the languages of modern
Europe, especially our own, it has mostly disappeared,
probably because with the advance of intelligence it was
no longer found necessary.

The facts in this chapter will have given the reader some idea how man has been and still is at work building up language. Any one who began by studying the grammars of such languages as Greek or Arabic, or even of such barbarous tongues as Zulu or Eskimo, would think them wonderfully artificial systems. Indeed, had one of these languages suddenly come into existence among a tribe of men, this would have been an event mysterious and unaccountable in the highest degree. But when one begins at the other end, by noticing the steps by which word-making and composition, declension and conjugation, concord and syntax, arise from the simplest and rudest beginnings, then the formation of language is seen to be reasonable, purposeful and intelligible. It was shown in the last chapter that man still possesses the faculty of bringing into use fresh sounds to express thoughts, and now it may be added that he still possesses the faculty of framing these sounds into full articulate speech. Thus every human tribe has the capabilities which, had they not inherited a language ready-made from their parents, would have enabled them to make a new language of their own.

CHAPTER VI

LANGUAGE AND RACE

THE next question is, What can be learnt from languages as to the history of the nations speaking them, and the races these nations belong to ?

In former chapters, in dividing mankind into stocks or races according to their skulls, complexions, and other bodily characters, language was not taken into account as a mark of race. In fact, a man's language is no full and certain proof of his parentage. There are even cases in which it is totally misleading, as when some of us have seen persons whose language is English, but their faces Chinese or African, and who, on inquiry, are found to have been brought away in infancy from their native countries. It is within every one's experience how one parent language disappears in intermarriage, as where persons called Boileau or Muller may be now absolutely English as to language, in spite of their French or German ancestry. Now not only individuals but whole populations may have their native languages thus lost or absorbed. The negroes shipped as slaves to America were taken from many tribes and had no native tongue in common, so that they came to talk to one another in the language of their white masters, and there is now to be seen the curious spectacle of black woolly-haired families talking broken-down dialects of English, French, or Spanish. In our own country the Keltic language of the Ancient Britons has not long since fallen out of use in Cornwall, as in time it will in Wales. But whether the Keltic language is spoken or not, the Keltic blood remains in the mixed population of Cornwall, and to class the modern Cornishmen as of pure English race because they speak English would be to misuse the evidence of language. Much bad anthropology has been made by thus carelessly taking language and race as though they went always and exactly together. Yet they do go together to a great extent. Although what a man's language really proves is not his parentage but his bringing-up, yet most children are in fact brought up by their own parents, and inherit their language as well as their features. So long as people of one race and speech live together in their own nation, their language will remain a race-mark common to all. And although migration and intermarriage, conquest and slavery interfere, from time to time, so that the native tongue of a nation can never tell the whole story of their ancestry, still it tells a part of it, and that a most important part. Thus in Cornwall the English tongue is a real record of the settlement of the English there, though it fails to tell of the Keltic race who were in the land before them, and with whom they mixed. In a word, the information which the language of a nation gives as to its race is something like what a man's surname tells as to his family, by no means the whole history, but one great line of it.

It has next to be seen what the languages of the world can show as to the early history of nations. Great care has to be taken with the proofs of connexion between languages. It is of little use to compare two languages as old-fashioned philologists were too apt to do when, if they found half-a-dozen words at all similar, they took these without more ado to be remnants of one primitive tongue, the origin of both. In the more careful philological comparisons of the present day many similarities of words have to be thrown aside as not proving connexion at all. In any two languages a few words are sure to be similar by mere accident, as where, in the Society Islands, *tiputa* means a cloak, like *tippet* with us. Words must only be compared when there is a real correspondence of meaning as well as sound, or the way would be opened for fancies like that of a writer who connects the well-known Polynesian word *tabu*, sacred, with *tabut*, the Arabic name of the ark of the covenant, apparently because that was a very sacred object. Also, words imitated from nature prove nothing in this way, as where the Hindus and the savages of Vancouver's Island both call a crow *kaka*, this being not because their languages are connected, but because it is the bird's cry. What is most important of all is to make

sure that the words compared really belong to the old
stock of the language they are found in. Before now a
writer has proved to his own satisfaction that Turkish,
Arabic, and Persian are all branches of one primitive
language, his argument being that the Turks call a man
adam, as the Arabs call the first man, and a father *pader*,
which is like the Persian word. The fact is true enough,
but what the argument omits to notice is that the
Turks have been for ages enriching their own barbaric
language by taking words from the cultured Arabic
and Persian, and *adam* and *pader* are such lately borrowed
words, not philologically Turkish at all. Borrowed
words like these are indeed valuable evidence, but what
they prove is not the common origin of languages; it is
intercourse between the nations speaking them. They
often give the clue to the country from which some new
produce was obtained, or some new instrument, or idea,
or institution, was learnt. Thus in English it is seen
by the very words how Italy furnished us with *opera*,
sonata, *chiaroscuro*, while Spain gave *gallina* and *mulatto*,
how from the Hebrews we have *sabbath* and *jubilee*, from
the Arabs *zero* and *magazine*, while Mexico has supplied
chocolate and *tomato*, Haiti *hammock* and *hurricane*, Peru
guano and *quinine*, and even the languages of the South
Sea Islands are represented by *taboo* and *tatoo*. But in
all this there is not one particle of evidence that any one
of these languages is sprung from the same family with
any other.

When two languages have such a common descent,
the philologist is not content to ascertain it by merely
looking for a few words of similar sound. Indeed he
expects to find that the words of the ancestral language
will not only have changed in its descendant languages,
but that they will often have changed according to
different rules. Thus he knows that according to the
rule called Grimm's law, the English *ten*, *tame*, should
appear in German with a different initial, *zehn*, *zahm*,
while again these should be represented in Latin by
decem, *domare*. With the same regularity of change, the
sound which in some of the Polynesian languages is *k*,
in others has become *t*; thus the word man, in the
Sandwich Islands *kanaka* (whence our sailors call any
South Sea Islander a *kanaker*), appears in New Zealand
under the form of *tangata*. Going beyond the sound of
words into their structure, the comparative philologist
reckons that, when two languages are allied, they ought

to show such similarity in the roots and in the putting together that neither chance nor borrowing can account for the resemblance. In the first chapter, for another purpose, examples were given of languages continuing to show their intimate connexion while diverging from their parent tongues. The reader may find it worth while to look back to these illustrations (p. 6) before going on to the following sketch of the families of language belonging to the various races of man.

The languages of white men mostly belong to two great families, the Aryan and Semitic. First as to the Aryan family, called also Indo-European, which takes in the languages of part of South and West Asia, and almost the whole of Europe. The original tongue whence these are all descended may be called the Primitive Aryan. What the roots of this ancient language were like, and how they were put together into words, the student may gain an idea from Greek and Latin, but a still better from Sanskrit, where both roots and inflexions have been kept up in a more perfect and regular state. As a rough illustration of the way in which words of our familiar European languages may be discerned in Sanskrit, one line of the first hymn of the Veda is here given, where the worshippers entreat Agni, the divine Fire, that he will be approachable to us as a father to a son, and will be near for our happiness :

Sa nah pitâ-iva sûnave Agne su-upâyanah bhava : sachasva nah svastaye.

Here may be more or less clearly made out words connected with Latin, Greek, and English *nos*, *pater*, *son*, *ignis*, *up*, *be*, *sequi*, *euestō*, and others. Though the original Aryan is a lost language, philologists try to reconstruct it by comparing its oldest and most perfect descendants, Sanskrit, Old Persian, Greek, Latin, Old Russian, Gothic, Old Irish, &c. Granting that a primitive Aryan tongue once existed, there must once have been a nation who spoke it, and whose descendants carried it down to later ages. It is hard to draw any certain bodily picture of the primitive Aryans themselves (see page 88), for in their course of migration and conquest they so mingled with other races, that now the nations united by Aryan speech range through the utmost varieties of white men, from the Icelander to the Hindu. A well-known theory is that the early home of the Aryans was in Inner Asia, in the regions of the Oxus and Yaxartes, for here the practicable way of migration for nomads with flocks and herds lie open down into Persia on the one side, and India on the other. As India and Persia have preserved in their sacred languages the Aryan tongue in early forms, it has been judged that the land whence the invading Aryans came was not far off. But it may have been further east in Central Asia, or, as is the opinion of a modern school of anthropologists, in the regions of Northern Europe where the fair-complexioned Aryan nations congregate. In this home-land, wherever it may have been, the Aryans lived in barbaric but not savage clans, tilling the soil, and grazing their flocks and herds, a warlike folk skilled in many arts of life, a people able to make laws and abide by them, a religious people earnest in the worship of the sun, and sky, and fire, and waters, and with pious faith in the divine spirits of their ancestors. Carrying with them their language, laws, and religion, these nation-founders spread in radiating tracks of migration over South-West Asia and all Europe. Where they went they found the land peopled by Dravidians, Tatars, and doubtless many other stocks once spread far and wide, like the Basques, whose language still lingers in the Pyrenees. Where the old languages have vanished, the record of the early populations of Europe is only to be had from their tombs, and seen in the features of the present nations, which may be often more those of the original people than of the Aryan invaders. The earliest Aryan hordes who spread from their first centre may have been the ancestors of the Keltic nations, for their language has undergone most change, and they are found in the far west of Europe, as though they had been pressed on by the Teuton-Scandinavian tribes who followed them, distant kinsfolk but not friends. The ancestors of the Græco-Italian nations migrated till they reached the Mediterranean, and behind them came the Slavonic peoples who now occupy Eastern Europe. Thus much of the beginnings of the Aryan nations may be learnt from their languages and their places on the map. It is not in the earliest ages of history that they appear on the world-stage where Egyptians and Babylonians had long played the great parts. The Aryans become prominent within a thousand years before the Christian era, when in India there arises among them the religion of Buddha, now reckoned the most numerous in the world; when the Medes and Persians come into power, and Cyrus

appears with his conquering host; when the Greeks
bring their wondrous intellect to bear on art, science,
and philosophy; and the Romans set up the military
and legal system which gave them their empire. In
later ages our Teutonic nations, who made their first
appearance as the ravagers of culture, come to be its
promoters. The Aryan nations have kept up in the
modern world the career of conquest and the union with
other peoples which they began in præhistoric ages.
Outside the world known to the ancients, Aryan languages are now spoken on far continents and islands,
whether the men who speak them are white colonists
from Europe, who have slain or driven out the old
dwellers on the soil, or whether they have become blended
with the native nations as in Mexico and Peru.

To proceed now to the languages of the next family,
the Semitic, an idea of these can be most easily gained
from Hebrew. Any student seriously bent on the science
of language should learn at least enough Hebrew to spell
out a few chapters of Genesis, for all the other languages
commonly taught in England being of the Aryan family,
this will serve to bring his mind out of that groove, by
familiarizing him with speech of a different material.
A very moderate number of roots, mostly of three consonants, by altering their internal vowels and changing
their affixes, are made to form the greater part of the
language so regularly that Hebrew dictionaries are
arranged throughout by the roots. Thus from the root
m-l-ch are derived verb and noun forms with the sense
of reigning, as *mâlach* = he reigned, *mâlchû* = they
reigned, *yimloch* = he shall reign, *timloch* = thou shalt
reign, *melech* = king (familiar in the name of *Melchi-
zedek*, " king of righteousness "), *melâchim* = kings,
malchenû = our king, *malchâh* = queen, *mamlâchâh* =
kingdom, and so on. The principal languages belonging
to the Semitic family are the Assyrian, Hebrew and
Phœnician, Syrian, Arabic, and Ethiopic. The Assyrian
of the Nineveh inscriptions and the Arabic spoken by the
desert Beduins between them best represent the original
language they are all descended from. The ancient or
modern peoples speaking Semitic tongues belong mainly
to the dark-white race, the type in which they agree
being now most plainly seen in the Jewish countenance,
with its aquiline nose, full lips, and curly black hair.
Yet by features alone it would not have been possible to
distinguish the Jews, Assyrians, and Arabs, among the

mass of dark-white nations. Here is seen the value of
language, which comes in to show that a certain group
of nations are connected by common ancestry from an
ancient people, who spoke the lost tongue whence Arabic
and Hebrew are offshoots, and who in the ages when
history begins were dwelling in South-West Asia, and
sending forth their migrating tribes to found new nations,
whose acts in the world form one of the great chapters of
history. The conquering Assyrians took up and carried
on the older Chaldæan civilization. The Phœnicians
became the great merchants of the old world, with
trading colonies along the Mediterranean and commerce
in the far East; nor was it only stuffs and spices that they
carried, but they spread arts and thoughts into new
regions, and in their hands the clumsy hieroglyphic
writing became the alphabet. The Israelites, though as
a nation they never reached such power or culture,
made their conquests in the world of religion, and while
the crowd of deities worshipped in Assyrian and Phœnician temples vanished away, the worship of Jehovah
passed on into Christianity, and overspread the world.
Latest, the warrior-tribes of Arabia carried the banner
of their prophet among the nations around, and founded
the faith of Islam, a civilizing power in the Middle Ages,
and even in these days of its decay an influence across
the world from Western Africa to the islands of the far
East.

The language of the ancient Egyptians, though it
cannot be classed in the Semitic family with Hebrew,
has important points of correspondence, whether due
to the long intercourse between the two races in Egypt,
or to some deeper ancestral connexion; and such
analogies also appear in the Berber languages of North
Africa. These difficult questions can merely be mentioned here. Attempts have been made, though with
little result, to prove the Aryan and Semitic languages
themselves to be descended from a single parent tongue.
If it is so, then ages of change have so wiped away the
traces of common origin that philological comparison
fails to substantiate them. While speaking of the
Aryan and Semitic families of language, it should be
noticed that many philologists connect them as belonging
to one class, as being " inflecting " languages, or such
as can blend their roots and affixes, and alter the roots
themselves internally so that, as the beginner in Greek
grammar well knows, it is often no easy matter to see

where the root ends and the termination begins. The inflecting families have certainly a power of compact word-formation which has done much to give expressiveness and accuracy to such poetical and philosophical languages as Greek and Arabic. But the distinction is by no means clear between the structure of such inflecting languages and the agglutinating languages of other nations, as the Tatars. Could the Aryan and Semitic families be both traced back to the same family, this would not prove the whole white race to have had one original language, for the Georgian of the Caucasus, the Basque of the Pyrenees, and several more would still lie outside, apparently unconnected with either of the great families, or with one another.

In the middle and north of Asia, on the steppes or among the swamps and forests of the bleak north, wandering hordes of hunters or herdsmen show the squat-built brown-yellow Tatar or Mongolian type, and speak languages of one family, such as Manchu and Mongol. Although principally belonging to Asia, these Tatar or Turanian languages have established themselves in Europe. At a remote period, rude Tatar tribes had spread over northern Europe, but they were followed up and encroached on by the invading Aryans, till now only much-mixed outlying remnants of them, Esths, Finns, Lapps, are found speaking Tatar languages. In later ages, history records how armies of Tatar race, Huns and Turks, poured into Europe in their turn, subduing the Aryan peoples, so that now the Hungarian and Turkish languages remain records of these last waves of invasion from Central Asia. The Tatar hordes are first heard of in history as barbarians, as many tribes are still, but their chief nations becoming Buddhists, Mohammedans, or Christians, have adopted the civilization belonging to these religions. The Tatar languages are of the kind called agglutinative, forming words by putting first the root, which carries the sense, and is followed by suffixes strung on to modify it. Thus in Turkish the root *sev*, to love, makes *sevishdirilmediler*, they were not to be brought to love one another. In some languages of this class, a remarkable law of vowel-harmony compels the suffix to conform its vowel to that of the root it is attached to, as if to make clear to the hearer that it belongs to it; thus in Hungarian *ház* = house, forms *házam* = my house, but *szék* = chair, forms *székem* = my chair.

The dense population of South-East Asia, comprising the Burmese, the Siamese, and especially the Chinese, shows a type of complexion and feature plainly related to the Tatar or Mongolian, but the general character of their language is different. The Chinese language is made up of monosyllables, each a word with its own real or grammatical sense, so that our infant-school books in one syllable give some notion of Chinese sentences. Other neighbouring languages share this habit of using monosyllables, and as this limits them to an inconveniently small number of words, they have taken to the expedient of making the musical pitch or intonation alter the meaning, as in Siamese, where the syllable *ha*, according to the notes it is intoned on, means a pestilence, or the number five, or the verb to seek. Thus the intoning which in England serves to express emotion or distinguish question from answer is turned to account in the far East for making actually different words, an example how language catches at any available device when a means of expression is wanted. Looking on the map of Asia at this south-east group of nations, it is plainly not by accident that the people of such neighbouring districts should have come to talk in words of one syllable, but the habit seems to have come from a common ancestral source, and gives the whole set of languages a family character. These monosyllabic languages are often used to illustrate what the simple childlike constructions of man's primitive speech may have been like. But it is well to mention that Chinese or Siamese, simple as they are, must not be relied on as primitive languages. The childlike Chinese phrases may be not primitive at all, but may come of the falling away of older complicated grammar, much as our own English tends to cut short the long words and drop the inflexions used by our ancestors. Chinese simplicity of grammar by no means goes with simplicity of thought and life. The Chinese nation, like the Egyptian and the Babylonian, had been raised to a highly artificial civilization in ages before the Phœnicians and Greeks came out of barbarism. It is not yet clear to what race the old Babylonians belonged who spoke the Akkadian tongue, but this shows analogies which may connect it with the Tatar or Mongolian languages.

The Malays and Polynesians   , a varied and mixed population of partly Mongoloid race, are united over their immense ocean-district half round the globe by languages of one family, the Malayo-Polynesian, to which the Melanesian languages largely belong. The parent tongue of this family may have belonged to Asia, for in the Malay region the grammar is more complex, and words are found like *tasik* = sea and *langit* = sky, while in the distant islands of New Zealand and Hawaii these have come down to *tai* and *lai*, as though the language became shrunk and formless as the race migrated farther from home, and sank into the barbaric life of ocean islanders.

The continent of India has not lost the languages of the tribes who were in the land before the Aryan invasion gave rise to the Hindu population. Especially in the south whole nations, though they have taken to Hindu civilization, speak languages belonging to the Dravidian family, such as Tamil, Telugu, and Canarese. The importance of this element of Indian population may be seen by these non-Aryan tongues still extending over most of the great triangle of India south of the Nerbudda, besides remnants in districts to the north. Yet Aryan dialects are spoken in India by many mixed tribes who may have little of Aryan blood. In the forests of Ceylon are found the only people in the world leading a savage life who speak an Aryan language akin to ours. These are the Veddas or " hunters," shy wild men who build bough huts, and live on game and wild honey, the children, as it seems, of forest-natives mingled with Singhalese outcasts whose language in a broken-down state they speak.

Among negroid peoples, whether or not the Andamaners and Papuas are connected by race with the African negroes, their languages show no connexion. Nor do all African negroes speak languages of one family, but some, such as the Mandingo, seem separate from the great language-family of Central and South Africa, named the Bantu from tribes calling themselves simply " men " (*ba-ntu*). One of the chief peculiarities of the Bantu languages is their working (just unlike the Tatar languages) by putting prefixes in front. Thus the African magician is called *mganga*, the plural of which is *waganga*, magicians. The Kafirs of a certain district bear the well-known name of the *basuto*, which is a plural form, a single native being called *mosuto*, while his country is *lesuto*, his language *sesuto*, and his character or quality *bosuto*. In South Africa lives a very different language-family, the Hottentot-Bushman, remarkable for the way

in which " clicks," much like what among us nurses
make to children and coachmen to horses, do duty as
consonants in words. Lastly, turning to America, the
native languages fall into a variety of families. Some
of these are known to English readers by a word or two,
as the Eskimo of the Arctic coasts by the name of the
kayak or single boat on which our sport canoes are
modelled; the Algonquin which prevailed from New
England to Virginia at the time of the early colonists,
and whence we have *moccasin* and *tomahawk*; the
Aztec of Mexico known by the *ocelot* and the *cacao-*
bean; the Tupi-Carib of the West Indies and the Brazilian
forests, the home of the *toucan* and *jaguar*; lastly the
Quichua or Peruvian, the language of the *inca*.
    In concluding this account of the chief families of
language, it is to be noticed that there are many more,
some consisting of only a few dialects or a single one.
Altogether a list of fifty or a hundred might perhaps be
made, of which no one has been satisfactorily shown to
be related to any other. It may, indeed, be expected
that often two or three which now seem separate may
prove on closer examination to be branches of one family,
but there seems no prospect of the families all coming
together in this way as offshoots of one original language.
The question whether there was one primitive speech,
or many, has been in past times most useful in encouraging the scientific comparison of languages. Both
theories claim to account for the actual state of language
in the world. On the one hand it may be argued that
the languages descended from the primitive tongue have
branched off so far apart as often no longer to show their
connexion; on the other hand, if there were many
primitive languages, of which those that survived have
given rise to families, this would come to much the same
state of things. But if, as seems likely, the original
formation of language did not take place all at once, but
was a gradual process extending through ages, and not
absolutely stopped even now, then it is not a hopeful
task to search for primitive languages at all (see page 104).
In the present improved state of philology it answers
better to work back from known languages to the lost
ancestral languages whence they must have come down.
It has been seen that this study leads to excellent results
as to the history, not only of the languages themselves,
but of the nations speaking them, as when it gives the
clue to the peopling of the South Sea Islands, or proves

some remote ancestral connexion between the ancient Britons and the English and Danes who came after them to our land. Yet though language is so valuable a help and guide in national history, it must not be trusted as if it could give the whole origin of a race, or go back to its beginning. All negroes do not speak languages of one family, nor all yellow, or brown, or white men. In exploring the early life of nations, their languages may lead us far back, often much farther than historical records, but they seem hardly to reach anywhere near the origins of the great human races, still less to the general origin of mankind.

CHAPTER VII

WRITING

TAUGHT as we are to read and write in early childhood, we hardly realize the place this wondrous double art fills in civilized life, till we see how it strikes the barbarian who has not even a notion that such a thing can be. John Williams, the South Sea Island missionary, tells how once being busy carpentering, and having forgotten his square, he wrote a message for it with a bit of charcoal on a chip, and sent this to his wife by a native chief, who, amazed to find that the chip could talk without a mouth, for long afterwards carried it hung by a string round his neck, and told his wondering countrymen what he saw it do. So in South Africa a black messenger carrying a letter has been known to hide it under a stone while he loitered by the way, lest it should tell tales of him, as it did of whatever was going on. Yet the art of writing, mysterious as it seemed to these rude men, was itself developed by a few steps of invention, which if not easy to make, are at any rate easy to understand when made. Even uncivilized races have made the first step, that of picture-writing. Had the missionary merely made a sketch of his L-square on the chip, it would have carried his message, and the native would have understood the whole business as a matter of course. Beginning at this primitive stage, it will be possible to follow thence through its whole course the history of writing and printing.

Fig. 47 shows a specimen of picture-writing as used by the hunting tribes of North America. It records an expedition across Lake Superior, led by a chief who is shown on horseback with his magical drumstick in his hand. There were in all fifty-one men in five canoes, the first of them being led by the chief's ally, whose

name, Kishkemunazee, that is, Kingfisher, is shown by
the drawing of this bird. Their reaching the other side
seems to be shown by the land-tortoise, the well-known
emblem of land, while by the picture of three suns
under the sky it is recorded that the crossing took three
days. Now most of this, childlike in its simplicity,
consists in making pictures of the very objects meant
to be talked of. But there are devices which go beyond
this mere imitation. Thus when the tortoise is put to
represent land, it is no longer a mere imitation, but has
become an emblem or symbol. And where the bird is
drawn to mean not a real kingfisher, but a man of that
name, we see the first step toward phonetic writing
or sound-writing, the principle of which is to make a

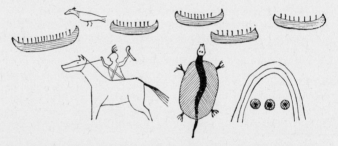

Fig. 47.—Picture-writing, rock near Lake Superior (after Schoolcraft).

picture stand for the sound of a spoken word. How
men may have made the next move toward writing
may be learnt from the common child's game of *rebus*,
that is, writing words " by things." Like many other
games, this one keeps up in child's sport what in earlier
ages was man's earnest. Thus if one writes the word
" water-man " by a picture of a water-jug and a man,
this is drawing the meaning of the word in a way hardly
beyond the American Indian's picture of the kingfisher.
But it is very different when in a child's book of puzzles
one finds the drawing of a water-can, a man being shot,
and a date-fruit, this representing in rebus the word
" can-di-date." For now what the pictures have come
to stand for is no longer their meaning, but their mere
sound. This is true phonetic writing, though of a rude
kind, and shows how the practical art of writing really

came to be invented. This invention seems to have been made more than once, and in somewhat different ways. The old Mexicans, before the arrival of the Spaniards, had got so far as to spell their names of persons and places by pictures, rebus fashion. Even when they began to be Christianized, they contrived to use their picture-writing for the Latin words of their new religion. Thus they painted a flag (*pan*), a stone (*te*), a prickly-pear (*noch*) (Fig. 48), which were together

pa-   te   noch   te.

FIG. 48.—*Pater noster* in Mexican picture-writing (after Aubin).

pronounced *pa-te-noch-te*, and served to spell *pater noster*, in a way that was tolerably exact for Mexicans who had no *r* in their language. In the same way they ended the prayer with the picture of water (*a*), and aloe (*me*), to express *amen*.

This leads on to a more important system of writing. Looking at the ordinary Chinese characters on tea-chests or vases, one would hardly think they ever had to do with pictures of things. But there are fortunately pre-

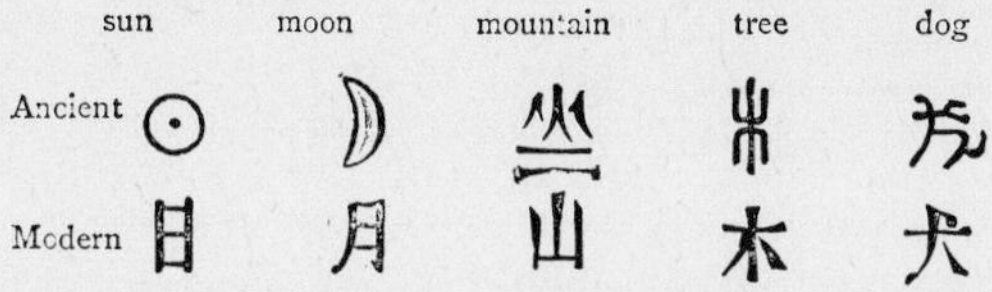

	sun	moon	mountain	tree	dog
Ancient					
Modern					

FIG. 49.—Chinese ancient pictures and later cursive forms (after Endlicher).

served certain early Chinese characters, known as the " ancient pictures," which show how what were at first distinctly formed sketches of objects came to be dashed off in a few strokes of the rabbit's-hair pencil, till they passed into the meaningless-looking cursive forms now in use, as is seen in Fig. 49.

The Chinese did not stop short at making such mere pictures of objects, which goes but little way toward writing. The inventors of the present mode of Chinese writing wanted to represent the spoken sounds, but here they were put in a difficulty by their language

consisting of monosyllables, so that one word has many
different meanings. To meet this they devised an
ingenious plan of making compound characters, or
" pictures and sounds," in which one part gives the
sound, while the other gives the sense. To give an idea
of this, suppose it were agreed that a picture of a box
should stand for the sound *box*. As, however, this sound
has several meanings, some sign must be added to show
which is intended. Thus a key might be drawn beside
it to show it is a *box* to put things in, or a leaf if it is to
mean the plant called *box*, or a hand if it is intended
for a *box* on the ear, or a whip would show that it was
to signify the *box* of a coach. This would be for us a
clumsy proceeding, but it would be a great advance
beyond mere picture-writing, as it would make sure at
once of the sound and the meaning. Thus in Chinese,
the sound *chow* has various meanings, as ship, fluff,
flickering, basin, loquacity. Therefore the character

舟　翢　焀　洀　誂

| ship | fluff | flickering | basin | loquacity |

FIG. 50.—Chinese compound characters, pictures and sounds.

which represents a ship, *chow*, which is placed first in
Fig. 50, is repeated afterwards with additional characters
to show which particular meaning of *chow* is intended.
A recognizable pair of feathers is placed by it to mean
chow = fluff; next, the sign of fire makes it *chow* =
flickering; next, the sign of water makes it *chow* =
basin; and lastly, the character for speech is joined to
it to make *chow* = loquacity. These examples, though
far from explaining the whole mystery of Chinese writing,
give some idea of the principles of its sound-characters
and keys or determinative signs, and show why a Chinese
has to master such an immensely complicated set of
characters in order to write his own language. To have
introduced such a method of writing was an effort of
inventive genius in the ancient Chinese, which their
modern descendants show their respect for by refusing
to improve upon it. At the same time it is not entirely
through conservatism that they have not taken to
phonetic writing like that of the western nations, for
this would, for instance, confuse the various kinds of
chow which their present characters enable them to keep

separate. But the Japanese, whose language was better
suited than the Chinese for being written phonetically,
actually made themselves a phonetic system out of the
Chinese characters. Selecting certain of these, they cut
them down into signs to express sounds, one to stand
for *i*, another for *ro*, another for *ha*, &c. Thus a set of
forty-seven such characters (which they call accordingly
the *iroha*) serve as the foundation of a system with
which for centuries Japanese has been written and its
dictionaries arranged by sound.

Next, as to the cuneiform writing, such as is to be
seen at the British Museum on the huge man-headed
bulls of Nineveh, or on the flat baked bricks which were
pages of books in the library of Sennacherib. The marks
like wedges or arrow-heads arranged in groups and rows
do not look much like pictures of objects. Yet there is
evidence that they came at first from picture-writing;
for instance, the sun was represented by a rude figure
of it made by four strokes arranged round. Of the
groups of characters in an inscription, some serve directly
to represent objects, as man, woman, river, house, while
other groups are read phonetically as standing for
syllables. The inventors of this ancient system appear
to have belonged to the Akkadian group of nations, the
founders of early Babylonian civilization. In later ages
the Assyrians and Persians learned to write their languages by cuneiform characters, in inscriptions which
remain to this day as their oldest records. But the
cuneiform writing was cumbrous in the extreme, and
had to give way when it came into competition with the
alphabet. To understand the origin of that invention,
it is necessary to go back to a plan of writing which
dates from antiquity probably even higher than the
cuneiform of Babylonia, namely, the hieroglyphics of
Egypt.

The earliest known hieroglyphic inscriptions of Egypt
belong to a period approaching 4000 B.C. Even at this
ancient time the plan of writing was so far developed
that the scribes had the means of spelling any word
phonetically, when they chose. But though the Egyptians had thus come to writing by sound, they only
trusted to it in part, combining it with signs which are
evidently remains of earlier picture-writing. Thus the
mere pictures of an ox, a star, a pair of sandals, may
stand for ox, star, sandals. Even where they spelt
words by their sounds, they had a remarkable way of

adding what are called determinatives, which are pictures
to confirm or explain the meaning of the spelt word.
One short sentence given as an example from Renouf's
Egyptian Grammar, shows all these devices.   The meaning is : " I (am) the Sun-god coming forth from the

N K one	sun god one	P R walk	M	horizon T one	R	X F T.	enemy pl. F
nuk	ra netar	per coming forth	em	xut horizon	er against	xeftu—f enemies—his	
I	sun god		from				

horizon against his enemies."   Here part of the pictures
of animals and things are letters to be read into Egyptian
words, as shown underneath.   But others are still real
pictures, intended to stand for what they represent.
The sun is shown by his picture, with a one-mark below,
and followed by the battle-axe, which is the symbol of
divinity, while farther on comes a picture of the horizon
with the sun on it.   Beside these, some of the figures
are determinative pictures to explain the words, the
verb to walk being followed by an explanatory pair of
legs, and the word enemy having the picture of an
enemy after it, and then three strokes, the sign of
plurality.   It seems that the Egyptians began with mere
picture-writing like that of the barbarous tribes of
America, and though in after ages they came to use
some figures as phonetic characters or letters, they never
had the strength of mind to rely on them entirely, but
went on using the old pictures as well.   How they were
led to make a picture stand for a sound is not hard to
see.   In the figure a character may be noticed which is
read R.   This is an outline of an open mouth, and
indeed is often used to represent a mouth; but the
Egyptian word for mouth being RO, the sign came to
be used as a character or letter to spell the sound RO
or R wherever it was wanted.   So much of the history
of the art of writing may thus be read in a single
hieroglyphic sentence.

These carefully drawn hieroglyphic or " sacred-sculp-
ture " pictures, used as they were for the solemn records
of church and state, were kept up for sacred purposes
into the time of the Greek dynasty, and even the Roman

empire in Egypt. Indeed after the secret of deciphering them had been lost for many ages, the names of Ptolemy and Cleopatra were among the first identified by Dr. Thomas Young. But from very ancient times the Egyptian scribes, finding the elaborate pictures too troublesome for business writing on papyrus, brought them down (much as the Chinese did theirs) to a few quick strokes. These were the " hieratic " characters, a few of which are seen in the second column of Fig. 51 following their hieroglyphic originals. Yet even when they used these, the Egyptian scribes never freed themselves from the trammels of their early picture-writing, so as to do away with the unnecessary multitude of phonetic signs, and drop the determinative pictures as useless. This great move was made by foreigners.

Tacitus, in a passage of his *Annals* describing the origin of letters, says that the Egyptians first depicted thoughts of the mind by figures of animals, which oldest monuments of human memory are to be seen stamped on the rocks, so that they (the Egyptians) appear as the inventors of letters, which the Phœnician navigators brought thence to Greece, obtaining the glory as if they had discovered what they really borrowed. This account may be substantially true, but it does not give the Phœnicians credit for their practical good sense, which they were able to follow, being strangers and not bound by the sacred traditions of Egypt. Possibly the Phœnicians (or some other Semitic nation), when they learnt the Egyptian hieroglyphics, saw that the picture signs mixed with the spelt words had become mere surplusage, and that all they really wanted was a small number of signs to write the sound of their words with, and thus may have been invented the earliest so-called Phœnician alphabet. Some of its letters may have been actually copied from the Egyptian characters, as is seen by Fig. 51, which shows a selection from the compared set drawn up by De Rougé, so arranged as to pass from the original Egyptian hieroglyphic to its hieratic form in the current writing, and thence to the corresponding letter of the Phœnician alphabet, with its value in our letters and examples of similar letters in other well-known forms of the alphabet.

It seems to have been about the tenth century B.C. that the original alphabet was made, forms of which were used by the Moabites, Phœnicians, Israelites, and other nations of the Semitic family to write their lan-

guages. A curious proof that it was among these Semitic
nations that the *alphabet* was first shaped has come
down to us in its name. To understand this, it has to
be noticed that the letters were named each by a word
beginning with it. The Hebrew forms of these names
are familiar to English readers from Psalm cxix., where
they stand in their order *aleph* or " ox " for *a, beth* or
" house " for *b, gimel* or " camel " for *g,* and so on.

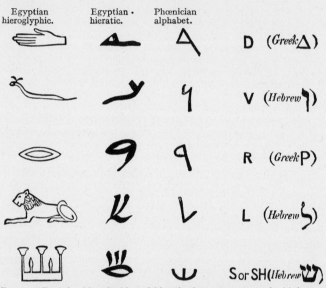

FIG. 51.—Egyptian hieroglyphic and hieratic characters compared with letters
of Phœnician and later alphabets (after De Rougé).

This is a natural way of naming letters; indeed our
Anglo-Saxon ancestors had another such set of names
belonging to the rune-letters they used in old times,
calling their letter *b, beorc* or " birch," their letter *m,
man,* their letter *th, thorn.* Now what confirms the
history that the Phœnicians had the alphabet first and
the Greeks learnt the art of writing from them is that
the Greeks actually borrowed the Phœnician names for
the letters, which were like the Hebrew ones just given,
and which in Greek passed into the well-known forms
alpha, beta, gamma, &c. Thence comes the word *alphabet,*

which thus preserves the traces of the letters having been made and named by the Phœnicians, having passed from them to the Greeks and Latins, and at last came down to us. It is interesting to look through a book of alphabets, where not only may be traced the history of the Greek and Latin letters, and others plainly related to them, such as the Gothic and Slavonic, but it may even be made out that others at first sight so unlike as the Northmen's runes and the Sanskrit characters, must all be descendants of the primitive alphabet. Thus the Brahman writes his Veda, the Moslem his Koran, the Jew his Old and the Christian his New Testament, in signs which had their origin in the pictures on temple walls in ancient Egypt.

Such changes, however, have taken place in writing, that it often requires most careful comparison to trace them. If one showed a Chinese an English note scribbled in modern handwriting, it would not be quite easy to prove to him that the characters were derived from old Phœnician ones such as those in Fig. 51. Our running-hand must be traced back through copybook-hand, and from small letters to Roman capitals, and so farther back. Readers will find this worth doing as an exercise. They may also be recommended to look at old-fashioned English writing, such as a Parish Register of the 16th century, which will show how much more the writing of that period was like the crabbed hand in which it is still thought proper to write German. We English fortunately learnt a simpler and better style from the Italian writing-masters, who taught us the " Roman hand " which Malvolio recognizes in *Twelfth Night.* Alterations in letters were not only made for convenience, but also for decoration. Thus among the tribes of the Middle Ages there arose fanciful varieties such as what we call Old English and Black Letter, and still use for ornamental purposes. This style of manuscript being in fashion when printing was introduced in Europe, English books were at first printed in it, as many German books are still. One has only to read a page of a German book so printed to satisfy oneself how great a gain of clearness it was to discard these letters with forms broken by unmeaning lines, and return to the more distinct Latin letters we now use.

Beside these general changes of alphabet, the history of writing shows how from time to time alterations have been made as to particular letters. The original

Phœnician alphabet was weak in vowels, in a way which
the learner of Hebrew can understand when he tries to
read it without the vowel points, which are more modern
marks put on for the benefit of those who do not know
the language well enough to tell how each word should be
pronounced. The Phœnician alphabet did not altogether
suit the writers of Greek and Latin, who altered some
letters and made new ones in order to write their languages more perfectly, and thus other nations have
made free in adding, dropping, and altering letters and
their sounds, to get the means required for each to
express its own tongue. To such causes may be traced
letters not known to the primitive alphabet, such as
Greek Ω and English W, which are explained by their
names of Omega or " great-O," and " double-U." The
digamma or F fell out of use in Greek, and the two
valuable Anglo-Saxon *th*-letters, ð and þ, are lost to
modern English. The letters H and X are examples of
letters which in Greek served purposes other than those
English uses them for. By arranging their alphabets
to suit the sounds of their languages, nations contrive
with more or fewer letters to spell with some accuracy,
Italian managing this fairly with twenty-two letters,
while Russian uses thirty-six. English has an alphabet
of twenty-six letters, but works them without regular
system, so that our spelling and pronunciation disagree
at every turn. One cause of this state of things has
been the attempt to keep up side by side two different
spellings, English and French, as where *g* is used to
spell both the English word *get* and the French word
gentle. Another cause has been the attempt to keep up
ancient sounds in writing, although they have been
dropped in speaking; thus in *throuGH, casTle, scene*, the
now silent letters are relics of sounds which used to be
really heard in Anglo-Saxon *thurH*, Latin *casTellum*,
Greek *sKēnē*. What makes this the more perplexing
is that in many words English writing does simply
try to spell what is actually spoken; English *tail* does
not keep up the lost guttural of Anglo-Saxon *tægel*, nor
does English *palsy* retain letters for the sounds that
have vanished in its derivation from French *paralysie*.
Our wrong spelling is the result not of rule but of want
of rule, and among its most curious cases are those
where the grammarians have managed to put both sound
and etymology wrong at once, writing *island, rhyme,
scythe*, where their forefathers rationally wrote *iland*,

rime, sithe. It is reckoned that on an average, a year
of an English child's education is wasted in overcoming
the defects of the present mode of spelling.

The invention of writing was the great movement
by which mankind rose from barbarism to civilization.
How vast its effect was may be best measured by looking
at the low condition of tribes still living without it,
dependent on memory for their traditions and rules of
life, and unable to amass knowledge as we do by keeping
records of events, and storing up new observations for
the use of future generations. Thus it is no doubt
right to draw the line between barbarian and civilized
where the art of writing comes in, for this gives permanence to history, law, and science. Such knowledge
so goes with writing that, when a man is spoken of as
learned, we at once take it to mean that he has read
many books, which are the main source men learn from.
Already in ancient times, as compositions of value came
to be written, there sprang up a class of copyists or
transcribers, whose business was to multiply books. In
Alexandria or Rome one could go to the bibliopole or
bookseller and buy a manuscript of Demosthenes or
Livy, and in later ages the copying of religious books,
splendidly illuminated, became a common occupation,
especially in monasteries. But manuscripts were costly,
only the few scholars could read them, and so no doubt
it would have remained had not a new art come in to
multiply writing.

This was a process simple enough in itself, and indeed
well known from remote ages. Every Egyptian or
Babylonian who smeared some black on his signet-ring
or engraved cylinder, and took off a copy, had made
the first step towards printing. But easy as the further
application now seems to us, no one in the Old World
saw it. It appears to have been the Chinese who
invented the plan of engraving a whole page of characters
on a wood-block and printing off many copies. They
may have begun as early as the sixth century, and at
any rate in the tenth century they were busy printing
books. The Chinese writing, from its enormous diversity
of characters, is not well suited to printing by movable
types, but there is a record that this plan was early
devised among them, having been carried on with
separate terra-cotta types in the eleventh century.
Moslem writers early in the fourteenth century describe
Chinese printing, so that it was probably through them

that the art found its way to Europe, where not long afterwards the so-called " block-books," printed from whole page wood-blocks after the Chinese manner, make their appearance, followed by books printed with movable types. Few questions have been more debated by anti-quaries than the claims of Gutenberg, Faust, and the others to their share of honour as the inventors of print-ing. Great as was the service these worthies did to the world, it is only fair to remember that what they did was but to improve the practical application of a Chinese invention. Since their time progress has been made in cheapening types, making paper by machinery, improv-ing the presses, and working them by steam-power, but the idea remains the same. Such is, in few words, the history of the art of printing, to which perhaps, more than to any other influence, is due the difference of our modern life from that of the Middle Ages.

In examining these methods of writing, we began with the rude hunter's pictures, passing on to the Egyptian's use of a picture to represent the sound of its name, then to the breaking down of the picture into a mere sound-sign, till in this last stage the connexion between figure and sound becomes so apparently arbitrary, that the child has to be taught, this sign stands for A, this for B. In curious contrast with this is the modern invention of the phonograph, where the actual sound spoken into the vibrating diaphragm marks indentations in the travelling strip of tinfoil, by which the diaphragm can be afterwards caused to repeat the vibrations and re-utter the sound. When one listens to the tones coming forth from the strip of foil, the South Sea Islander's fancy of the talking chip seems hardly unreasonable.

CHAPTER VIII

ARTS OF LIFE

THE arts by which man defends and maintains himself, and holds rule over the world he lives in, depend so much on his use of instruments, that it will be well to begin with some account of tools and weapons, tracing them from their earliest and rudest forms.

Man is sometimes called, to distinguish him from all lower creatures, the " tool-using animal." This distinction holds good in a general way, marking off man with his spear and hatchet from the bull goring with his horns, or the beaver carpentering with his teeth. But it is instructive to see how plainly the ape tribes, coming nearest to ourselves in having hands, have also rudiments of the implement-using faculty. Untaught by man, they defend themselves with missiles, as when orangs in the durian trees furiously pelt passers-by with the thorny fruit. The chimpanzee in the forests is said to crack nuts with a stone, as in our Zoological Gardens monkeys are often taught to do by the keepers, where they take readily to the use of these and more difficult implements, as soon as the thought has been put into their minds.

The lowest order of implements are those which nature provides ready-made, or wanting just a finish; such are pebbles for slinging or hammering, sharp stone splinters to cut or scrape with, branches for clubs and spears, thorns or teeth to pierce with. These of course are oftenest found in use among savages, yet they sometimes last on. in the civilized world, as when we catch up any stick to kill a rat or snake with, or when in the south of France women shell the almonds with a smooth pebble, much as the apes at Regent's Park would do. The

higher implements used by mankind are often plainly
improvements on some natural object, but they are
adapted by art in ways that beasts have no notion of, so
that it is a better definition of man to call him the
" tool-maker " than the " tool-user." Looking at the
various sorts of implements, we see that they were not
invented all at once by sudden flashes of genius, but
evolved, or one might almost say grown, by small successive changes.   It will be noticed also that the instrument which at first did roughly several kinds of work,
afterwards varied off in different ways to suit each
particular purpose, so as to give rise to several different
instruments.   A Zulu seen at work scraping the stick
that is to be the shaft of his assegai, with the very iron
head that is to be fixed on it, may give an idea what
early tool-making was like, before men clearly understood
that the pattern of instruments suitable for a lance-head
was not the best for cutting and scraping.   We should
be horrified at the thought of the blacksmith pulling out
one of our teeth with his pincers, as our forefathers
would have let him do ; the forceps we expect the dentist
to use is indeed a variety of the smith's tool, but it is a
special variety for a special purpose.   Thus in the history
of instruments, the tools of the mechanic cannot well be
kept separate from the weapons of the hunter or soldier,
for in several cases it will be seen that both tool and
weapon had their origin in some earlier instrument that
served alike to break skulls and coco-nuts, or to hack
at the limbs of trees and of men.
    Among the simplest of weapons is the thick stick or
cudgel, which when heavier or knobbed passes into the
club.   Rude champions have delighted in the ferocious
roughness of such a gnarled club as Hercules in the
pictures carries on his shoulder, while others spent their
leisure hours in elegant shaping and carving, like that
of the South Sea Island clubs to be seen in museums.
From savage through barbaric times the war-club lasted
on into the Middle Ages of Europe, when knights still
smashed helmets in with their heavy maces.   Mostly
used as a weapon, it only now and then appears in
peaceful arts, as in the ribbed clubs with which the
Polynesian women beat out bark cloth.   It is curious to
see how the rudest of primitive weapons, after its serious
warlike use has ceased, survives as a symbol of power,
when the mace is carried as emblem of the royal
authority, and is laid on the table during the sitting of

Parliament or the Royal Society. While the club has been generally a weapon, the hammer has been generally an implement. Its history begins with the smooth heavy pebble held in the hand, such as African blacksmiths to this day forge their iron with, on another smooth stone as anvil. It was a great improvement to fasten the stone hammer on a handle; this was done in very ancient times, as is seen by the stone heads being grooved or bored on purpose (see Fig. 54 *i*). Though the iron hammer has superseded these, a trace of the older use of stone remains in our very name *hammer*, which is

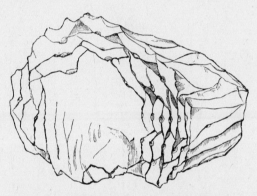

FIG. 52.—Gunflint-maker's core and flakes (Evans).

the old Scandinavian *hamarr*, meaning both rock and hammer.

From beating we come to hacking and cutting. At the earliest times known of man's life on the earth, his pointed and edged instruments of sharp stone are among his chief relics. Even in the mammoth-period he had already learnt not to be content with accidental chips of flint, but knew how to knock off two-edged flakes. This art of flaking flint or other suitable stones is the foundation of stone-implement making. Perhaps the best idea of it may be gained from the Suffolk gunflint makers who at this day carry on the primæval craft, though with better tools and for so different a purpose. Fig. 52 shows a gunflint-maker's core of flint, with the flakes replaced where he has knocked them off, and the mark of the blow is seen which brought away each flake. The flakes made by Stone Age men for instruments may be three-sided like the Australian flake in Fig. 53 *b*. But the more convenient flat-backed shape *a, c*, has been used from the earliest known times. The flint core, Fig. 54 *f*, with the flakes *e* taken from it, shows how by previous flaking or trimming it was prepared for the new flake to come off with a suitable back. The finest flakes are those not struck off, but forced off by pressure with a flaking-tool of wood or horn. The neat Danish flake, Fig. 53 *c*, was no doubt

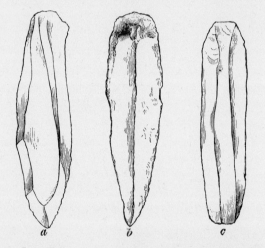

FIG. 53.—Stone Flakes :—*a*, Palæolithic; *b*, Modern Australia; *c*, Ancient Denmark.

made so, and the still more beautiful sharp flakes of obsidian with which the native barbers of Mexico, to the astonishment of Cortes' soldiers, used to shave. A stone flake just as struck off may be fit for use as a knife, or as a spear-head like that in Fig. 58 *a*; or by further chipping it may be made into a scraper, spear-head, arrow-head, or awl, like those in Fig. 54.

The oldest known tribes of men have left in the drift gravels of the quaternary or mammoth-period not only rough flakes like Fig. 53 *a*, but the stone implements already mentioned in the first chapter, of which the drawing is here repeated in Fig. 55. It is not clear

whether any of them were fixed in handles, but there
are specimens found which have only one end chipped

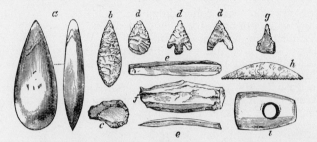

FIG. 54.—Later Stone Age (neolithic) implements. *a*, stone celt or hatchet; *b*,
flint spear-head; *c*, scraper; *d*, arrow-heads; *e*, flint flake-knives; *f*, core
from which flint-flakes taken off; *g*, flint-awl; *h*, flint saw; *i*, stone hammer-
head.

to a point, but the other end of the flint left smooth, so
that they were evidently grasped in the hand to hack
with. When edged all round, as in the figure, this type

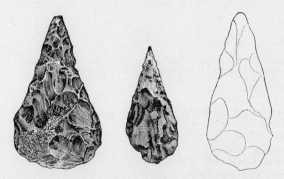

FIG. 55.—Earlier Stone Age (palæolithic) flint picks or hatchets.

would pass into the celt, with its broad end used for
chopping. There is nothing to show that the men of
the old drift-period ever ground a stone implement to
an edge. Thus their stone implements were far inferior
to the neatly-shaped and sharp-edged ground celts of

the later Stone Age, Fig. 54 *a*, Fig. 56 *a*. The word celt used for the various chisel-like instruments of rude and ancient tribes is a convenient term, taken from Latin *celtis*, a chisel, in the Vulgate translation of Job xix. 24, "vel celte sculpantur in silice"; "or that they were graven with a chisel (*celte*) in the rock." It is uncertain whence Jerome got the word, which he uses elsewhere, and which has passed on his authority into later language. It may be worth while to mention that the name of the implements called *celts* has nothing to do with the name of the people called *Celts or Kelts*. A stone celt only requires a handle to make it into a

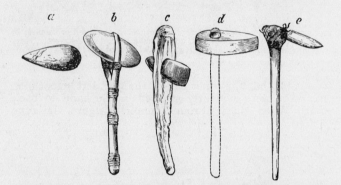

Fig. 56.—Stone Axes, &c. *a*, polished stone celt (England); *b*, pebble ground to edge and mounted in twig handle (modern Botocudo, Brazil); *c*, celt fixed in wooden club (Ireland); *d*, stone axe bored for handle (England); *e*, stone adze (modern Polynesia).

hatchet. This was done very simply by the forest Indians of Brazil, who would pick up a suitable water-worn pebble, rub one end down to an edge, and bind it in a twig, Fig. 56 *b*. Another rude way of mounting a celt was to stick it into a club, so as to form a woodman's or warrior's axe such as *c*, which shows one dug out of a bog in Ireland. The most advanced method was to drill a hole through the stone blade to take the handle as in *d*. When the stone blade is fixed with the edge across, the tool becomes a carpenter's adze, as *e*, which is the instrument used by the canoe-building Polynesians.

When metal came into use, the forms of the stone implements were imitated in copper, bronze, or iron, and though the patterns were of course lightened and

otherwise improved to suit the new material, it may be
plainly seen that the stone hatchets and spear-heads in
museums are the ancestors (so to speak) of the metal
ones made ever since.   But also the use of metal brought
in new and useful forms which stone was not suited to.
An idea of these important changes may be gained by
careful looking at the series of metal cutting-instruments
in Fig. 57.   We begin with *a*, which is an Egyptian
bronze battle-axe, not very far changed from the stone
hatchet.   But *b*, the bronze falchion, carried also by
Egyptian warriors, is a sort of axe-blade with the handle
not at the back, but shifted down; this convenient
alteration could not have been made in the stone hatchet,

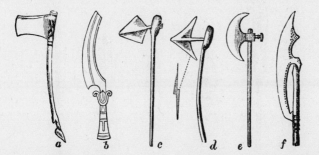

FIG. 57.—*a*, Egyptian battle-axe; *b*, Egyptian falchion; *c* and *d*, Bechuana
    battle-axes; *e*, English horseman's axe (16th century); *f*, German pole-axe
    (15th century).

which would have broken in the shank at the first blow,
while in metal it answers perfectly.   In *c* and *d* is seen
a remarkable transformation of another kind, where in
Africa the iron spear-blade passes into the battle-axe,
retaining (as if to show its history) the ogee-section
originally characteristic of the missile weapon.   The
battle-axes thus developed show resemblance to the
familiar European form *e*, which however seems to have
arisen in a different way, being developed from the
hatchet.   The pole-axe *f* shows further modification,
the lower point of the blade being actually attached to
the haft, so as to give greater length and strength to the
cutting edge.   These instances will serve to give an idea
of the varied lines of growth by which edged weapons
have assumed their modern shapes.   Yet through all it

seems clear that these instruments, whether tools or
weapons, or such as, like the bill-hooks of the early
English and the modern Malays, served alike for peace
and war, may have all originated from early metal
instruments, themselves derived from still earlier instruments of stone.

From the early stone spear-heads another set of
weapons seem to have gradually arisen, as may be seen
in Fig. 58. Looking at the spear from the Admiralty
Islands, *a*, the head of which is a large flake of obsidian,
it is plain that such a spear, when the shaft is broken

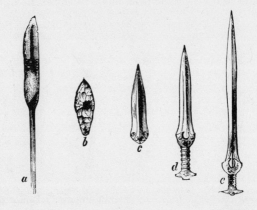

FIG. 58.—*a*, Stone spear-head (Admiralty Is.); *b*, stone spear-head or dagger-
blade (England); *c*, iron spear-head knife (Africa); *d*, bronze dagger; *e*,
bronze leaf-shaped sword.

off short, becomes a dagger. The daggers made by
these natives are in fact shaftless spear-heads, and one
often cannot tell whether the flint blades of shapes like
b, which are dug up in Europe, were intended for mounting as spears or as daggers. Now the brittleness of
stone was against the use of stone blades more than a
few inches long, but when metal came in, the blades
could be made long, taper, and sharp, thus developing
into two-edged daggers of deadly effect. In old Egyptian
pictures warriors are seen armed with spear and dagger,
these two weapons having blades of similar shape, so
that the dagger may be described as a large spear-head
with a hilt to grasp in the hand. It seems as though

the metal dagger, by further lengthening, passed into the two-edged sword, a weapon impossible in stone. To give an idea how this may have come about, Fig. 58 shows specimens, *d* and *e*, from the bronze-period of Northern Europe. Straight two-edged swords may of course be used for cut or thrust, or both. But on placing side by side a one-edged sabre and a two-edged broadsword or rapier, it will not be seen that though both are called swords, and are fitted up with similar hilts, hand-guards, and sheaths, they are nevertheless two weapons of separate nature, the sabre having passed into a form admirably suited for a cutting stroke, while the rapier retains the character of a thrusting weapon, which it inherits from the original spear. This last spear-type, of which one modern development is the bayonet, has mostly served for warlike purposes. Yet it is not unknown as a peaceful implement, as may be seen in African two-edged knives, which are evidently derived from spear-heads; one of these is represented by *c* in the figure, and also in the instrument which our surgeons, conscious of its original model, call the little spear or *lancet*.

To proceed to other kinds of tools. Thorns, pointed splinters of bone, or flint flakes worked to a point (Fig. 54 *g*), served early tribes of men as borers. The saw probably invented itself from a jagged flint flake, which afterwards became the more artificial flint saw, Fig. 54 *h*. Thus the men of the Stone Age had in rude and early forms some of the principal tools, which were improved upon in the ages of metal. It is interesting to look in Wilkinson's *Ancient Egyptians* at the contents of the Egyptian carpenter's tool-basket, where the bronze adze, saw, chisels, &c., show traces of likeness to the old stone implements. On the other hand, this Egyptian set of tools, and still more those of the ancient Greek and Roman carpenters, come remarkably near those we are using at this day. One difference which kept the ancient carpenters below ours was that they had not got beyond nails, never having seized the idea of the screws which are so essential to modern construction, nor of such tools as the screw-auger and gimlet, which depend on the screw for their action. ' Among the ancient cultured nations of Egypt and Assyria, handicrafts had already come to a stage which could only have been reached by thousands of years of progress. In museums may still be examined the work of their joiners, stone-

cutters, goldsmiths, wonderful in skill and finish, and
often putting to shame the modern artificer. Of course
these results were obtained by the ancient craftsman
with what we should consider a wasteful expenditure of
labour. The use of steel and other improvements have
given the modern workman great advantages, and, what
is more, the modern world has utterly outstripped the
ancient in the use of machines, as will be more fully
seen presently when the examination of the simpler
instruments has been gone through.

To continue the survey of weapons. The cudgel or
club is hurled by the hunter or warrior, as when the
Zulu will bring down an antelope at a surprising distance
with a throw of his round-headed club or knob-kerry,
and the Turk till modern times used to throw his mace
in battle. The sporting use outlasts the warlike, and
even in England the fowler's throwing-cudgel is not
unknown in country parts, where it is called a *squoyle*.
A flat thin club made curved or crooked by following
the branch it is cut out of has been liked by sportsmen
of various nations for its destructive whirling flight, as
where the old Egyptian fowler may be seen in the
pictures flinging his flat curved throw-stick into the
midst of a flight of wild-duck. The Australians not
only throw wooden clubs and blades as weapons in this
ordinary way, but make and throw with surprising skill
a peculiar light curved blade which has been called the
" come-back " boomerang, which veers in its course and
returns to the thrower, as may be seen by flipping
cardboard boomerangs with their arms slightly bent out
of the plane. Again, it is evident that stones flung by
hand must have been among man's first weapons. A
simple instrument for lengthening the arm and accumu-
lating momentum is the sling, which is so generally
known even among the lowest tribes of man that it is
probably of great antiquity.

The rudest spear, which is a mere pointed stick, is
known everywhere in the savage world, the point being
often hardened by thrusting it into the fire. Of spears,
whether such clumsy sticks or more artificially pointed
weapons, the heavier kinds serve for thrusting and the
lighter for throwing, while intermediate sizes are fit for
both purposes. It is obvious how, to prevent the spear
from coming out of the wound, it came to be barbed.
Another device, known widely among rude hunters and
fishers, is to put the point loosely on to the shaft, attach-

ing it by a cord of some length which uncoils when the point sticks in the animal and the shaft drops off, so that the struck beast cannot break away the shaft but drags it trailing, or the fish is held and marked down by the floating wood. The distance to which the spear can be hurled by hand is much increased by using a spear-thrower, acting like a sling. In Captain Cook's time the New Caledonians slung their spears with a short cord with an eye for the finger, while the Roman soldiers had a thong (*amentum*) made fast to their javelins near the middle of the shaft for the same purpose. But wooden spear-throwers from one to three feet long, grasped at one end and with a peg or notch at the other to take the butt of the spear, have been more favoured with savage and barbaric races. Thus Fig. 59 shows the Australian spear-thrower. This looks a more primitive instrument than the bow, which indeed was not known to these rude savages. It seems as though with

FIG. 59.—Australian spear thrown with spear-thrower (after Brough Smyth).

the progress of weapons the spear-thrower was discarded, for it is not found among any nation higher than the old Mexicans; there is a fine specimen in the British Museum of this " atlatl," of which Spanish writers mention the effectiveness. The bow and arrow (as General Pitt-Rivers suggests) may very likely have grown out of a simpler contrivance, the spring-trap set in the woods by fitting a dart to an elastic branch, so fastened back as to be let go by a passing animal, in whose track it discharges the weapon. However invented, the bow came into use in ages before history. Its arrow is a miniature of the full-sized javelin, and the old stone arrow-heads found in most regions of the world (see Fig. 54 *d*) show the existence of the bow-and-arrow in the Stone Age, though hardly back to the drift-period. The art of feathering the arrow goes back as far as history, and we know not how much farther. The simplest kind of long-bow is like that we still use in the sport of archery, made of one piece of tough wood. Fig. 60 *a* shows a long-bow of the forest-tribes of South

America, unstrung, with its string hanging loose. What may be called the Tatar or Scythian bow is formed of several pieces of wood or horn, united with glue and sinews. Shorter than the long-bow, it gets its spring by being bent outside-in to string it; thus the concave side of the Tatar bow *b* when unstrung (as shown by the dotted lines in the figure) becomes the convex side when strung. Bows of this class belong especially to

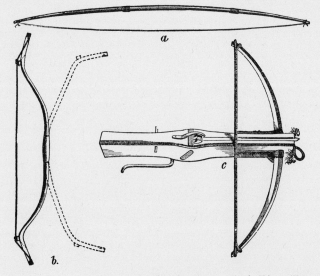

FIG. 60.—Bows. *a*, South American long-bow (unstrung); *b*, Chinese (Tatar bow; *c*, European cross-bow.

northern regions where there is a scarcity of tough wood suited to making long-bows in one piece. As a warlike weapon the bow lasted on in Europe through the Middle Ages, and as late as 1814 the world looked on with wonder to see the Kalmuk cavalry ride armed with bows-and-arrows through the streets of Paris. A further step in the history of the bow was to mount it on a stock, so as to take aim at leisure and touch a trigger to let go the string. Thus it became the cross-bow, which seems to have been invented in the East,

and was known in Roman Europe about the sixth
century. In the figure, *c* represents it in its perfected
form with a winch to draw the bow, as soldiers used it
in the sixteenth century. Cross-bows are still made in
Italy for shooting birds with a bolt or pellet.

To understand the next great move in missile weapons,
it is necessary to look back to savage life. The blow-
tube, through which the forest Indian of South America
blows his tiny poisoned plug-darts, or the
similar Malay weapon called the sumpitan, may have
been easily invented wherever long large reeds grew.
With simple darts or pellets the blow-tube served for
shooting birds, and it is often kept up as a toy, as in
our boys' peashooters. When, however, gunpowder was
applied in warfare, its use was soon adapted to make
the blow-tube an instrument of tremendous power, when
instead of the puff of breath in a reed, the explosion of
powder in an iron barrel drove out the missile. In the
early guns of the Middle Ages, the powder was fired by
putting a coal or match to the touchhole, as continued
to be done till lately with cannon. For hand-guns, this
early match-lock was followed by the wheel-lock. This
led up to the flint-lock, which it is curious to compare
with the cross-bow, for the bent bow released by the
trigger, which in the cross-bow did the actual work of
shooting out the missile, has now come down, in the
form of a spring and trigger, to the subordinate use of
striking the light to ignite the powder which actually
propels the ball. In more modern guns, the trigger
and spring still remain, the improvement lying in the
use of fulminating silver in the cap, ignited by the blow
of the hammer. The rifling of the barrel by means of
grooves, though introduced to prevent it from fouling,
renews in its effect the ancient plan of feathering the
arrow to cause it to rotate, this giving increased steadi-
ness of flight. The modern conical shot shows a partial
return from the spherical bullet towards the ancient
bolt or arrow, and at last breech-loading goes back to
the old plan of putting the arrows in at the butt-end of
the savage blow-tube.

As thus plainly appears, the ingenuity of man has
been eminent in the art of destroying his fellow-men.
In surveying the last group of deadly weapons, from
the stone hurled by hand to the rifled cannon, there
comes well into view one of the great advances of culture.
This is the progress from the simple tool or implement,

such as the club or knife, which enables man to strike or cut more effectively than with hands or teeth, to the machine which, when supplied with force, only needs to be set and directed by man to do his work. Man often himself provides the power which the machine distributes more conveniently, as when the potter turns the wheel with his own foot, using his hands to mould the whirling clay. The highest class of machines are those which are driven by the stored-up forces of nature, like the saw-mill where the running stream does the hard labour, and the sawyer has only to provide the timber and direct the cutting.

As to how simple mechanical powers were first learnt, it is of no use to guess in what rude and early age men found that stones or blocks too weighty to lift by hand could be prized up and moved along with a stout stick, or rolled on two or three round poles, or got up a long gentle slope more easily than up a short steep rise. Thus such discoveries as those of the lever, roller, and inclined plane, are quite out of historical reach. The ancient Egyptians used wedges to split off their huge blocks of stone, and one wonders that, knowing the pulley as they did, it never appears in the rigging of their ships (see Fig. 71). A draw-well with a pulley is to be seen in the Assyrian sculptures, where also a huge winged bull is being heaved along with levers, and dragged on a sledge with rollers laid underneath.

The wheel-carriage, which is among the most important machines ever contrived by man, must have been invented in ages before history. To see what constructive skill the leading nations had already attained to in times we reckon as of high antiquity, it is worth while to examine closely the Egyptian war-chariots, with their neatly-fitted and firmly-tired spoke-wheels turning on their axles secured by linch-pins, while the body, pole, and double harness show equal technical skill. In looking for some hint as to how wheel-carriages came to be invented, it is of little use to judge from such high skilled work as was turned out by these Egyptian chariot-builders, or by the Roman *carpentarii* or carriage-builders from whom our *carpenters* inherit their name. But, as often happens, rude contrivances may be found which look as though they belonged to the early stages of the invention. The plaustrum or farm-cart of the ancient world in its rudest form had for wheels two solid wooden drums near a foot thick, and made from a tree-trunk

cut across, which drums or wheels did not turn on the
axle but were fixed to it; the axle was kept in place
by wooden stops, or passed through rings at the bottom
of the cart, and went round together with its pair of
wheels, as children's toy carts are made. It is curious
to notice how, under changed conditions, the builders
of railway-carriages have returned to this early construction. In the ancient cart, Fig. 61, the squared end of
the axle shows that it must turn with the wheels. In
such countries as Portugal the old classic bullock-cart
on this principle is still to be seen, and it has been
reasonably guessed that such carts tell the story how
wheel-carriages came to be invented. Rollers were early

Fig. 61.—Ancient bullock-waggon, from the Antonine Column.

used, on which a block of stone or other heavy weight
was trundled. Suppose such a roller made of a smoothed
tree-trunk to be improved by cutting the middle part
smaller, so that it became an axle and pair of broad
wheels in one piece, then, by making this axle work
underneath the rudest framework, the simplest imaginable wheel-carriage is made. If the first notion of a
cart were suggested, the wheels might afterwards
be made separately and pinned on to the square axle,
and provided with tires. Then, for light wheels and
smooth ground, the wheels would at last be made to
turn on fixed axles. This is only conjecture, but at
any rate it puts clearly before our minds what the
nature of a carriage is.

Another ancient machine is the mill. The rudest
tribes of savages had a simple and effective means ready

to hand for powdering charcoal and ochre to paint
themselves with, or for the more useful work of bruising
wild seeds gathered for food.   The whole apparatus consists of a roundish stone held in the hand, and a larger
hollowed stone for a bed.   It is curious to notice how
closely our pestle and mortar still keeps to this primitive
type.   Now any one using the pestle and mortar may
notice that it works in two ways, the stuff being either
pounded by striking, or ground by rubbing against the
side of the mortar.   When people took to agriculture,
and grain became a chief part of their food, and mealing
it the women's heavy work, forms of mealing-stones
came into use suited not for pounding but for grinding
only, and doing this more perfectly.   An example may
be seen in Fig. 62, a rude ancient corn-crusher dug up

FIG. 62.—Corn-crusher, Anglesey (after W. O. Stanley).

in Anglesey, the stone muller or roller having its sides
hollowed for the hands of the grinder, who worked it
back and forward on the bed-stone.   The perfection of
such a corn-crusher may be seen in the " metate " with
its neatly shaped bed and rolling-pin of lava, with which
the Mexican women crush the maize for their corn-cakes
or tortillas.   But it is by one stone revolving upon the
other that grain is best ground, and here we have the
principle of the mill.   The quern or hand-mill of the
ancient world in its simple form consisted of two circular
flat mill stones, the upper being turned by a handle,
while the grain was poured in through the hole in the
centre, and came out as meal all round the edge.   This
early hand-mill has lasted on into the modern world, and
Fig. 63 shows " two women grinding at the mill," as
they might be seen in the Hebrides in the last century;
the long stick, which hangs from a branch above, has
its end in a hole in the upper stone, and a cloth is spread

on the ground to catch the meal. The quern is still used in north Scotland and the islands. If the reader will notice the construction of a modern flour-mill, it will be seen that the neatly faced and grooved millstones are now of great weight, and the upper one balanced on the pivot which gives it rapid rotation from below by means of water or steam-power, but, notwithstanding these mechanical improvements, the essential principle of the primitive hand-mill is still there.

FIG. 63.—Hebrides women grinding with the quern or hand-mill (after Pennant).

Another group of revolving tools and machines begins with the drill. The simplest mode of twirling the boring-stick between the hands is to be seen in fire-making (Fig. 72). In this clumsy way rude tribes know how to bore holes through hard stone by patiently twirling a reed or stick with sharp sand and water. This primitive tool was improved both for making fire and boring holes, by winding round the stick a thong or cord, which by being pulled backward and forward worked the drill, as the ancient shipwrights boring their timbers are described in the Odyssey (ix. 384). The ingenious

plan of using a bow with its string to drive the drill, so
that one man can manage it, was already known in the
old Egyptian workshops, but the still more perfect
Archimedean drill is modern. The turning-lathe seems
to have had its origin in the drill. To those who have
only seen the lathe in its improved modern forms this
may not be clear, but it is seen by looking at the old-
fashioned pole-lathe with which the turner used to shape
his wooden bowls and chair-legs, which were made to
revolve by a cord pulled up and down, on somewhat
the same principle as the Homeric drill. The foot-lathe,
with its crank and continuous revolution, superseded
this, to be itself encroached upon by the introduction
of steam-power for driving, and even for applying the
tool in the self-acting lathe.

In examining these groups of instruments and
machines, the development of many of them has been
traced back till their origins are lost in dim præhistoric
ages, or to where ancient history can show them arising
from a fresh idea or a new turn given to an old one.
It is seldom possible to get at the real author of an
ancient invention. Thus no one knows exactly when
and how that wonderful mechanical contrivance, the
screw, appeared. It was familiar to the Greek mathematicians, and the screw linen-presses and oil-presses of
classic times look almost modern in their construction.
In the period of ancient civilization there appear the
beginning of that immense change which is remodelling
modern life, by inventions which set the forces of nature
to do man's heavy work for him. This great change
seems to have been especially brought on by contrivances
to save the heavy toil of watering the fields. A simple
hand-labour contrivance of this kind is the shadoof of
the Nile valley, where a long pole with a counterpoise
at one end is supported on posts, and carries a bucket
hanging to the longer end to dip up water from below.
One need not travel to the East to watch this old contrivance, for it is to be seen at work in our brickfields.
For irrigation, it was mechanically an improvement on
this to set a gang of slaves to turn a great wheel with
buckets or earthen jars at its circumference, which rose
full from the water below, and as they turned over
emptied themselves into a trough at a higher level. But
when such a wheel was built to dip in a running stream,
then the current itself would turn the wheel, and thus
would come into existence the noria or irrigating water-

wheel often mentioned in ancient literature, and to be
seen still at work both in the East and in Europe. By
these or some similar steps of invention the water-wheel
was made a source of power for doing other work, such
as grinding corn, instead of the women at the quern or
the slaves at the treadmill, or the mill-horse in his
everlasting round. As the Greek epigram says, " Cease
your work, ye maids who laboured at the mills, sleep
and let the birds sing to the returning dawn, for Demeter
has bidden the water nymphs to do your task; obedient
to her call, they throw themselves on the wheel and
turn the axle and the heavy mill." The classical corn-
mill, with the cog-wheels driven by the water-wheel,
may have been a good deal like the water-mills still
working on our country streams. Such machinery was
early applied to grinding corn, and afterwards to other
manufactures, so that now the word mill no longer
means a grinding-mill only, but is also used where
machinery is driven by power for other purposes. It
was a great movement in civilization for the water-mill
and its companion contrivance the wind-mill to come
into use as force-providers, doing all sorts of labour,
from the heaviest work of the European factory down
to turning the Tibetan prayer-wheels, which go round
repeating for ever the sacred Buddhist formula. Within
the last century the civilized world has been drawing
an immense supply of power from a new source, the
coal burnt in the furnace of the steam-engine, which is
already used so wastefully that economists are uneasily
calculating how long this stored-up fossil force will last,
and what must be turned to next—tide force or sun's
heat—to labour for us. Thus, in modern times, man
seeks more and more to change the labourer's part he
played in early ages, for the higher duty of director or
controller of the world's force.

CHAPTER IX

HAVING, in the last chapter, examined the instruments used by man, we have next to look at the arts by which he maintains and protects himself. His first need is to get his daily food. In tropical forests, savages may easily live on what nature provides, like the Andaman Islanders, who gather fruits and honey, hunt wild pigs in the jungle, and take turtle and fish on the coast. Many forest tribes of Brazil, though they cultivate a little, depend mostly on wild food. Of such the rude man has no lack, for there is game in plenty and the rivers swarm with fish, while the woods yield him a supply of roots and bulbs, calabashes, palm-nuts, beans, and many other fruits; he collects wild honey, birds' eggs, grubs out of rotten wood, nor does he despise insects, even ants. In less fertile lands savage life goes on well while game and fish abound, but when these fail it becomes an unceasing quest for food, as where the Australians roam over their deserts on the look-out for every eatable root or insect, or the low Rocky Mountain tribes gather pine-nuts and berries, catch snakes, and drag lizards out of their holes with a hooked stick. The Fuegians wander along their bleak inhospitable shores feeding mostly on shell-fish, so that in the course of ages their shells, with fish-bones and other rubbish, have formed long banks above high-water mark. Such shell-heaps or " kitchen-middens " are found here and there all round the coasts of the world, marking the old resorts of such tribes; for instance on the coast of Denmark, where archæologists search them for relics of rude Europeans, who, in the Stone-age, led a life somewhat like that of Tierra del Fuego. Hunting and fishing go

on through all levels of society, beginning with the
savages who have no other means of subsistence, till at
last among civilized nations game and fish hardly do
more than supplement the more regular supplies of grain
and meat from the farm.   Looking at the devices of the
hunter and fisher, it will be seen how thoroughly most of
them belong to the ruder stages of culture.

The natives of the Brazilian forests, to whom tracking
game is the chief business of life, do it with a skill that
fills with wonder the white men who have watched them.
The Botocudo hunter, gliding stealthily through the
underwood, knows every habit and sign of bird and beast;
the remains of berries and pods show him what creature
has fed there; he knows how high up an armadillo
displaces the leaves in passing, and so can distinguish
its track from the snake's or tortoise's, and follow it to
its burrow by the scratches of its scaly armour on the
mud.   Even the sense of smell of this savage hunter is
keen enough to help him in tracking.   Hidden behind the
trunk of a tree, he can imitate the cries of birds and
beasts to bring them within range of his deadly poisoned
arrow, and he will even entice the alligator by making
her rough eggs grate together where they lie under leaves
on the river-bank.   If an ape he has shot high in the
boughs of some immense tree remains hanging by its
tail, he will go up after it by a hanging creeper where no
white man would climb.   At last, laden with game and
useful forest things, such as palm-fibre to make hammocks, or fruit to brew liquor, he finds his way back to
his hut by the sun and the lie of the ground, and the
twigs that he bent back for way-marks as he crept
through the thicket.   In Australia, the native hunter
will lie in wait behind a screen of boughs near a water-
hole till the kangaroos come to drink, or will track one in
the open for days, camping by his little fire at night to
be ready for the pursuit again at dawn, keeping unseen
and to the leeward till at last he can creep near enough
to hurl his spear, seldom in vain.   When the natives
hunt together, they will put up brush-fence in two long
wings converging towards a pit, and so drive the kangaroo
into it; or they will form a great hunting party for a
battue, surrounding half a mile of bush-land, and with
shouts and clatter of weapons driving all the game to
the centre where they can close round and despatch
them with spears and waddies.   In fowling the Australians show equal expertness.   A native will swim under

water breathing through a reed, or will merely cover his head with water-weed till he gets among a flock of ducks, which one by one he noiselessly pulls under and tucks into his belt. This shows in a simple form a kind of duck-hunting which is found in such distant parts of the world, that travellers have been puzzled to guess whether the idea spread from one tribe to another, or was invented many times. It may be seen on the Nile, where a harmless-looking calabash floats in among the water-fowl, with a swimming Egyptian's head inside. The Australian hunter takes the wallaby (a small kangaroo) by fastening to a long rod like a fishing-rod a hawk's skin and feathers, making the sham bird hover with its proper cry till it drives the game into a bush where it can be speared. Of devices of stalking with an imitated animal, one of the most perfect is that of the Dogrib Indians, when a pair of hunters go after reindeer; the foremost carries a reindeer's head, while in the other hand he has a bunch of twigs against which he makes the head rub its horns in a lifelike way, and the two men, walking as the deer's fore and hind legs, get among the herd and bring down the finest. In England, till of late years, fowlers used to hide behind a wooden horse moved along on wheels, and a relic of this survives in the phrase " to make a *stalking-horse* of one," often now used by people who have no idea what the word meant.

Hunting with dogs was very ancient, and was found among uncivilized tribes; thus the Australians seem to have trained the dingo or native dog for the chase, and most of the North American Indians had their native hunting-dogs. Still, dogs were not so universal among rude tribes as they have been since European breeds were carried all over the world; for instance, the natives of Newfoundland seem to have had no dogs. The largest and fiercest animal whose instinct of prey man has thus taken advantage of is the hunting-leopard or cheetah, which in India or Persia is carried in an iron cage to the field and let loose upon the deer; when it has pounced on the game the huntsman draws it off with the taste of blood and gives it a leg for its share in the partnership. Already in classic times there is mention of birds of prey trained to strike game-birds or drive them into the net, or to pounce on hares. Hawking or falconry reached its height as a royal sport in mediæval Tartary, where Marco Polo describes the Great Khan going out, borne by two elephants in his litter hung with cloth of gold and covered with lion-skins, to see the sport of his ten thousand falconers flying their hawks at the pheasants and cranes. From the East hawking spread over Europe. It was familiar to our early English ancestors, and if one had to paint a symbolic picture of the Middle Ages, one could hardly choose more characteristic figures than the knight and lady riding out with their hooded hawks on their fists. Since then falconry has all but died out in Europe, and nowadays the traveller may best see it in the Asiatic district where it first came up, Persia or the neighbouring countries. In such sports the quest of food (now often contemptuously called " pot-hunting ") becomes subordinate to the excitement of the chase. It was so especially where fleet animals like the deer were hunted on horseback, till at last the royal stag-hunt became a court ceremony with its cavalcades and its great officers of state in splendid uniforms. Such pageantry is, indeed, declining in modern Europe, but the place it used to hold in English court life is shown by noblemen still occupying in the Royal household the places of Master of the Buckhounds and Hereditary Grand Falconer.

The modern hunter has a vastly increased power of killing game, from the use of fire-arms instead of the bow and spear which came down from savage times. The effect of bringing in guns is seen among the native American buffalo-hunters. They were always reckless in destruction when they once came within reach of the herds, but now with the help of the white man and the use of his rifles there is such slaughter that travellers have found the ground and air for miles foul with the carcases of buffalo killed merely for the hides and tongues. In the civilized world, what with killing off game, and what with the encroachment of agriculture on the wild lands, both the supply and the need of game for man's subsistence have much lessened. But the hunter's life has been from the earliest times man's school of endurance and courage, where success and even trial gives pleasure in one of its intensest forms. Thus it has come to be kept up artificially where its practical use has fallen away. In civilized countries it is seen at its best where it keeps closest to barbaric fatigue and danger, like grouse-shooting in Scotland, or boar-hunting in Austria, but at its meanest, where it has come down to shooting grain-fed pheasants as tame as barn-door fowls.

Next, as to trapping game. This was seen in a

curiously simple form in Australia, where a native
would lie on his back on a rock in the sunshine with a bit
of fish in his hand, pretending to be fast asleep, till some
hawk or crow pounced on the bait, only to be itself
pounced on by the hungry man, who broiled and ate it
then and there. A plan of taking game which must
have readily suggested itself to rude hunters was the
pitfall, in its simplest shape a mere hole too deep for a
heavy beast to get out of when it has fallen in. The
savage trapper will dig such a pit, and cover it with
brushwood or sods, as in Africa the bushmen take the
huge hippopotamus and elephant, while in fur-countries
the hunters arrange their pitfalls in various ways, the
most artificial plan being to cover them with a wooden
floor which upsets when trodden on. The word *trap*,
meaning originally step (like German *treppe*), may have
come from its usually being some contrivance for the
game to tread on. It is so not only with the pitfall,
but with other common kinds of trap, which, when the
animal steps on the catch, drop down on it, or pull a
noose round it, or let fly a dart at it, all which are plans
known in the uncivilized world. The art of catching
birds and beasts with a noose, held in the hand or fastened
to the end of a stick, is universal. Perhaps the most
skilful noosing is that done on horseback by the herdsmen
of Mexico, though it should be noticed that their *lazo*
is not a native American invention; it was brought over
by the Spaniards with its name, which is simply Latin
laqueus, a rope. To use the noose for trapping purposes,
it is only necessary to set it in the track where game pass,
for them to run their heads into, as the North American
Indians do. But the noose may also be attached to a
bough bent back so as to spring up when an animal
touches it, and catch him. Or a spear may be arranged
as the savages of the Malay Peninsula do it, with an
elastic bamboo so bent back that when released by the
animal it will spear him. The suggestion has been
already mentioned (p. 89) that such a spring-trap first
led to the invention of the bow and arrow. Actual bows
and arrows are set as traps in such countries as Siberia,
and the spring-gun is a modern improvement on these.

Lastly, the net is one of the things known to almost all
men, so far as history can tell. The native Australians
net game like ancient Assyrians or English poachers, and
are not less skilled in netting wild fowl. To see this art
at its height we may look at the pictures of fowling scenes

on the monuments of ancient Egypt, which show the great clap-nets taking geese by scores; even the souls of the dead are depicted rejoicing in this favourite sport in the world beyond the tomb.

Among the various arts of the fisherman, one common among rude tribes was easily hit upon. Every day at the turn of the tide at river-mouths and on low shores, and inland near streams after a flood, fish are left behind in the shallow pools. Led by this experience, the savage has wit enough to assist nature, as where the Fuegians put up stake fences on the coast at low-water mark, while in South Africa near the rivers large flats are walled in with loose stones ready for the floods. Thus our fish-weirs and fish-dams are no novelties in civilization. Nor is the device of drugging or narcotizing fish a civilized invention, but to be seen in perfection among the tropical forest-tribes of South America, who use for the purpose a score or so of different plants. There is nothing surprising, however, in its being known to men so rude, for it must often occur by accident, from the branches or fruit of the right kind of euphorbia or paullinia falling into some forest pool, an experiment which the observant native would not be slow to try again. Next, a mode of fishing usual among savages, is spearing, the spear for this being barbed, and often made more effective by the head spreading into several barbed prongs. An account of a native Australian fishing describes him lying athwart his bark canoe, with his spear-point dipping into the water ready to go down without splashing, and, what is more remarkable, the fisherman keeping his own eyes under water, so that not only the ripple does not disturb his view, but his aim is not interfered with by the refraction of light which makes it so difficult for a man out of the water to hit an object below the surface. The wilder races also know well how after dark fish come to a light, so that salmon-spearing by torchlight, now that it is no longer so frequent in Scotland or Norway, may be seen in all its picturesqueness among the Indians of Vancouver's Island. Shooting fish with the bow and arrow, which many low tribes do with wonderful dexterity, may be counted as a variety of fish-spearing. The fish-hook is a contrivance not known to all savage tribes, but some have it, as the Australians who cut their hooks out of shell, and are even known to fish with a hawk's claw attached to a line. ·The ancient Egyptian would sit like a modern European angler by a canal or pond, fishing with rod and line; his hook was of bronze. The Greeks used artificial flies for " dapping," if not for throwing. On the whole it is remarkable how little modern fishermen have moved from the methods of the rudest and oldest men. The savage fish-spear, with its three or four barbed prongs, is curiously like that our sailors still use, and call a fish-gig. Only we make the head of iron, not of wood and fish-teeth. So it is with the harpoon used by American whalers, with its loosely fitting point which comes off when the fish is struck, only remaining attached by a long cord to the floating shaft; this is copied, but with a steel point, from the bone-headed harpoon of the Aleutian Islanders. Our fishermen carry on their business on a large scale, with their steam-trawlers and seines which sweep a whole bay, but their net-fishing is much of the same kinds as may be found among the peoples from whom we have here taken our early examples of spearing and angling.

Thus man, even while he feeds himself as the lower animals do, by gathering wild fruit and catching game and fish, is led by his higher intelligence to more artificial means of getting these. Rising to the next stage, he begins to grow supplies of food for himself. Agriculture is not to be looked on as a difficult or out-of-the-way invention, for the rudest savage, skilled as he is in the habits of the food-plants he gathers, must know well enough that if seeds or roots are put in a proper place in the ground they will grow. Thus it is hardly through ignorance, but rather from roving life, bad climate, or sheer idleness, that so many tribes gather what nature gives, but plant nothing. Even very rude people, when they live on one spot all the year round, and the climate and soil are favourable, mostly plant a little, like the Indians of Brazil, who clear a patch of forest round their huts to grow a supply of maize, cassava, bananas, and cotton. When we look at the food-plants of the world, it appears that some few are grown much as in their wild state, like the coco-nut and bread-fruit, but most are altered by cultivation. Sometimes it is possible to find the wild plant and show how man has improved it, as where the wild potato is found growing on the cliffs of Chile. But the origin of many cultivated plants is lost to tradition and has become a subject for tale-tellers. This is the case with those edible grasses which have been raised by cultivation into the cereals, such as wheat, barley, rye, and by their regular and plentiful supply have become the mainstay of human life and the great moving power of civilization. It is clear that the development of these grain-plants from their wild state was before the earliest ages of history, which throws back the beginnings of agriculture to times older still. How ancient was the first tilling of the soil, is shown by ancient Egypt and Babylonia, with their governments and armies, temples and palaces, for it could have been only through carrying on agriculture for a long series of ages that such populations could have grown up so closely packed together as to form a civilized nation. Plants, when once brought into cultivation, make their way from people to people across the globe. Thus the European conquerors of America carried back the maize or Indian corn which had been cultivated from unknown antiquity over the New World, and which now furnishes the Italian peasant with his daily meal of polenta or porridge; it is grown even in Japan, and down to the south of Africa, where it is the " mealies " of the colonist. An English vegetable garden is a curious study for the botanist who assigns to each plant its proper home, and to the philologist who traces its name. Sometimes this tells its story, fairly, as where *damson* and *peach* describe these fruits as brought from Damascus and Persia. But the *potato*, brought over in Queen Elizabeth's time, seems to have borrowed the name of another plant botanically different, the *batata*, or sweet-potato. The luscious tropical *ananas* has lost its native Malay name except among botanists, and has taken the name of the common fir-cone or *pine-apple*, which in shape it so closely resembles.

By noticing how rude tribes till the soil, much is to be learnt as to the invention of agricultural implements. Wandering savages like the Australians carry a pointed stick to dig up eatable roots with, as in Fig. 64 *a*. Considering how nearly planting a root is the same work as digging one up, it is likely that a tribe beginning to till the soil would use their root-digging sticks for the new purpose; indeed, a pointed stake has been found as the rude husbandman's implement both in the Old and New World. It is an improvement on this to dig with a flat-bladed tool like a spear, sword, or paddle, and thus we have the civilized spade. A more important tool, the hoe, is derived from the pick or hatchet. The wooden picks of the New Caledonians serve both as weapons and for planting yams, while the African's

hatchet—an iron blade stuck in a club—only has to
have the blade turned across to become his hoe. It
is curious to find in Europe the rudest imaginable hoe,
less artificial than the elk's shoulder-blade fastened to a
stick, with which the North Ameri-
can squaws hoed their Indian corn.
This is the Swedish " hack," Fig.
64 *b*, a mere stout stake of spruce-
fir with a bough sticking out at the
lower end cut short and pointed.
With this primitive implement in
old times fields were tilled in Sweden,
and it was to be seen in forest farm-
houses within a generation or two.
Swedish tradition records the steps
by which agriculture improved. The
wooden hack was made heavier and
dragged by men through the ground,
thus ploughing a furrow in the
simplest way; then the implement
was made in two pieces, with a
handle for the ploughman and a
pole for the men to drag by, the
share was shod with an iron point,
and at last a pair of cows or mares
were yoked on instead of the men.
This seems nearly the way in which,
thousands of years earlier, the hoe
first passed into the plough. Fig.
65 is from a picture of agriculture in ancient Egypt. Here the
labourer is seen following the plough
to break up the clods with his
peculiar hoe, with its long, curved,
wooden blade roped to the handle.
Now looking at the plough itself, it
is seen to be such a hoe, rope and
all, only heavier and provided with
a pair of handles for the ploughman
to guide and keep it down, while a

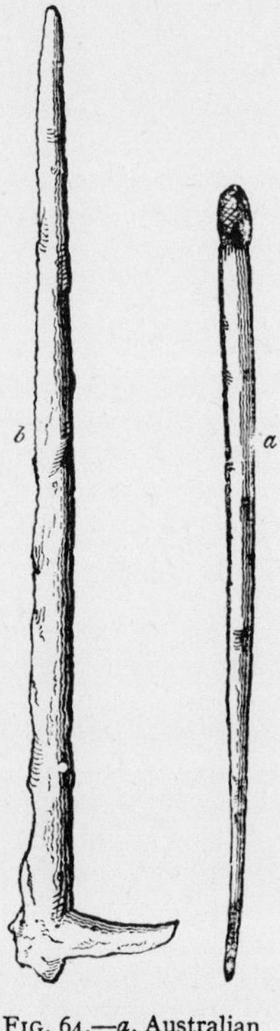

FIG. 64.—*a*, Australian
digging-stick;
b, Swedish wooden hack.

yoke of oxen drag it through the ground. The valley
of the Nile was one of the districts where high agriculture earliest arose, and in the picture here copied we
may almost fancy ourselves seeing at its birth the great
invention of the plough. To arm it with a heavy metal
ploughshare, to shape this so that it shall turn the sod

over in a continuous ridge, to fix a coulter or " knife " in front to give the first cut, and to mount the whole on wheels; all these were improvements known in Rome in the classical period. In modern times we have the self-acting plough no longer needing the ploughman to follow at the plough-tail, and the steam-plough has a more powerful draught than oxen or horses. Yet those who have looked at the earlier stages can still discern in the most perfect modern plough the original hoe dragged through the ground.

There survives even now in the world a barbaric mode of bringing land under cultivation, which seems to show us man much as he was when he began to subdue the primæval forest, where till then he had only wandered, gathering wild roots and nuts and berries. This primitive

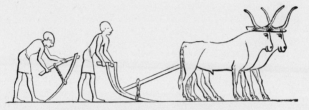

Fig. 65.—Ancient Egyptian hoe and plough.

agriculture was noticed by Columbus, when landing in the West Indies he found the natives clearing patches of soil by cutting the brushwood and burning it on the spot. This simple plan, where the wood is not only got out of the way, but the ashes serve for dressing, may still be seen among the hill-tribes of India, who till these plots of land for a couple of years and then move on to a new spot. In Sweden this brand-tillage, as it may be called, is not only remembered as the old agriculture of the land, but in outlying districts it has lasted on into modern days, giving us an idea what the rough agriculture of the early tribes may have been like when they migrated into Europe. It is not to be supposed, on looking at an English farm of the present day, that its improvements were made all at once. The modern farming system has a long and changing history behind it. One interesting point in its growth is that in long-past ages much of Europe was brought under cultivation by village-communities. A clan of settlers would possess them-

selves of a wide tract of land, and near their huts they
would lay out great common fields, which at first they
perhaps tilled and reaped in common as one family.
It became usual to parcel out this tillage land every few
years into family lots, but the whole village-field was still
cultivated by the whole community, working together
in the time and way settled by the village elders. This
early communistic system of husbandry may still be
seen not much changed in the villages of such countries
as Russia. Even in England its traces have out-lasted
the feudal system, and remain in the present days of
landlord and tenant. In several English counties there
may still be noticed the boundaries of the great common-
fields, divided lengthwise into three strips, which again
were divided crosswise into lots, held by the villagers;
the three divisions were managed on the old three-field
system, one lying fallow while the other two bore two
kinds of crops.

Next, as to the history of domesticating animals for
food. The taming of sociable creatures like parrots and
monkeys is done by low forest tribes, who delight in
such pets; and very rude tribes keep dogs for guard and
hunting. But it marks a more artificial way of life when
men come to keep and breed animals for food. The
move upwards from the life of the hunter to that of the
herdsman is well seen in the far north, the home of the
reindeer. Among the Esquimaux the reindeer was only
hunted. But Siberian tribes not only hunt them wild,
but tame them. Thus the Tunguz live by these herds,
which provide them not only with milk and meat, but
with skins for clothing and tents, sinews for cord, bone
and horn for implements, while as they move from place
to place the deer even serve as beasts of draught and
burden. Here is seen a specimen of pastoral life of a
simple rude kind, and it is needless to go on describing
at length the well-known life of higher nomad tribes,
who shift their tents from place to place on the steppes
of Central Asia or the deserts of Arabia, seeking pasture
for their oxen and sheep, their camels and horses. There
is a strong distinction between the life of the wandering
hunter and the wandering herdsman. Both move from
place to place, but their circumstances are widely
different. The hunter leads a life of few appliances or
comforts, and exposed at times to starvation; his place
in civilization is below that of the settled tiller of the
soil. But to the pastoral nomad, the hunting which is

the subsistence of the ruder wanderer has come to be only an extra means of life. His flocks and herds provide him for the morrow, he has valuable cattle to exchange with the dwellers in towns for their weapons and stuffs, there are smiths in his caravan, and the wool is spun and woven by the women. What best marks the place in civilization which the higher pastoral life attains to, is that the patriarchal herdsman may belong to one of the great religions of the world; thus the Kalmuks of the steppes are Buddhists, the Arabs are Moslems. A yet higher stage of prosperity and comfort is reached where the agricultural and pastoral life combine, as they already did among our forefathers in the village communities of old Europe just described. Here, while the fields were cultivated near the village, the cattle pastured in summer on the hills and in the woodlands belonging to the community, where also the hunter went for game, while nearer home there were common meadows for pasture and to provide the hay for the winter weather, when the cattle were brought under shelter in the stalls. In countries so thickly populated as ours is now, the last traces of the ancient nomad life disappear when the herds are no longer driven off to the hills in summer.

After the quest of food, man's next great need is to defend himself. The savage has to drive off the wild beasts which attack him, and in turn he hunts and destroys them. But his most dangerous foes are those of his own species, and thus in the lowest known levels of civilization war has already begun, and is carried on against man with the same club, spear, and bow used against wild beasts. General Pitt-Rivers has shown how closely man follows in war the devices he learnt from the lower animals; how his weapons imitate their horns, claws, teeth, and stings, even to their venom; how man protects himself with armour imitated from animals' hides and scales; and how his warlike stratagems are copied from those of the birds and beasts, such as setting ambushes and sentinels, attacking in bodies under a leader, and rushing on with war-cries to the fight.

We have already in the last chapter examined the principal offensive weapons. The daubing on of venom to make them more deadly is found among low tribes far over the world. Thus the Bushman mixes serpent's poison with the euphorbia juice, and the South American native poison-maker, prepared by a long fast for the mysterious act, concocts the paralysing *urari* or *curare* in the secret depths of the forest, where no woman's eye may fall on the fearful process. Poisoned arrows were known to the ancient world, as witness the lines which tell of Odysseus going to Ephyra for the man-slaying drug to smear his bronze-tipped arrows; but Ilos would not give it, for he feared the ever-living gods. Thus it seems that in early ages the moral sense of the higher nations had already condemned the poisoned weapons of the savage, with something of the horror Europeans now feel in examining the Italian bravo's daggers of the Middle Ages, with their poison-grooves imitated from the serpent's tooth.

How the warrior's armour comes from the natural armour of animals is plainly to be seen. The beast's own hide may be used, as where one sees in museums the armour of bear-skins from Borneo, or breastplates of crocodile's skin from Egypt. The name of the *cuirass* shows that it was at first of leather, like the *buff* jerkin. The Bugis of Sumatra would make a breastplate by sewing upon bark the cast-off scales of the ant-eater, overlapping as the animal wore them; and so the natural armour of animals was imitated by the Sarmatians, with their slices of horses' hoofs sewed together in overlapping scales like a fir-cone. Such devices, when metal came in, would lead to the scale armour of the Greeks, imitated from fish-scales and serpent-scales, while their chain-mail is a sort of netted garment made in metal. The armour of the Middle Ages continued the ancient kinds, now protecting the whole body with a suit from head to foot (*cap-à-pie*) of iron scales, or mail (that is, meshes), or of jointed plates of iron copied from the crab and lobster, such as the later suits of armour which decorate our manorial halls. With the introduction of gunpowder, armour began to be cast aside, and, except the helmet, what remains of it in military equipment is more for show than use. The shield also, once so important a part of the soldier's panoply, has been discarded since the days of musketry. Our modern notion of a shield is that of a large screen behind which the warrior can shelter himself, but this does not appear to have been the original intention. The primitive shield was probably the parrying-shield, used like the narrow Australian parrying-stick, which is only four inches across in the middle where it is grasped, but with which the natives ward off darts with wonderful dexterity. The small round Highland target, one of the varieties of shield

which remained latest in civilized Europe, is made to
be thus dexterously handled as a weapon of defence, to
ward off javelins, or parry the thrust of spear or sword.
It is easy to see that such parrying-shields belong to
the early kind of warfare where the battle was a skirmish,
and every warrior took care of himself. But when
fighting in close ranks began, then the great screen-
shields would come in, serving as a wall behind which
the old Egyptian soldiers could ensconce themselves,
or the Greek or Roman storming-party creep up to the
foot of the wall in spite of stones and darts hurled
down on them.

The savage or barbarian is apt to fall on his enemy
unawares, seeking to kill him like a wild beast, especially
where there is bitter personal hatred or blood-vengeance.
But even among low tribes we find a strong distinction
drawn between such manslaughter and regular war,
which is waged not so much for mutual destruction as
for a victory to settle a quarrel between two parties. For
instance, the natives of Australia have come far beyond
mere murder when one tribe sends another a bunch of
emu-feathers tied to the end of a spear, as a challenge to
fight next day. Then the two sides meet in battle array,
their naked bodies terrific with painted patterns, brand-
ishing their spears and clubs, and clamouring with taunts
and yells. Each warrior is paired with an opponent, so
that the fight is really a set of duels, where spear after
spear is hurled and dodged or parried with wonderful
dexterity, till at last perhaps a man is killed, which
generally brings the fray to an end. Among the rude
Botocudos of Brazil, a quarrel arising from one tribe
hunting hogs on another's ground might be settled by
a solemn cudgelling-match, where pairs of warriors
belaboured one another with heavy stakes, while the
women fought by scratching faces and tearing hair, till
one side gave in. But if in such an encounter the beaten
party take to their bows and arrows, the scene may
change into a real battle. When it comes to regular
war, the Botocudos will draw up their men fronting the
enemy, pouring in arrows, and then rushing together
with war-whoops to fight it out tooth and nail, killing
man, woman, and child. They make expeditions to
plunder the villages of their settled neighbours, and
when enemies are near in the forest they will stick
splinters in the ground as caltrops to lame them, and
shoot from ambush behind fallen trunks or shelters of

boughs. The slain in battle they will carry off to cook
and devour at the feast, where with wild drunken dancing
their warlike zeal is inflamed to frenzied rage. Thus to
excite courage is the purpose of the frantic war-songs
and war-dances, which are common to mankind, among
savages and even far more cultured nations. Low
tribes also keep up the fierce hatred and pride of battle
by trophies of the enemy—his head dried and hung as
an ornament of the hut, or his skull fashioned into a
drinking-cup. The wars of the North American Indians
have picturesque incidents often described in our books,
the braves smoking in solemn council of war, the declaration of war by the bundle of arrows wrapped in a rattlesnake's skin, or the blood-red war-hatchet struck into
the war-post, the recruiting-feast where the dog was eaten
as emblem of fidelity, the war-party creeping through
the woods in single line (which we thence call " Indian
file "), the stealthy attack on the enemy's camp or village,
the wild scalp-dance of the returning victors, the tortur-
ing of the captives at the stake, where the very children
were set to shoot arrows at the helpless foe, who bore his
torments without a groan, boasting of his own fierce
deeds and taunting his conquerors in his death-agony.
Indian war was " to creep like a fox, attack like a panther,
and fly like a bird." Yet at times the warriors of two
tribes would meet in fair battle, standing to watch duels
between pairs of champions, or all rushing together in a
general melée.

In the warfare of rude races, it is to be noticed how
fighting for quarrel or vengeance begins to pass into
fighting for gain. Among some tribes the captives,
instead of being slain, are brought back for slaves, and
especially set to till the ground. By this agriculture is
much increased, and also a new division of society takes
place, to be seen still arising among such warlike tribes
as the Caribs, where the captives with their children
come to form an hereditary lower class. Thus we see
how in old times the original equality of men broke up,
a nation dividing into an aristocracy of warlike freemen,
and an inferior labouring caste. Also forays are made
for the warriors to bring home wives, who are the slaves
and property of their captors. Milder imitation of this
hostile wife-capture appears in the custom, widely
prevailing among the ruder peoples of the world, and
lasting on even among the more civilized, of carrying off
brides from families at peace, as a recognized mode of

marriage. As property increases, there appears with it
warfare carried on as a business, by tribes living more or
less by plunder, glorying in their murderous profession,
and despising the mean-spirited farming villagers whose
labour provides them with corn and cattle. A perfect
example of such a robber-tribe were the Mbayas of
South America, whose simple religion it was that their
deity, the Great Eagle, had bidden them live by making
war on all other tribes, slaying the men, taking the
women for wives, and carrying off the goods.

War among civilized nations differs from that of savage
tribes in being carried on with better weapons and
appliances, and by warriors being trained to fight in
regular order. The superiority of a regular army to a
straggling savage war-party may be well seen by looking
at the pictures in Wilkinson's *Ancient Egyptians* of
troops marching in rank and step to sound of trumpet,
especially noticing the solid phalanx of heavy infantry
with spear and shield. The strength of such Egyptian
solid squares of 10,000 men is described in the Cyropædia
(probably with truth as to military tactics if not to
actual history), how they could not be broken even by
the victorious Persians, but amid the rout of man and
horse the survivors still held out, sitting under their
shields, till Cyrus granted them honourable surrender.
An Egyptian army had its various corps divided into
companies, and commanded by officers of regular grades.
In battle the heavy immovable phalanx held the centre,
the archers and light infantry in the wings acted in line
or open order, there were bodies of slingers, and the
noble warriors drove their chariots into the thick of the
opposing host. This military efficiency was attained by
having a standing army formed by a regular military
class, trained from youth in the art of war, and maintained by eight acres of land assigned to every soldier.
From an early time also we find the Egyptians employing
foreign mercenary troops, whose peculiar costumes and
faces are conspicuous in the battle-pictures. Thus also
the Assyrian war-scenes show that their military system
was on a level with that of Egypt. The rise of the
science of war to a higher stage belongs to Greece, and
the whole history of its growth is told in Greek literature.
Beginning with the Iliad, the descriptions there show
war and armies in a state more barbaric than in Egypt,
with little discipline and less generalship, and encounters
of Greek and Trojan champions with the armies looking

on as savages would do. But when we come to later ages of Greek history, it is seen that they had by that time not only learnt what the older civilization had to teach, but had brought their own genius to develop it further. Their corps of all arms, archers, charioteers, cavalry, and the phalanx of spearmen, were disciplined and ranged in order of battle much after the ancient Egyptian and Assyrian manner. But whereas in old times a battle had been a trial of mere strength between two armies drawn up facing one another, the military historian, Xenophon, describes the change made in the art of war by the Theban leader, Epaminondas, when at Leuktra, with forces fewer than the Spartans, he charged with his men in column fifty deep against their twelve deep right wing, and by breaking them threw the whole line into disorder, and won the battle. At Mantineia, carrying out this plan yet more skilfully, he arranged his troops in a wedge-shaped body with the weaker divisions slanting off behind so as to come up when the enemy's front was already broken. In such ways was developed the science of military tactics, which made skilful manœuvring as important as actual fighting. The Romans, a nation drilled to battle and conquest, came at last to rule the world by the mere force of military discipline. In the Middle Ages the introduction of gunpowder increased the killing-power of troops whose artillery from bows and arrows became muskets and heavy cannon. The reader's attention has been already drawn to the military scenes of Egypt and Assyria. If now, fresh from watching the manœuvres of a modern army in sham fight, he will look at these pictures to see war as it was three or four thousand years ago, he will observe how substantially the new system is founded on the old, with developments due to two new ideas, namely, tactics and the use of fire-arms.

Somewhat the same lesson may be learnt by comparing the older and ruder kinds of fortification and siege with those of modern times. Tribes at the level of the Kamchatkans and the North American Indians knew how to fortify their villages with embankments and palisades. In ancient Egypt and Assyria and neighbouring countries, strong and high fortress-walls and towers were defended by archers and slingers, and attacked by storming-parties with scaling-ladders. Old sieges were unscientific, as is so curiously seen in the Homeric poems, where the Greeks encamp over against Troy, but seem to have no notion of regularly investing it, much less of attack by sap and trench. The Greeks and Romans came on to use higher art in fortification and siege, and there appear among them machines of war such as the ancient battering-ram, heavy and skilfully engineered, while contrivances of the nature of huge bows like the catapult led up to the cannon of later ages which superseded them.

Lastly, looking at the army system as it is in our modern world, one favourable change is to be noticed. The employment of foreign mercenary troops, which almost through the whole stretch of historical record has been a national evil alike in war and peace, is at last dying out. It is not so with the system of standing armies which drain the life and wealth of the world on a scale more enormous even than in past times, and stand as the great obstacle to harmony between nations. The student of politics can but hope that in time the pressure of vast armies kept on a war-footing may prove unbearable to the European nations which maintain them, and that the time may come when the standing army may shrink to a nucleus ready for the exigencies of actual war if it shall arise, while serving in peace-time as a branch of the national police.

CHAPTER X

ARTS OF LIFE—(*continued*)

We have next to examine the dwellings of mankind. Thinking of the nests of birds, the dams of beavers, the tree-platforms of apes, it can scarcely be supposed that man at any time was unable to build himself a shelter. That he does not always do so is mostly because while on the move from place to place he may be content to sleep in the open, or take to the natural shelter of a tree or rock. Therefore, though evidence happens to remain of ancient savage races having dwelt much in natural sheltering-places, it must not be thence inferred that these rough folk, even the contemporaries of the mammoth, were too helpless to build themselves huts when it suited them. Rock-shelters under the cliffs were in Europe the resort of the ancient savages, as is proved by the bones and flint flakes and other remains that are found lying there in the ground. Caves are ready-made houses for beast or man. It has been already mentioned (p. 24) how, in such countries as England and France, caverns were the abodes of the old tribes of the reindeer and mammoth period, and the Bushmen of South Africa are a modern example of rude tribes thus given to dwelling in caves in the rocks. But caverns are so convenient that they are now and then still used in the civilized world, and most of us have seen some cave in a cliff forming the back of a fisherman's cottage, or at least a storehouse. It is not so much with these natural dwellings that we are here concerned as with artificial structures, however rude, set up by man for his shelter.

In the depths of Brazilian forests, travellers have come

upon the dwellings of the naked Puris, which are not even huts, only sloping screens made by setting up a row of huge palm-leaves some eight feet long, leaning against a cross-pole. Being put up to windward, this shelters the lazy Indian as he lolls in his hammock slung between two trees, and with the dense foliage overhead life is not comfortless on fine days, though in bad weather the family and dogs have to crouch defenceless round the wood fire on the ground. Even in these tropical forests, what is generally met with is a real hut, though it may be such a rude one as the Botocudos make with these same great palm-leaves, sticking a number of them with their stalks in the ground in a circle, and bringing their points together, so as to form a roof overhead. The Patachos go to work more artificially, bending together young growing trees and poles stuck in the ground, so that by binding their tops together they form a framework which is then thatched over with large leaves. Much the same lesson in primitive architecture may be learnt from the natives of Australia, among whom a party camping out will be content to set up a line of leafy boughs in the ground to form a screen or break-wind for the night; but when they take the pains to interlace such boughs overhead, the screen becomes a hut, and where they stay for a while they will make a regular framework of branches, covering them in with sheets of bark, or leaves and grass, and even laying on sods or daubing the outside with clay. The invention of the simple round hut is thus easily understood. It is plain, too, how a conical hut, when roving tribes like the American Indians carry from place to place its poles and skins or sheets of bark, becomes in fact a portable tent, and this shows how tents came to be invented. The more cultured herdsmen of the East carry for their tent-coverings sheets of felted hair or wool, and we ourselves use for temporary shelter tents of canvas. Indeed one has only to look at the common bell-tent of the soldier to see that it is a transformed savage hut. Now the circular hut, whether beehive or conical, is low to creep into and small to lie or crouch in. More room is often got by digging the earth out some feet deep within, but a greater improvement in construction is to raise the hut itself on posts or a wall, so that what was at first the whole house now becomes the roof. Thus is built the round hut with its side-posts filled in with wattle and mud, or its solid earthen wall carrying the thatched roof which may reach beyond in shady eaves. Such were in ancient times common peasants' dwellings in Europe, as they still are in other quarters of the world, and indeed we perhaps keep up a memory of them in the round thatched summer-houses in our gardens, which are curiously like the real huts of barbarians. Next, as African travellers remark, one great sign of higher civilization is when people begin to build their houses square-cornered instead of round. The circular hut to be easily built must be small, and room is best gained by building the house oblong, with a ridge pole along the roof where the sloping poles from the sides meet. By being able to build to any required length, it became possible for many families, often twenty, to live together in village-houses as rude peoples often do. In barbaric countries spacious houses are built with the roofs carried on lofty posts with cross-timbers, or on solid walls of earth or stones; in fact they are constructed on much the same principles as our modern houses, though more rudely.

It does not seem difficult to make out how stone and brick architecture came into use. Where wood is scarce, men readily take to building walls of stone, turf, or earth. Thus the Australians are known to build shelters by heaping up loose stones as a wall, and roofing with sticks laid across. Rough stones, though they make good embankments and low walls, would be too unsteady for high walls, except slaty and stratified slabs which form natural building-stones. With mere stones out of the ground dwellings would hardly be built of a higher kind than the curious beehive-houses of the Hebrides, whose small rudely vaulted chambers are formed by the piled stones overlapping inwards till they almost meet above, and covered in with growing turf, so that they look like grassy hillocks with passages for the dwellers to creep in. This primitive building is very ancient, and though such houses are no longer made the old ones still serve as shealings in summer. The ancient Scotch underground dwellings or " weems " (*i.e.* caves) have chambers of rough stones, and remind antiquaries of Tacitus' account of the caves dug by the ancient Germans and heaped over with dirt, where they stored their grain and took refuge themselves from the cold, and in time of war from the enemy. When the craft of the mason is brought in, buildings of a higher order begin. The stones may at first be merely trimmed to fit one another like the pieces of a mosaic, as in the so-called Cyclopean stone-work of old Etruscan and Roman walls. But the world soon adopts a higher way, not arranging the plan to suit the stones, but shaping the stones to fit the work, especially using rectangular blocks of stone to lay down in regular courses of masonry. In ancient Egypt, the masons hewed and smoothed even granite and porphyry to a finish which is envied by the architects of our own day, and the pyramids of Gizeh are as wonderful for the fine masonry of their slopes, chambers, and passages, as for their prodigious size. Our modern notion of a stone building is that the blocks of stone are to be fixed together with a layer of mortar to bind them, but in the old and beautiful architecture of Egypt and Greece the faced stone blocks lie on one another, having no cement to hold them, and needing none. Clamps of metal were used when required to hold the stones together. Cement or mortar (so called from the mortar or trough in which it was mixed) was also well known in the ancient world. The Roman builders not only used the common lime-and-sand mortar, which hardens by absorbing carbonic acid from the air, but they also knew how by adding volcanic ash or pozzolana to make a water-resisting cement, whence the name of " Roman cement " given to a composition used by our masons. Mention has been already made of the practice of coating the sides of the savage bough-hut with clay. The ancient people who built their settlements on piles out in the Swiss lakes used to do this, as is proved by bits of the clay coating which were accidentally baked when the huts were burnt down, and fell into the water, where they may still be found, showing the impressions of the long-perished reed cabins on which the moist clay was plastered. We still have something of the kind in what cottage-builders call " wattle and daub." One also sees now and then in an English country lane a cottage or cowhouse which is a relic of another sort of primitive architecture, its walls being simply built of " cob," that is, clay mixed with straw. Such hut-walls of clay or mud are very usual in dry climates such as Egypt, where they are cheaper and better than timber. This being so, there is no difficulty in understanding how sun-dried bricks· came into use, these being simply convenient blocks of the same mud or loam mixed with straw which was used to build the cottage walls. These sun-dried bricks were used in the East from high antiquity. Some of the

Egyptian pyramids still standing are built of them, and the pictures show how the clay was tempered and the large bricks formed in wooden moulds much as in modern brickfields. With these the architects of Nineveh built the palace walls ten or fifteen feet thick, which were panelled with the slabs of sculptured alabaster. For such sun-dried bricks, clay and water form a sufficient cement. Building with mud-bricks, which indeed suits the climate well, goes on in these countries as of old. They were used also in America, and to this day the traveller in such districts as Mexico will often find himself lodged in a house built of them, and wondering whether he may account by Spanish-Moorish influence for its being like an Eastern caravanserai, or whether mud-brick villages came by natural invention to be so alike on both sides of the world. Baked bricks seem to have been a later invention, easy enough to nations who baked earthen pots, but only wanted in more rainy climates. Thus the Romans, whom mere mud-bricks would not have suited, carried to great perfection the making of kiln-burnt bricks and tiles.

For ordinary house-building, we now have recourse to the mason or bricklayer to build the walls, and tiles or slates are an improvement on the old thatch. But we so far keep to the old wooden architecture, that the floors and the timbering of the roof are still wood-work. For tombs and temples, however, built to last for ages, means were early wanted of roofing over spaces with the bricks or stones themselves without trusting to wooden beams. There are two modes of doing this, the false arch and the real arch, which are both ancient. The false arch is an arrangement which would occur to any builder, in fact it is what children make in building with wooden bricks, when they set them overlapping more and more till the top ones come near enough for one brick to cover the gap. Passages and chambers roofed in like this with projecting blocks of stone may be seen in the pyramids of Egypt, in ancient tombs of Greece and Italy, in the ruined palaces of Central America; and thus are built the domes of the Jain temples in India. It does not follow that the architects were ignorant of the real arch; they may have objected to it from its tendency to thrust the walls out. It is not known exactly how and when the arch was invented, but the idea might present itself even in roofing over doorways with rough stones. In the tombs of ancient Egypt real arches are to be seen, con-

structed in mud-bricks, or later in stone, by architects
who quite understood the principle. Yet though the
arch was known in what we call ancient times, it was not
at once accepted by the world. It is remarkable that
the Greek architects of the classic period never took to
it. It was left to the Romans, who applied it with admirable skill, and from whose vaulted roofs, bridges, and
domes, those of the mediæval and modern world are
derived.

In thus looking over the architcture of the world, we
see that its origins lie too far back for history to record its
beginning and earliest progress. Still there is reason to
believe that, in architecture as in other arts, man began
with the simple and easy before he came on to the complex
and difficult. There are many signs of stone architecture
having grown out of an earlier wooden architecture.
Thus, on looking at the Lykian tombs in the entrance-hall
of the British Museum, it will be seen that though they
are of hewn stone their forms are copied from wooden
beams and joists, so that the mason shows by his very
patterns that he has taken the place of an earlier carpenter.
Even in the early stone-work of Egypt, traces of wooden
forms are to be seen. In India there are stone buildings
whose columns and architraves are not less plainly
copied from wooden posts and horizontal beams resting
on them. It is possible that, when men first took to
setting up stone columns and supporting stone blocks
upon them, this idea may have come into their minds
from the wooden posts and beams they had been used to.
But when it is said, as it often has been, that the porticos
of Greek temples are copies in stone of older wooden
structures, practical architects object that the Parthenon
is not really like carpenter's work. Indeed it is known
that the Greeks did not invent their own column-archi-
tecture, but, taking the idea of it from what they saw in
Egypt and other countries, carried it out according to
their own genius.

After dwellings, we come to examine clothing. It has
first to be noticed that some low tribes, especially in the
tropical forests of South America, have been found by
travellers living quite naked. But even among the
rudest of our race, and in hot districts where clothing is
of least practical use, something is generally worn, either
from ideas of decency or for ornament. Where little
or no clothing is worn, it is common to paint the body.
The Andaman islanders, who plaster themselves with a

mixture of lard and coloured earth, have a practical
reason for so doing, this coat of paint protecting their
skin from heat and mosquitos; but they go off into love
of display when they proceed to draw lines on the paint
with their fingers, or when a dandy will colour one side
of his face red and the other olive-green, and make an
ornamental border-line where the two colours meet down
his chest and stomach. Among the relics of the ancient
cave-men of Europe are hollowed stones, which were their
primitive mortars for grinding the ochre and other
colours for painting themselves. Indeed, few habits
mark the lower stages of human life so well as the
delight in body-patterns of bold spots and stripes in
striking colours, familiar to us in pictures of Australians
dancing at a corroboree, or Americans working themselves up to frenzy in the scalp-dance. The primitive
sign of mourning also makes its appearance where savage
mourners blacken (or whiten) themselves over. In the
higher civilization, faded beauties may still make a poor
attempt to revive youthful bloom with touches of red
and white. But the ancient war-paint is now looked
down on as a sign of utter barbarism; so much so that
the ancient Britons, though a nation of considerable
civilization, have been treated by many historians as
mere savages because they kept up this rude practice,
as Cæsar says, staining themselves blue with woad, and
so being of horrider aspect in war. Among ourselves
the guise which was so terrific in the Red Indian warrior
has come down to make the circus-clown a pattern of
folly. It is very likely that this paint-striped face may
represent a fashion come down from the ancient times
when paint was worn by the barbarians of Europe, much
as certain figures used in Chinese ritual have paint-
streaked faces, doubtless keeping up what was once an
ordinary decoration. When the skin is tattooed, the
chief purpose of this is no doubt beauty, as where the
New Zealander had himself covered with patterns of
curved lines such as he would adorn his club or his canoe
with; it was considered shameful for a woman not to
have her mouth tattooed, for people would say with
disgust " she has red lips." Tattooing prevails as widely
among the lower races of the world as painting, and the
fashionable designs range from a few blue lines on the
face or arms, up to the flower-patterns with which the
skins of the Formosans are covered like damask. Where
the art is carried to perfection, as in Polynesia, the skin

is punctured, and the charcoal-colour introduced, by tapping rows of little prickers. But a rougher mode is common, as in Australia or Africa, where gashes are made and wood-ashes rubbed in so that the wound heals in a knob or a ridge. Marks on the skin often serve other purposes than ornament, as in Africa, where a long scar on a man's thigh may mean that he has done valiantly in battle, or the tribe or nation a negro belongs to may be indicated by his mark; for instance, a pair of long cuts down both cheeks, or a row of raised pimples down his forehead to the tip of his nose. Higher up in civilization, tattooing still lasts on, as where Arab women will slightly touch up their faces, arms, or ankles with the needle, and our sailors amuse themselves with having an anchor or a ship in full sail done with gunpowder on their arms; but in this last case the original purpose is lost, for the picture is hidden under the sleeve. Naturally, as clothing comes more and more to cover the body, the primitive skin-decorations cease, for what is the use of adorning oneself out of sight?

The head is frequently cropped or shaved close as a sign of mourning. Some thus go bald always, as among the Andaman islanders; or let the hair grow in tonsure-fashion in a ring round the shaved crown, like the Coroado (that is, "crowned") Indian of Brazil; or wear a shaven head with a long scalp-lock or pigtail like the North American Indians, or the Manchus of Tartary, from whom the modern Chinese have adopted this habit. A curious mode of twisting the hair with strips of bark into hundreds of long thin ringlets is seen in the portraits of natives of Lepers' Island, Fig. 66.

Various tribes grind their front teeth to points, or cut them away in angular patterns, so that in Africa and elsewhere a man's tribe is often known by the cut of his teeth. Long finger-nails are noticed even among ourselves as showing that the owner does no manual labour, and in China and neighbouring countries they are allowed to grow to a monstrous length as a symbol of nobility, ladies wearing silver cases to protect them, or at least as a pretence that they are there (see the portraits of Siamese actresses in royal dress   ). Or the nails may be let to grow as a sign that the wearer leads a religious life, and does no worldly work, as in the accompanying figure of the hand of a Chinese ascetic, Fig. 67.

As any nation's idea of beauty is apt to be according to the type of their own race, they like to see their distinc-

tive features exaggerated. Looking at a Hottentot
face,   one understands why the mothers would
squeeze the babies' snub noses yet further in, while in
ancient times a little Persian prince would have a bold

Fig. 66.—Natives of Lepers' Island (New Hebrides)

aquiline nose shaped for him.   In
all quarters of the globe is found the custom of compres-
sing infants' heads by bandages and pads to make the
little plastic skull grow to an approved shape.   But as to
what that shape ought to be, tastes differ extremely.   In

the Columbia River district, some Flathead tribes will so
flatten out the forehead that the front faces look like a
pear with the large end uppermost, while neighbouring
tribes press in the upper part of the skull so that their
faces look like the pear with the small end up.   Hippokrates, the ancient physician, mentions the artificially
deformed skulls of the Makrokephali or " long-heads "

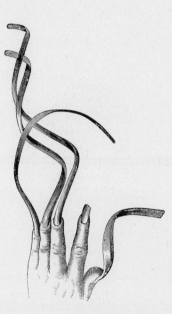

Fig. 67.—Hand of Chinese ascetic.

of the Black Sea district.   The genuine Turkish skull is
of the broad Tatar form, while the nations of Greece and
Asia Minor have oval skulls, which gives the reason why
at Constantinople it became the fashion to mould the
babies' skulls round, so that they grew up with the
broad head of the conquering race.   Relics of such
barbarism linger on in the midst of civilization, and not
long ago a French physician surprised the world by the
fact that nurses in Normandy were still giving the
children's heads a sugar-loaf shape by bandages and a

tight cap, while in Brittany they preferred to press it round. No doubt they are doing so to this day.

The propensity to beautify the body with ornaments belongs to human nature as low down as we can follow it. In South America the naked people were adorned with rings on legs and arms, and one tribe had as their only apparel a macaw's feather stuck in a hole at each corner of their mouths, and strings of shells hanging from their noses, ears, and under-lips. This latter case is a good example of the ornaments being fastened into the body, which is pierced or cut to receive them. Various tribes wear labrets or lip-ornaments, some gradually enlarging

Fig. 68.—Botocudo woman with lip- and ear-ornaments.

the hole through the under-lip till it will take a wooden plug two or three inches across, as in the portrait (Fig. 68) of a woman of the Botocudos, a Brazilian tribe who owe their name to this labret, which the Portuguese compared to a *botoque* or bung. Ear-ornaments, as the figure shows, are put in the same way in the lobe of the ear, which they stretch so that when the disc of wood is taken out it falls in a loop and even reaches the shoulder. Thus it is possible that there may be some truth in the favourite wonder-tale of the old geographers, about the tribes whose great ears reached down to their shoulders, though the story had to be stretched a good deal farther when it was declared that they lay down on one ear and covered themselves with the other for a blanket. The

great interest to us in these savage ornaments is in the
tendency of higher civilization to give them up.   In
Persia one still finds the nose-ring through one side of a
woman's nostril, but European taste would be shocked
by this, though it allows the ear to be pierced to carry
an ear-ring.   As to ornaments which are merely put on,
they are mostly feathers, flowers, or trinkets worn in
the hair, or strung-ornaments or rings on the neck, arms,
and legs.   In what remote times man had begun to take
pleasure in such decorations may be seen by the peri-
winkle-shells bored for stringing found in the cave of
Cro-Magnon, which no doubt made necklaces and bracelets for the girls of the mammoth-period.   In the modern
world necklaces and bracelets remain in unchanged use,
though anklets, such as the bangles of the Hindu dancing-
girl, have of course disappeared from the costume of
civilized wearers of shoes and stockings.   It would not
suit our customs to keep an affectionate memory of dead
relatives by wearing their finger and toe bones strung as
beads, as the Andaman women do, but our ladies keep
in fashion barbaric necklaces of such things as shells,
seeds, tigers' claws, and especially polished stones.   The
wearing of shining stones as ornaments lasts on, whether
they have come to be precious pearls or rubies, or glass
beads which are imitation stones.   Where metal becomes
known it at once comes into use for ornament, and this
reaches its height where amused travellers describe
some Dayak girl with her arms sheathed in a coil of stout
brass wire, or some African belle whose great copper rings
on her limbs get so hot in the sun that an attendant
carries a water-pot to sluice them down now and then.
To see gold jewelry of the highest order, the student
should examine that of the ancients, such as the Egyptian,
Greek, and Etruscan in the British Museum, and that of
mediæval Europe.   The art seems now to have passed
its prime, and become a manufacture, of which the best
products are imitations from the antique.   The cutting
of precious stones such as diamonds into facets is, however, a modern art.   As to finger-rings, if their use arose
out of the signet rings of Egypt and Babylon, then the
few which are still engraved as seals keep up the original
idea, while those which only carry pearls or diamonds
have turned into mere ornaments.

To come now to clothing proper.   The man who wants
a garment gets it in the simplest way when he takes the
covering off a tree or a beast, and puts it on himself.

The bark of trees provides clothes for rude races in many districts, as for instance in the curious use which natives of the Brazilian forests have long made of the so-called " shirt-tree " (lecythis). A man cuts a four or five feet length of the trunk, or a large branch, and gets the bark off in an entire tube, which he has then only to soak and beat soft and to cut slits for armholes, to be able to slip it on as a ready-made shirt; or a short length will make a woman's skirt. The wearing of bark has some-times been kept up as a sign of primitive simplicity. Thus in India it is written in the laws of Manu that when the grey-haired Brahman retires into the forest to end his days in religious meditation, he shall wear a skin or a garment of bark. A ruder people, the Kayans of Borneo, while in common life they like the smart foreign stuffs of the trader, when they go into mourning throw them off and return to the rude native garment of bark-cloth. In Polynesia the manufacture of *tapa* from the bark of the paper-mulberry was carried to great perfection, the women beating it out with grooved clubs into a sort of vegetable felt, and ornamenting it with coloured patterns rubbed on. The people were delighted with the white paper of the Europeans, and dressed themselves in it as a fine variety of tapa, till they found that the first shower of rain spoilt it. Leaves, also, are made into aprons or skirts which clothe various rude tribes. Not only are there " leaf-wearers " in India, but at a yearly festival in Madras the whole low-caste population cast off their ordinary clothing, and put on aprons of leafy twigs.

The skin garments worn by the savages of the ancient world have rotted away these many thousand years, but we may see how generally they used to be worn by the vast numbers of skin-dressing implements of sharp stone (see Fig. 54 c) found in the ground. Till lately the Patagonians, when they came on their journeys to a place where suitable flint or obsidian was to be found, would load themselves with a supply of lumps to chip into these primitive currier's scrapers. Savages, that their fur robes or deer-skin shirts should not dry stiff, know how to dress the leather skilfully by such processes as rubbing in fat or marrow, and suppling with the hands; they also smoke it, to keep. Thus the North Americans know how to prepare deer-skin for garments into something like what we call chamois leather. But it hardly seems as though the lower races had taught themselves the process of actual tanning with bark or galls, where the tannic acid forms in the substance of the skin insoluble compounds which resist change for ages, so that the beautiful cut and embossed work in tanned leather from ancient Egypt may still be seen perfectly preserved in our museums. In such riding countries as Mexico, suits of leather are still worn, while in Europe the buff jerkin and the huntsman's buckskins are disappearing; but it is still everywhere acknowledged that there is nothing like leather for covering the feet. In wearing furs, our height of luxury keeps curiously close to the savage fashion of the primitive world.

Plaiting and matting are arts of such simplicity that they are known to savages. In hot countries matting is convenient for dress, as when South Sea Islanders make gowns of plaited grass, and the old art still provides the civilized world with hats and bonnets of straw or chip. Next, if we pull a scrap of woven cloth to pieces, we see that it is in fact a piece of matting done with thread. Therefore, to understand weaving, we have to begin with the making of string or thread. All mankind can twist string, but some peoples do it in a lower way than others, taking vegetable fibre, wool, or hair, and twisting it by rolling between their flat palms, or with one hand on the thigh. Our shoemakers still keep up this ancient process, which it is worth the reader's while to imitate, by twisting two strands of tow, and then rolling these into one with the reverse movement. At any rate he will find how much practice he would take to do it as cleverly as the Australians when they have the women's hair cut to furnish a supply of fishing-lines, or the New Zealanders when they run out a handful of native flax by inches into a neat and perfect cord. But the higher nations use a mechanical contrivance, the spindle, for thread-making, and the question is how this came to be invented. Fig, 69 shows what may have happened. At *a* is figured a cross-stick, forming a simple reel or winder, on which the Australians wind their hair-string just mentioned. Now if it had occurred to one of these savages to secure his thread by drawing it into a split at the end of the stick, he might have seen that by giving the hanging reel a twirl he could make it twist a new strand for him much faster than he could do between his hands. The Australian never saw how to do this. But looking at *b* in the figure, which represents an ancient Egyptian woman spinning, it is evident that such a

spindle as she is working with may have been invented
by turning a mere reel to this new use. Such spindles
were known over the ancient civilized world, and among
the commonest objects dug up near old dwellings are the
spindle-whorls of stone or terra-cotta, like great buttons,
which with a stick through the middle formed the whole
simple implement. Spindles may still be seen in the
hands of peasant women in Italy or Switzerland. It
teaches at once the permanence and the development of
machinery, to watch in the factory the action of the
spinning-frame which combines the ancient implement
with modern appliances, a hundred spindles in a row

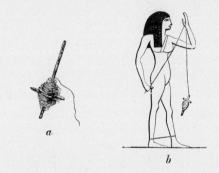

FIG. 69.—*a*, Australian winder for hand-twisted cord; *b*, Egyptian woman
spinning with the spindle.

being driven rapidly by steam-power, and all tended by
a single operative.

The next point is how people provided with thread or
yarn taught themselves to weave it into cloth. As has
just been said, cloth is a sort of matting made with
threads, but as these cannot be held stiff like rushes, a
number of them may be stretched in a frame to form a
warp, and then the cross-thread or woof worked in and
out with the fingers, or on a stick, as the Mexican girl is
doing in Fig. 70. This toilsome method still suits the
difficult patterns of the tapestry-weaver. But time-
saving contrivances were invented very early. The
ancient Egyptian pictures already show the alternate
threads of the warp being lifted by cross-bars, so as to
allow the woof-thread carried by a shuttle to be sent
right across the piece of cloth at one throw. The looms

of classic Greece and Rome were much the same, and
little improvement was made in the machine during the
Middle Ages. Indeed in out-of-the-way places such as
the Hebrides, the tourist may still see the old cottage-loom
which, except in being horizontal so that the weaver sits
to it instead of standing, hardly differs from the loom at
which Penelope may be imagined weaving the famous
shroud that she undid at night. Only about a century
ago improvement began again, when the "flying shuttle"
was invented, which instead of being thrown by hand,
was driven swiftly across by a pair of levers or artificial
arms. Of late years this improved loom has passed
into the power-loom, the steam-engine now doing the
hard labour instead of the weaver's hands and feet. The

FIG. 70.—Girl weaving. (From an Aztec picture.)

ingenious device of the Jacquard loom, with its perforated
cards arranging the threads, has made it possible to
weave even landscapes and portraits.

The primitive *tailor* or "cutter" (*tailleur*) had not
only to cut his skin or bark into shape, but to join pieces
by means of sinew or thread. This art of sewing makes
its appearance among savages, and is seen in its rudest
form among the Fuegians who pierce their guanaco-
skins with a pointed bone, push the thread through, and
make a tie at each hole. Among tribes who have only
such bone awls, or stiff thorns, to work with, sewing cannot get beyond the shoemaker's fashion of first making
a row of holes and then pushing and pulling the thread
through. But bone needles with eyes are found in the
reindeer-caves of France, so that possibly the seamstresses
of the mammoth-period may already have known how

to stitch and embroider their soft skins. When the metal-period began, bronze needles came into use such as are to be seen in museums, and in modern times the fine steel needles have become an example how finish and cheapness may be gained by division of labour, one set of workpeople being entirely occupied in grinding the points, another in drilling the eyes, and so on. But the sewing-needle is still in principle that of the ancient world, and hand-sewing, after holding its place for thousands of years, has suddenly had to compete with the work of the new sewing-machine, which runs its more rapid seams in a mechanically different way.

Next, as to the shape of garments. If we knew of no costume but what we commonly wear now, we might think it more a product of mere fancy than it really is. But on looking carefully at the dresses of various nations it is seen that most garments are variations of a few principal kinds, each made for a particular purpose in clothing the body. The simplest and no doubt earliest garments are wraps wound or hung on the body, and by noticing how there are worn it may be guessed how they led to the later use of garments fitted to the wearer's shape. To begin with the simplest mantles, a skin or blanket with a hole through the middle forms a ready-made garment of the poncho kind. When one throws a rug or blanket over one's shoulders, it becomes a garment which requires fastening in front, or on one shoulder, to leave the arm free. This fastening may be done with a thorn or bone pin, the primitive *brooch*, that is, " skewer " (French *broche*); we now use the word brooch to mean the more civilized metal pin with a safety-clasp, the Latin *fibula* or " fixer." Now if one stands thus draped in a blanket or sheet, one has only to raise the arms to show how naturally sleeves came to be made by sewing together under the arms. Next, putting the blanket over the head and holding it under the chin, it is seen how the part over the head will make a hood, which can be thrown back when not wanted. When it was found convenient to make the hood separate, there arose various kinds of head-covering, whose baggy shape often shows their origin, for instance the pointed " fool's-cap." When the mantle thrown over the shoulders is short, it forms the *cape* or *cope*; when long, it becomes the *cloak*, which owes its name to its likeness to a bell (French *cloche*). For convenience, many varieties of the mantle are cut into shape, as for instance

the toga in which the ancient Roman draped himself
was rounded off. But ever since the invention of
weaving certain garments had been worn just as they
came from the loom, such as the Scotch plaid, and that
ancient Eastern wrapper which we still know by its
Persian name of *shawl* (*shâl*). Such woven garments
are apt to keep a mark of their origin in the fringe, which
in its original form is the ends of the warp-threads left on
by the weaver, and when these threads are tied together
in bundles they give rise to tassels. Another great
group of garments are tunics, seen in a simple form in
the chiton of ancient Greek female dress, which has been
compared to a linen sack open at both ends, and was held
up by a brooch on each shoulder, leaving openings for the
arms. The tunic, closed at the shoulders and generally
provided with sleeves, is the most universal of civilized
garments, whether worn hanging loose like a shirt, or
drawn in at the waist by a girdle or belt. In its various
forms it is seen as the tunic of the Roman legionary and
the " red shirt " of the Garibaldian volunteer, the coat
of the mediæval noble, the smock-frock of the English
peasant, the blouse of the French workman, and, lastly,
it led to our modern coats and waistcoats, which are
tunics made to open in front and close with buttons.
One of the great steps in personal cleanliness and therefore in culture made by our forefathers, was the adoption
of a linen tunic next the skin, the " short " garment, or
shirt. Again, a piece of cloth wrapped round the body
and held up by a girdle forms the skirt or kilt, and the
way in which Eastern women fasten their skirts together
between the feet, for conveience of walking, shows how
trousers were invented. Many ancient nations wore
trousers, as the Sarmatians, whose modern-looking
costume may be seen on Trajan's column, and the Gauls
and Britons, so that it is a mistake to call the present
Highland costume the " garb of old Gaul." The classic
Greeks and Romans looked on the *braccæ* or *breeches*
as belonging to barbarism, but their opinion has not
been accepted by the civilized world.

These remarks may lead readers to look attentively
into books of costume, which indeed are full of curious
illustrations of the way in which things are not invented
outright by mere fancy, but come by gradual alterations
of what was already there. To account for our present
absurd " chimney-pot " hat, we must see how it came by
successive changes from the conical Puritan hat and the

slouched Stuart hat, and these again from earlier forms.
The sense of the hat-band must be found in its once having been a real cord to draw in the mere round piece of
felt which was the primitive hat; and to understand
why our hat is covered with silk nap, it must be remembered that this is an imitation of the earlier beaver-fur
hat, which would stand rain. Even the now useless
seams and buttons on modern clothes (see   p. 12)
are bits of past history.

This chapter may be concluded with an account of
boats and ships. He who first, laying hold of a floating
bough, found it would bear him up in the water, had
made a beginning in navigation. Naturally, history
has kept no record of the origin of such an art. Yet the
rudest forms of floats, rafts, and boats, may still be seen
in use among savages, and even the civilized traveller
coming to a stream or lake may be glad to make shift
with a log or a bundle of bulrushes to help him across,
and carry his gun and clothes over dry. Comparing
these rough-and-ready means with the contrivances
made with skill and care for permanent use, a fair idea
may be had of the stages through which the shipwrights'
art grew up.

The mere float comes lowest, as where a South Sea
Island child goes into the water with an unhusked
coco-nut to hold on by; or a Hottentot will swim his
goats across the river, supporting his body by sprawling
on one end of a drift-log of willow, which he calls his
" wooden-horse." Australians have been known to
come out to our ships sitting astride logs pointed at the
ends, and paddling with their hands, while native fishermen of California will sit on a bundle of rushes tied up in
the shape of a sailor's hammock. Rude as these are,
they at any rate show that the makers have noticed the
advantage which the craft with a sharp bow has over the
blunt-ended log in getting through the water. In all
quarters of the globe, men improve on the float by
making it hollow for buoyancy; it thus becomes a boat.
One way of doing this is to scoop out a log. Anyone
who happens to have been up country in America may
have paddled himself in such a " dug-out " across a
pond or river; and, after experience of the care required
to keep a cylinder from rolling over in the water, he will
know how great an improvement it was in boat-building
when a keel was put on to steady the craft. To savages
with their stone hatchets, the hollowing out of a log is a

laborious business when the wood is of a hard kind, and they are apt to use fire to help them, setting the tree-trunk alight along the proper line and hacking away the burning wood. Columbus was struck with the size of such vessels made by the natives of the West Indies, mentioning in his letters many canoes of solid wood, " multas scaphas solidi ligni," some so large as to hold seventy to eighty rowers. The Spaniards adopted their Haitian name *canoa*, whence our *canoe*. Yet this *dug-out*, or *monoxyle* (" one-log "), to use its Greek name, was well known in other barbaric countries, and had been common in Europe in ages before history, as may be seen by the specimens in museums, preserved by the peat or sand in which they were found imbedded. Even the Latin word *scapha*, used above, carries the record of this early boat-building; it is Greek *skaphē*, which corresponds so exactly in meaning to the term " dug-out," as to be an evident relic of the time when boats were really scooped out of solid trunks; related to these words are English *skiff* and *ship*, so that the line of connexion in names runs through from first to last. Another very simple way of making a boat is that seen among the Australians, where a man will strip a sheet of bark off the stringy-bark tree, tie it together at the ends, and paddle off in this improvised bark-canoe. If, however, it is to be used more than once, he sews the ends together, and puts in stretchers or cross-pieces of wood to keep it in shape. Thus appears the bark-canoe, not unknown in Asia and Africa, and attaining in North America its greatest perfection, with its framework of cedar and sheathing of sheets of birch-bark sewed together with fibrous cedar-roots. Such canoes are still in full use in districts like the Hudson's Bay territory, being well suited to a broken navigation where rapids make it needful to carry boat and cargo overland, or a " portage " has to be made from one river to another. The principle of skin-canoes is much the same, using hide for bark. North American Indians crossing rivers have been known to turn the skins of their tents into vessels by means of a few twigs to keep them stretched. Scarcely above this are the round skin-covered boats of boughs of Mesopotamia, and the portable coracles of the ancient Britons; on the Severn and the Shannon fishermen still go down to the river carrying on their backs their coracles, now made of tarred canvas on a frame, but modelled on the ancient type. The Esquimaux kayak has its framework of bone or drift-wood on which are stretched the seal-skins which convert it into a water-tight life-buoy, in which the skin-clad paddler can even turn over sideways and bring his boat up right on the other side. Our modern so-called canoes are imitations of this in wood.

Next, when the barbaric shipwright comes to improving a dug-out canoe by sewing or lacing on a strip of thin board as a gunwale, or making his whole boat by sewing thin boards together over the ribs, instead of skins or sheets of bark, he brings his vessel a stage nearer to our boats. From Africa across to the Malay Archipelago, such sewn ships used to be, and often still are, the ordinary native craft. The South Sea Island canoes, thus laced together with sinnet or coco-nut fibre braid so neatly that the joints hardly show, are marvels of barbaric carpentry. In the gulf of Oman, men used to go across to the coco-nut islands with their tools, cut down a few palms, make the wood into planks, sew these together with cord made from the bark, make sails of the leaves, load the new-made ships with the nuts, and set sail.

Before coming to the ships of civilized nations, let us look back for a moment to the ruder floats. Two or three logs fastened together form a raft, which though clumsy to move has the advantage of not upsetting, and carrying a heavy load. At the time of the discovery of Peru, the Spaniards were amazed to meet with a native raft out in the ocean, and with a sail set. The rafts which bring goods down the Euphrates and Tigris are buoyed with blown sheep-skins; at the end of the voyage the raft is broken up and the wood sold, so that only the empty skins have to go back to serve another time. With still more perfect economy, the rafts down the Nile are buoyed with earthen pots for sale in the bazaar, so that nothing goes back. Timber-rafts, like those on the Rhine, are well arranged for merely floating down stream. But when a raft has to be driven through the water by oars or sails, its resistance is excessive, and it has occurred to the Fijians and other islanders that a raft formed by two parallel logs united by cross-poles and carrying a raised platform, would go more easily. Looking at this simple contrivance, it has been reasonably thought that it led up to the invention of the outrigger canoe, known in ancient Europe, and now prevailing in the Pacific and as far as Ceylon. One of the two logs is now represented by the canoe, the second remaining as the outrigger log, fastened to the ends of the two projecting poles, so as to steady the whole in rough weather. Or indeed the two logs may both become canoes, and the platform be retained; thus we have the Polynesian double-canoe, whose principle has been lately turned to account in the double-steamboat to smooth the passage between Dover and Calais.

Next, as to the ways by which boats are propelled through the water. The origin of rowing is plainly shown by the Australian straddling his pointed log and paddling with his hands, or by the fisherman of the Upper Nile propelling with his feet the bundle of stalks he sits astride on. The primitive wooden paddle, imitating the form and doing the work of the flat hand or foot, is well known to savages, who mostly use the single paddle with a blade or shovel end; the double-ended paddle, such as our canoeists have borrowed from the Esquimaux, is a peculiar improved form. The paddle used free-handed to dig or sweep at the water is best suited to the narrow bark-canoe or hollowed trunk, but for larger craft it is a rude contrivance as compared with the civilized oar, which is a lever pulled against a fulcrum so as to use more of the rower's force, and in a steadier pull. The difference between barbaric and civilized knowledge of mechanical principles is well seen by comparing a large South Sea Island canoe, with twenty paddlers shovelling the water, to one of our eight-oared launches. Of sails, perhaps the simplest idea is to be seen in Catlin's sketch of North American Indians standing up each in his canoe, holding up his blanket with outstretched arms with its lower end tied to his leg, and so going before the wind. The rudest regular sail used anywhere is a mat or cloth held up by two sticks as stays at the upper corners and made fast below, or supported by an upright pole and cross-piece, the primitive mast and yard. It is so common for the lower tribes of men never to sail their boats, that it is difficult to imagine that their ancestors ever knew how. Surely they would have kept it up, for the art of saving so much labour with so little pains would not easily have fallen out of mind. It seems more likely that the invention of the sailing vessel belongs to a period when civilization was far advanced. Yet this period was very ancient.

Up to this point, in making out how the simpler kinds of boats came into existence, history gives no help. Not

only does their origin mostly lie beyond record, but by
the time we come fairly into history we find the ancient
nations knowing how to build vessels of more advanced
order, framed with keel and ribs, and sheathed with
nailed planks, in fact the direct predecessors of our own
ships. Egypt, or somewhere else in that Old World
region of ancient culture, may have been the original
centre whence the higher shipwrights' craft spread over
the world. It is instructive to study the ancient
Egyptian vessel (Fig. 71) depicted on the wall of a
Theban tomb, and to see how far it already has in a
rudimentary state the parts which we recognise as
belonging to the fully-developed ship. As was common,

FIG. 71.—Ancient Nile-boat, from wall-painting, Thebes.

it was a combination of rowing-galley and sailing-ship.
The rowers sit on cross benches, pulling at the oars which
pass through loops, while at the stern is worked the great
steering-oar which is the ancestor of our *rudder* (this used
to be merely an oar, which its name originally meant,
like *ruder* in German). There is a mast held up by stays
and carrying yards, with ropes rigged to hoist them and
to furl the sail. The forecastle and poop are already
represented by raised structures on the deck. In the
Egyptian pictures of war-ships it is seen how these
served as stations for the archers, while the fighting-men
were also protected behind a bulwark, and there is even
the " crow's nest " on the top of the mast serving as a
place for slingers to hurl stones from at the enemy, from
which comes our " mast-head." Comparing with the

Egyptian vessels the ancient galleys and ships of the Mediterranean, whether Phœnician, Greek, or Roman, it is impossible to think these can have come into existence by separate lines of invention; the family likeness among them is too strong. Even farther off, the likeness of the craft still used in the Ganges to the ancient Nile-boats is surprising, and the eye of Osiris painted on the Egyptian funeral bark that carried the dead across the lake to the western burial-place may perhaps have first suggested the painting of eyes as ornaments on the bows of boats, from the barks in Valetta harbour in the west to the junks of Canton in the east. In following the course of development from the ancient to the modern ship, we notice that from time to time new appliances came in, as metal sheathing to protect the planks from the boring teredo, the iron fluked anchor instead of a great stone, the capstan for hauling, &c. More masts and spars now served to carry more sails, and tier above tier of rowers impelled the classic bireme and trireme. The war-galley lasted on into our own time in the Venetian navy, kept in use in spite of its bad sea-going quality for its power of dashing upon sailing-vessels helpless in a calm. The galley-slaves who laboured at the huge oars were captives or criminals, and, though the French galleys no longer remain for penal servitude, the term *galérien* or galley-slave still means a convict. The vast improvement of European sailing-vessels in the Middle Ages is in great measure due to an invention learnt from the far east—the mariner's compass. Ships, now able to steer their courses on long voyages out of sight of land, were improved in build and rigging, while the men-of-war with several decks armed with tiers of cannon became floating castles. Lastly, during the present century, steam-power has been applied to propel the ship from within, the paddle-wheel or screw in fact taking the place of the old banks of oars, and the changeable wind-power being now only turned to account as an occasional aid and means of saving fuel. It is needless to describe the changes which modern armour-plating and huge guns have made in the construction of ships of war, but even these still show plainly enough how they were formed by successive alterations from the primitive canoe.

CHAPTER XI

ARTS OF LIFE—(*concluded*)

THE subject next to be considered is Fire and its uses. Man understands fire and deals with it in ways quite beyond the intelligence of the lower animals. There is an old story how, in the forests of equatorial Africa, when travellers had gone away in the morning and left their fires burning, the huge manlike apes called pongos (probably our gorillas) would come and sit round the burning logs till they went out, not having the sagacity to lay more wood on. This story is often repeated to contrast human intelligence with the dulness of even the highest apes. Of course there had been forest-fires in ages before man, as when the trees had been set in flames by lightning or by a lava stream. But of all creatures man alone has known how to manage fire, to carry it from place to place with burning brands, and when it went out to produce it afresh. No savage tribe seems really to have been found so low as to be without fire. In the limestone caverns, among the relics of the mammoth period, morsels of charcoal and burnt bones are found imbedded, which show that even in that remote antiquity the rude cave-men made fires to cook their food and warm themselves by.

As to the art of producing fire, the savage way was mostly by the friction of two pieces of wood, and to this day travellers may now and then see the simple apparatus at work. The hand fire-drill consists of a stick like an arrow-shaft cut to a blunt point, which is twirled like a chocolate-muller between the hands (shifted up when they get too far down) with such speed and pressure as to bore a hole into an under-piece of wood, till the charred dust made by the boring takes fire. Fig. 72 shows a Bushman thus drilling fire while his companion attends to the tinder. The Polynesian way is different, pushing the pointed stick along a groove of its own making in the under-piece of wood. Either method will make fire in a few minutes, but knack and proper choice of wood are needed, and one of us will hardly succeed. For easier working, some nations have long had a mechanical improvement on the simple savage fire-drill, by driving it with a thong wound a couple of turns round the stick, and pulled to and fro; also, working it with a bow like the common bow-drill of our tool-shops is not unknown. In either case a top-piece is required to keep the drill down (not too hard) on its bearing.

Among civilized nations, the old fire-drill had already

FIG. 72.—Bushman drilling fire (after Chapman).

in ancient times been superseded in common use by better contrivances, especially the flint and steel. But although discarded from practical life, it has been kept up for ceremonial purposes. As has been already mentioned (p. 12), the Hindu fire-priest may be still seen " churning " with a fire-drill driven by a cord the divine fire for their sacrifices, thus religiously keeping to the old-fashioned instrument used in daily life by the early Aryans. The ancient Romans had such a survival of their past state of arts in the law that, if the vestal virgins let out the sacred fire, it was to be made afresh by drilling into a wooden board. The old art has even lasted on in Europe to our own day as the orthodox means of kindling the " need-fire," with which, when there was a murrain, the peasants in many parts used to light bonfires to drive the horses and cattle through, to save them from the pestilence. This rite, inherited from the religion of præ-Christian times, requires new wild-fire made by friction, not the tame fire of the hearth. The last need-fire on record in Great Britain is perhaps one that was made in Perth in 1826, but they may still be seen in Sweden and elsewhere when there is cholera or other pestilence about. In the last century there was a law passed forbidding the superstitious friction-fire in Jönköping, the very district now famous for its cheap *tandstickor* or tinder-sticks, that is, lucifer-matches. So curiously do the extremes of civilization come together in the world.

The fire-drill is a means of converting mechanical force into heat till the burning-point of wood is reached. But all that is really wanted is a glowing hot particle or spark, and this can be far more easily got in other ways. Breaking a nodule of iron pyrites picked up on the sea-shore, and with a bit of flint striking sparks from it on tinder, is a way of fire-making quite superior to the use of the wooden drill. It was known to some modern savages, even the miserable natives of Tierra del Fuego; to the præhistoric men of Europe, as appears from the bits of pyrites found in their caves; and of course to the old civilized world, as witness the Greek name of the mineral, *puritēs* or " fiery." Substitute for this a piece of iron, and we have the flint-and-steel, the ordinary apparatus of nations from their entry into the iron age till modern times. Yet even this has now been so discarded that the old-fashioned kitchen tinder-box with its flint and U-shaped steel, and damper for preparing the tinder from scraps of burnt linen to light the brimstone-match with, has become a curiosity worth securing when found by chance in some farmhouse. Mention need hardly be made here of the burning-lens and the concave mirror known in ancient Greece, nor of the wooden condensing syringe (much like that described in our books on physics) known in the Chinese region; these are rather curious than practically important. Quite otherwise with the invention of the lucifer-match, dating from about 1840. Its action depends on phosphorus igniting by being rubbed, the head of an ordinary lucifer being of an inflammable composition, containing chlorate or nitrate of potash, which is fired by particles of phosphorus mixed in with it; for the safety-match, these particles of phosphorus are put, not in the match-head, but on the rubber instead.

In the low levels of civilization the hut is often so small

that the fire has to be made outside. But when it becomes spacious enough, the fire of logs burns on the hard-trodden earth in the middle of the hut, the smoke finding its way out as it can by door and cracks. Those who have chanced to spend a night lying on the ground with their feet to the fire in such a dwelling know both what place the fire has in barbaric comfort, and how that comfort was increased when builders took the trouble to make a smoke-hole in the roof, and afterwards came to a real chimney. The history of artificial warming from this point lies so plainly before us as not to need a long description. From the fire of a few sticks on the cottage hearth, we come to the wide fire-places in the halls of country houses, with their fire-dogs, after the fashion of the Middle Ages. Then come the coal-fires in open grates, the closed stoves, and the arrangements for warming the house with currents of hot air, or circulating pipes of hot water.

From house-warming we come to cookery. The heat applied in cooking food, bursting the cells and softening the tissues so as to make it easier to chew, is an important aid to digestion, saving energy which would be wasted on assimilating raw flesh or vegetables. It would not indeed be impossible for man to live on uncooked food, and perhaps the nearest approach to this is found on some coral islands of the Pacific, where raw fish and coco-nuts form a great part of the native diet. Low tribes, especially half-starved wanderers of the deserts, such as the Australians, eat insects, grubs, shellfish, and small reptiles, raw as they find them; and Brazilian forest-men have been seen to imitate the ant-bear by poking a stick into an ant-hill, and letting the ants run up it into their mouths. These practices shock Europeans, who themselves however have no scruples as to oysters and cheese-mites, to which they happen to be accustomed. But these rude tribes know how to cook, as indeed all mankind do, the familiar definition of man as the " cooking animal " having no proved exception, ancient or modern. Civilized nations have come so thoroughly to this way of assisting nature, that they cook almost everything they eat, only keeping up primitive habits in eating nuts, berries, and other fruit raw as more pleasing to the taste. It has long been looked on as a sign of low culture to eat raw meat, like the Eurytanes of the interior of Greece whom Thukydides mentions as " most ignorant in their speech, and said to be raw-

eaters (ōmophagoi)." Even the native tribes of New
England were struck with this habit among the roving
race of the far north, whom they called accordingly
Eskimantsic or "raw-flesh-eaters," a name they still
bear in its French form *Esquimaux*.

The roughest ways of cooking are to be seen among
savages, who broil their meat on the burning logs, or
roast it stuck on the primitive spit, a pointed stake
planted sloping over the fire, or bury it in the hot embers
as boys do chestnuts or potatoes. From this latter mode
comes the invention of the oven, which in its simplest
form may be a pit dug in the ground, often lined with
baking-stones; when it has been heated by a wood-fire
within, the meat or vegetables are put in and covered up
with ashes. Brazilian tribes set up four posts with a
grating of branches across, on which they laid their game
and fish with a slow fire underneath. Meat prepared on
such a *boucan* will keep a long while; the pirates of the
West Indies used thus to prepare their stores of meat,
whence comes the word *bucaneer*. To the buffalo-
hunting tribes of North America belongs the invention of
pemmican, meat dried and pounded for keeping, while in
many parts of the world people know how to dry sheets
or strips of meat in the hot sun; this is called *jerked*
meat, and will keep. The use of hot stones in baking
has just been mentioned. From this the important art
of boiling food may have been derived. In many parts
of the world, among tribes who do not know how to
make an earthen pot, there is found the curious art of
stone-boiling, which is a sort of wet baking. The
Assinaboins of North America have their name, which
means "stone-boilers," from their old practice of digging
a hole in the ground, lining it with a piece of the
slaughtered animal's hide, and then putting in the meat
with water, and hot stones to boil it. Tribes of the far
West actually managed by means of red-hot stones to
boil salmon and acorn-porridge in their baskets made of
close-plaited roots of the spruce fir. The process of
stone-boiling has lasted on even in Europe where found
convenient for heating water in wooden tubs. Linnæus
on his northern tour found the Bothland people brewing
beer in this way, and to this day the "rude Carinthian
boor" drinks such "stone-beer," as it is called. As
soon as the cooks anywhere are provided with earthen
pots or metal kettles, boiling over the fire becomes easy.
Yet it is curious to notice the absence of boiled meats

from the feasts of the Homeric heroes, where there is so much about the joints stuck on spits to roast, and the vengeful Odysseus rolling to and fro on his bed is compared to an eager roaster turning a stuffed paunch before the blazing fire. Among the old Northmen it was otherwise, for it is told in the Edda how the warriors feast every night in Walhalla on the sodden flesh of the boar Sæhrimnir, who is daily boiled in the huge kettle, and comes to life again ready for the morrow's hunt.

The simplest ways of making bread, such as seem to have come in with the earliest cultivation of grain, answer so well for some purposes that they may still be seen almost unchanged. Thus in a north-country cottage the housewife moistens the oatmeal and kneads it into dough, which spread out thin is baked into oatcakes on the hot iron girdle (it used to be a hot stone); and the damper of the Australian colonist is as simply made with flour and water in thick cakes, baked in the embers. These take us back near the primitive stages of an art which almost more than any other has civilized mankind. Such unleavened bread being first in use, the invention of leavened bread would follow as a matter of course, by the sour dough on the uncleaned vessel fermenting into *leaven* (French *levain*, lightening), which starts fermentation through the fresh dough, disengaging bubbles of carbonic acid within it which expand it into a spongy mass. In later times the yeast from brewing was found to be a better means than leaven; and there are modern processes of introducing the gas by means of baking-powder (such as sal-aëratus or aërated salt, bicarbonate of soda), or the bread may be aërated by mixing the carbonic acid gas mechanically. The other great means of preparing farinaceous or starchy food is by boiling, which lets the starch out to mix with the water by bursting the tiny granules in which it is enclosed. Rice boiled whole furnishes about half the food of mankind, and among other staple articles of vegetable food are the various kinds of pap or porridge made with wheat, barley, oats, maize, sago, cassava, &c. Looking over a modern cookery-book, it is seen what an endless list of dishes and sauces have been contrived by clever cooks, to please the palate and make one wish for more. As to progress in cookery in this way, no doubt the moderns have left the ancients behind. But, after all, the main purpose of cooking food is to bring it into a proper condition for keeping up and working the human machine, body and mind. Examining it from this point of view, it is curiouś to notice what an old-world business it is. Its main processes of roasting, baking, and boiling, belong to the barbaric stage of culture, and had their origin in ages before history.

The liquors drunk by man may next be noticed. Savage tribes such as the Australians were water-drinkers when discovered by the Europeans, and even the Hottentots and North American Indians knew no fermented drinks. It is difficult to suppose that an indulgence so tempting would ever be forgotten, if once known; so that possibly the ancestors of these peoples may have from the first been ignorant of the art of fermenting liquor. But in most countries, especially where grain and fruit were cultivated, one would think that the process must sooner or later discover itself, by the accident of some suitable juice or mash being left to stand. In Mexico the milky juice of the aloe is fermented into pulque; in Asia and Africa palms are tapped for palm-wine or toddy; cider from apple-juice, and mead from honey and water, are well known; the Tatars ferment their mares' milk into kumiss. Especially liquors of the beer kind prevail widely; the first men-tioned in history is the beer brewed from barley by the ancient Egyptians, whence may perhaps be traced the ancient ale or beer of Europe; allied to it are the kvass or rye-beer of Russia, the pombe or millet-beer of Africa, the so-called rice-wine of the Chinese, the chicha made with maize or cassava by the natives of America. Wine seems not less ancient, and the Egyptian paintings show the vineyards, the wine-presses, the wine-jars; indeed, wine-making is still much what it was in those early ages of history. In ancient times it is curious to notice the frank undoubting delight of men in intoxicat-ing drink, as a divinely given means of drowning care and stimulating dulness into wild joy. They drank it solemnly in their religious feasts and offered it to their gods. The ancient bards of the Vedic hymns thought no ill in singing of Indra the Heaven-god, reeling drunk with the libations of the sacred soma poured out by his worshippers, and in later ages the Greeks chanted in bacchanal processions the praises of the beneficent Dionysos, who made all nations happy with the care-dispelling juice ᴜᴌ the grape. But in early times also there comes into view an opposite doctrine. The guardians of religion, sensible of the evil of drunkenness, begin to proclaim not only excess as hateful, but the very tasting of strong drink a sin. The Brahmans, although the libation of the soma remains by old tradition among their sacred rites, yet account the drinking of spirituous liquors one of the five great sins; while in the old rival religion of Buddha, one of the ten precepts or commandments which the novice promises to obey is that forbidding the use of intoxicating liquor. Though the religion of Mohammed arose in great measure out of Judaism and Christianity, he cast off their ancient honour for wine and its use in sacred rites, forbidding it as an abomination. It was not till the Middle Ages that distilled spirit, though more ancient in the East, came into use among the western nations. It was generally accepted as beneficial, as is well seen in the name of "water of life," Latin *aquavitæ*, French *eau-de-vie*, Irish *usquebaugh* (for shortness *whisky*). Alcoholic spirit is now produced in immense quantities from the refuse of wine-making, brewing, sugar-refining, &c. Its employment as an habitual stimulant is among the greatest evils of the modern world, bringing about in the low levels of the population a state of degradation hardly matched in the worst ages of history. On the other hand, modern civilized life has gained in comfort by taking to the use of warm slightly stimulant drinks. Tea, at first valued by the Buddhist monks in Central Asia as a drug to keep the ascetic awake for his nightly religious duties, seems to have been introduced as a beverage in China at about the Christian era, and has spread from thence all over the world. Coffee is at home in Arabia, and the world owes its general use to the Moslems. Chocolate was brought by the Spaniards from old Mexico where it was a favourite drink. With these, mention has to be made of tobacco, also an importation from America, where at the time of the discovery it was smoked by natives of both the north and south continent.

In here describing fires and fire-places (p.143), wood has been taken as the primitive fuel. Indeed, the fire of fallen boughs made at a picnic in the woods may take our minds fairly back to præhistoric life. When in the savage hut the logs are piled on the earthen floor, this simple hearth already becomes the gathering-place of the family and the type of home. But in treeless districts the want of fuel is one of the difficulties of life, as where on the desert plains the buffalo-hunter has to pick up for the evening fire the droppings which he calls "buffalo-

chips " or " bois de vache." Even in woodland countries,
as soon as people collect in villages, the fire-wood near
by is apt to run short. When some American Indians
were asked what reason they supposed had brought the
white men to their country, they answered quite simply
that no doubt we had burnt up all our wood at home, and
had to move. The guess was so far good that something
of the kind must really have happened had we depended
on the fuel from our forests and peat-bogs, for the supply
in England was giving out. Thus what was in old times
the forest-land of Kent and Sussex, and has still kept
its name of the Weald (*i.e.* wood), is not now well-
timbered, but this is because in Queen Elizabeth's time
it had been stripped to make charcoal for the iron
furnaces. Indeed, there then seemed danger that
as population increased and manufactures throve,
England might become like North China now, where in
the cold weather people huddle at home wrapped in
furs, fuel being too scarce except for the cooking-stove.
But instead of this coming to pass, there took place
an industrial change in England, which multiplied the
population and brought on our present prosperity. This
was the use of coal, on which our modern manufacturing
system depends. Even for household purposes the coal-
cellar has almost superseded the wood-stack, and the
blazing yule-log has become a picturesque relic of the
past. The very word *coal*, which in the English Bible
keeps its original sense of burning wood, has since been
usurped by the mineral. It must not, however, be
supposed that the use of coal was only discovered in
modern times. The Chinese have mined it from time
immemorial. In the thirteenth century, the famous
Venetian traveller, Marco Polo, related that in Cathay
there is a kind of black stones, which are dug out of
veins in the mountains, and burnt like faggots; and I
can tell you (he says) that, if you put them on the fire in
the evening so that they catch well, they will burn all
night and even be alight in the morning. That this was
told and received as a wonder in Europe, shows how
unfamiliar the use of coal then was. Though *lithanthrax*
or " stone-coal " was not unknown to the ancients, its
full importance to modern life only came gradually into
view. Having first been brought in for economy to
meet the scarcity of wood, it afterwards became, when
applied to the steam-engine, an almost boundless source
of power for all mechanical work. A steam-engine, for

every few shovelfuls of coal its furnace is fed with, will do the day's work of a horse.   Thus the yearly output of millions of tons of steam-coal in Great Britain alone furnishes a supply of force in comparison with which what was formerly available from windmills and water-mills and the labour of men and beasts was quite small, while the workman's task becomes more and more that of directing this brute force to grind and hammer, to spin and weave, to carry across land and sea.   It is like the difference between driving the waggon and carrying the sacks of corn to market on one's own back.   It is an interesting problem in political economy to reckon the means of subsistence in our country during the agricultural and pastoral period, and to compare them with the resources we now gain from coal, in doing home-work and manufacturing goods to exchange for foreign produce.   Perhaps the best means of realizing what coal is to us will be to consider that, of three English-men now, one at least may be reckoned to live by coal, inasmuch as without it the population would have been so much less.

The Australian savage would catch up a blazing brand from the camp-fire, to light him into the dark forest and scare away the demons.   Thus there is as yet no difference between his primitive means of artificial heat and light. The two begin to separate when resinous pine-splints or the like are set aside to serve as natural flambeaux, and from this the next step is to make artificial flambeaux, of which the commonest is the twist or *torch* (from Latin *torquere*) of oakum dipped in pitch or wax.   Till this century we used torches much as the ancient Romans did, but they are now seldom to be seen, and by their disuse the picturesque side of life loses many striking effects of torchlight glare and shadow on banquet and procession—the delight of painters and poets.   Not half the passers-by in old-fashioned streets now know that the extinguishers on the iron railings were to put out the links or torches carried to light the company to their coaches.   The candle looks as though it might have been invented from the torch.   The rushlight, made of the pith of the rush dipped in melted fat, was in common use in Pliny's time, as was also the wax or tallow candle with its yarn wick.   The old classic lamp was a flattish oval vessel with a nozzle (*i.e.*, nostril) at one end for the wick to come out at.   Simple as this construction is, it has had a long unchanged use.   Museums have few

Greek and Roman objects more plentiful than such earthenware lamps, nor more exquisite specimens of metal-work than the bronze ones; and to this day the traveller off the main road in Spain or Italy is lighted to his bedroom with a brass stand-lamp much after the manner of the ancients, with its pick-wick hanging to it by a chain. The lamp only came into its improved modern make about a century ago, when Argand let the air in from below, and put on the glass chimney to set up a draught. The gas-lamp is still later, only having come into practical use during the last sixty years. But it is curious to notice that natural gas-lighting had long been known in places where decomposing bituminous beds underground set free carburetted hydrogen. Thus at the famous fire-temples of Baku (west of the Caspian), a hollow cane was stuck in the ground near the altar, through which the gas rose and burnt at its mouth, while the pilgrim fire-worshippers prostrated themselves and adored the sacred flame. In China, at salt springs where such a supply of natural gas comes up, the practical-minded people have for ages laid it on through bamboos to boil the brine-kettles and light up the works. Of late in Pennsylvania, the example has been followed on an immense scale.

The examination here made of the modes of cooking requires some notice of vessels. For water-vessels men can make shift without the art of the potter, using joints of bamboo, coco-nut shells, calabash rinds, buckets scooped out of wood, pails of bark, bottles of skin. The horseman in desert regions carries his water-gourd at his saddle-bow, and even where a glass imitation has come in the French go on calling it a *gourde*, just as we keep up the name of the old leather *bottle* for the glass ones we use now. It was one of the greatest household inventions to make earthen pots to stand the fire for boiling. When and where pottery was invented is too far back to say. On the sites of ancient dwellings, wherever earthenware was in use, potsherds may be picked up in the ground. Where they are not to be found, as among the relics of tribes of the reindeer-period in the caves of France, it may be safely concluded that these early savages had not come so far in civilization. The same is true of the Australians, Fuegians, and many other modern savages who had no pottery, and no broken bits in their soil to show that their predecessors ever had. One asks, how did men first hit upon the idea of making an earthen pot?

It may not look a great stretch of invention, but invention moved by slow steps in early culture, and there are some facts which lead to the guess that even pots were not made all at once.   There are accounts of rude tribes plastering their wooden vessels with clay to stand the fire, while others, more advanced, moulded clay over gourds, or inside baskets, which being then burnt away left an earthen vase, and the marks of the plaiting remained as an ornamental pattern.   It may well have been through such intermediate stages that the earliest potters came to see that they could shape the clay alone and burn it hard.   This shaping was doubtless at first done by hand, as in America or Africa the native women may still be seen building up large and shapely jars or kettles from the bottom, moulding on the clay bit by bit.   So in Europe, as any museum of antiquities shows,

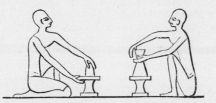

Fig. 73.—Ancient Egyptian Potter's Wheel (Beni Hassan).

the funeral urns and other earthen vessels of the stone and bronze ages were hand-made; and even now tourists who visit the Hebrides buy earthen cups and bowls of an old woman who makes them in ancestral fashion without a potter's wheel, and ornaments them with lines drawn with a pointed stick.   Yet the potter's wheel was known in the world from high antiquity. Fig. 73 represents Egyptian potters at work, as shown in the wall-paintings of the Tombs of the Kings.   It is seen that they turned the wheel by hand.   So the Hindu potter is described as now going down to the river side when a flood has brought him a deposit of fine clay, when all he has to do is to knead a batch of it, stick up his pivot in the ground, balance the heavy wooden table on the top, give it a spin round, and set to work. It was an improvement on this simplest wheel to work it from below by the foot, and in our potteries a labourer drives it with a wheel and band, but the principle

ARTS OF LIFE

152

remains unchanged. As we watch with untiring pleasure
the potter with this simple machine so easily bringing
shape out of shapelessness, we can well understand how
in the ancient world it seemed the very type of creation,
so that the Egyptians pictured one of their deities as a
potter moulding Man on the wheel. Fine art made
some of its earliest and most successful efforts in shaping
the earthen vase, engraving and moulding patterns or
figures on it, and painting it with pictures of gods and
heroes, or scenes from myth or daily life, so that much
of our knowledge of such nations as Etruscans and even
Greeks is derived from the paintings on their vases,
art-relics almost everlasting though so fragile. A great
part of the pottery of the world is still of the first and
simplest kind, mere baked clay (Italian *terra cotta*)
without glaze, like our flower-pots, and therefore porous.
To cure this fault, some people, as the Peruvians,
varnished it, while even the Greeks often burnt in bitu-
men. The great improvement of glazing, that is, melting
on a glassy coating in the furnace, was already known
in ancient Egypt and Babylonia, while in later ages
glazed earthenware reached high artistic excellence in
the Persian ware and the *majolica* (from Majorca). In
China a more perfect ware had been made above a
thousand years before European potters got at the secret
of imitating it. We call it *china*, or by the curious
name *porcelain*, which originally meant a kind of oriental
nacre or mother-of-pearl. China or porcelain dishes are
ordinarily manufactured from a mixture of fine white
kaolin or porcelain clay and felspar, which has to be
fired at a sufficiently high temperature to render it semi-
vitreous throughout, and translucent. The common
principle in the make of these two kinds of pottery,
glazed earthenware and Chinese or European china, lies
in the presence of the fusible glassy silicates, which form
a coating on the surface or are diffused through the
substance.

Glass is a mixture of silicates of two or more of the
bases : soda, potash, lime, lead oxide. There is a fanciful
story told by Pliny, describing its invention as having
taken place on a sandy shore of Phœnicia, where a ship
happening to be moored, the merchants, finding no
stones to boil their kettle on, brought on shore lumps of
nitre with which the ship happened to be laden, where-
upon the fire melted the silica and alkali into glass. But
the fact is that glass-making was an Egyptian art ages

before the rise of Phœnician commerce, and to all appearance the Phœnicians and other nations learnt it from thence. Fig. 74 shows an Egyptian glass-blower. Among other things he would have made flasks to be covered with reed, much like our present oil-flasks. The ancient Egyptians made glass beads, and variegated glass cups, which even the Venetian glassworks can hardly match. But modern Europe may claim the clever art of making crown glass for window-panes by twirling the red-hot blown globe till it opens in a circular sheet, and also the polishing of sheets of plate-glass, which make possible our great looking-glasses with their backs of brilliant tin amalgam.

Fire is so important a means in extracting metal from the ore and working it afterwards, that some account of the use of metal may properly come in this chapter. But

Fig. 74.—Ancient Egyptian Glass-blowing (Beni Hassan).

in thinking how men were led to the difficult processes of smelting ores to extract the metal, it has to be remembered that some metals are found in the metallic state. Thus the native copper near Lake Superior was used in long-past ages by the tribes then living in the country, who treated bits of the metal as a kind of malleable stone, hammering it cold into hatchets, knives, and bracelets. The same is true of gold, natural nuggets of which can be beaten cold into ornaments. It is only a guess that metal-working may have begun in this simple way; still it seems a likely guess. Iron also is found in the metallic state, especially in the aerolites or meteoric stones which fall on the earth from time to time. Though in many of these the metal is apt to shiver to bits under the hammer, there is some meteoric and other native iron fit to be made into implements when heated white-hot in the forge, and it can even be to some extent worked cold. Some of the ores of metal are themselves so metallic-looking that the smith would attempt to work them in the fire, and this may have led to proper smelting. Thus magnetic iron ore not only looks like iron, but can be heated in the forge, and then and there hammered into such things as horse-shoes.

It is a question whether men first worked copper or iron. In classic times, indeed, people felt certain that bronze was in use before iron. This bronze is an alloy of copper with about a ninth of tin to harden it, what an English mechanic would now call " gun-metal." An often-quoted line of Hesiod's tells how the men of old worked in bronze when as yet black iron was not; and Lucretius, the Epicurean poet, taught that after the primitive time when men fought with sticks and stones, iron and bronze were discovered, but bronze was known before iron. However, the Greeks and Romans did not really remember very ancient times, and in some countries the use of iron was early. Egyptian and Babylonian inscriptions make mention of iron as well as copper. A piece of wrought iron taken out of the masonry of the great pyramid may be seen in the British Museum, and there are Egyptian pictures even showing the blue steel which the butcher had hanging at his side to sharpen his knife on. Now what is to be particularly noticed is that the Egyptians, though they thus had iron, mostly made their carpenters' tools of bronze. Among the Homeric Greeks, the smiths knew of iron, and even of steel or steely iron, if one may judge so from the famous passage in the Odyssey (ix. 391) about the hissing of the axe as the smith dips it in the cold water to strengthen the iron. Yet all the while bronze was the ordinary material not only for the warrior's armour and shield, but for his spear and sword. Clearly we have here a state of arts very unlike our own now, and it is worth while to try to understand the difference. An instructive remark in Kaempfer's account of Japan near two centuries ago, may help to explain it, where he says that both copper and iron were smelted in the country, and were about the same price, so that iron tools cost as much as copper or brass ones. The state of things far back in the ancient world may have been something like this. Iron, though known, was hard to smelt from the ore, and Homer's calling it the " much-wrought iron " shows how difficult the smiths found it to forge. But copper was plentiful, one well-known source being the island of Cyprus, whence its name of *æs Cyprium* (*copper*). Tin had not to be fetched from the ends of the world; there were mines in Georgia, Khorassan, and elsewhere in inner Asia, where perhaps the discovery was made of using it to harden copper into bronze. When once this had been hit upon, the ease with which bronze could be melted, and such things as hatchets cast in stone moulds, would make it more convenient than iron to the ancient artificer. This may have been the real reason why the " bronze age " set in over a great part of Europe and Asia, and was only followed by the " iron age " when iron, coming to be better worked, cheaper and more plentiful, and steel especially being improved, brought out that superiority to bronze for tools and weapons which to us seems a matter of course. The remains of the lake-dwellings of Switzerland show how central Europe was one inhabited by rude tribes using stone implements, how at a later period bronze hatchets and spears prevailed, and lastly iron came in. Such, too, has been the history of the stone, bronze, and iron ages, traced by archæologists in the burial-places of old Scandinavia, whether the use of the new metals was learnt by the native nations or brought in by conquering invaders. Nations living in the bronze age are known to history, especially the Mexicans and Peruvians, whom the Spaniards at the conquest found working in bronze with some skill, but knowing nothing of iron; their state was like that of the Massagetæ of central Asia, described by Herodotus some two thousand years earlier. Most of Africa, on the other hand, seems to have had no bronze age, but to have passed directly from the stone age to the iron age. Iron-smelting seems to have come into Africa in the north, and only spread lately down to the Hotten-tots, who still remember in their stories the time when their ancestors used to cut down trees with stones. The Africans easily dig up their rich iron ore and smelt it with wood in simple furnaces which may be mere holes in the ground, the draught being generally by bellows. The primitive pair of bellows may there be seen, made of whole skins of goats or other animals, of which the one full of air is pressed or trodden on, while the empty one is pulled up to fill itself through a slit or valve. This shows iron-smelting not far from its rudest and probably earliest state. Among the various improvements which have now made iron more plentiful than in ancient times are the use of coke instead of charcoal for smelting; the introduction of cast iron, which seems old in China,

but was not common in England till the last century;
the use of machinery for rolling and forging. The
progress of steel-making has been such as lately to make
it possible for railways to be laid down with steel at a
penny a pound.

Other metals and their effect on civilization may be
spoken of briefly. Silver has from ancient times been
the companion of gold, as precious metals. Lead was
easily extracted, and served the Romans for roofs and
water-pipes. The alloy of copper and zinc was made
by the Romans not by fusing together the two metals,
but by heating copper with the zinc ore called calamine;
the result was brass, an inferior kind of bronze. Quicksilver was known to the ancients, who distilled it from the
red cinnabar, and understood its use in extracting gold
and silver, and for gilding. Of the many metals which
have become known in modern times some have practical
uses. Thus platinum is valuable for vessels which have
to bear extreme heat or resist the action of acids, and
aluminium is useful for its remarkable lightness. But
we still mostly depend on the metals whose origin is
lost in antiquity—iron, copper, tin, lead, silver, and gold.

The mention of these last precious metals leads us to
notice the important part which coin has had in developing civilization, and this again belongs to the general
history of trade or commerce. The modern Englishman,
accustomed to shops and counting-houses, hardly realizes
from what rude beginnings our complex commercial
system arose. It is instructive to see trade in its lowest
form among such tribes as the Australians. The tough
greenstone, valuable for making hatchets, is carried
hundreds of miles by natives who receive from other
tribes in return the prized products of their districts,
such as red ochre to paint their bodies with; they have
even got so far as to let peaceful traders pass unharmed
through tribes at war, so that trains of youths might be
met, each lad with a slab of sandstone on his head to
be carried to his distant home and shaped into a seed-
crusher. When strangers visit a tribe, they are received
at a friendly gathering or corrobboree, and presents
are given on both sides. No doubt there is a general
sense that the gifts are to be fair exchanges, and if either
side is not satisfied there will be grumbling and quarrel-
ling. But in this roughest kind of barter we do not yet
find that clear notion of a unit of value which is the great
step in trading. This higher stage is found among the

Indians of British Columbia, whose strings of haiqua-
shells, worn as ornamental borders to their dresses,
serve them also as currency to trade with, a string of
ordinary quality being reckoned as worth one beaver's
skin. In the Old World many traces have come down of
the times when value was regularly reckoned in cattle;
as where in the Iliad, in the description of the funeral
games, we read of the great prize tripod that was valued
at twelve oxen, while the female slave who was the second
prize was only worth four oxen. Here the principle of
unit of value is already recognized, for not only could
the owner of oxen buy tripods and slaves with them,
but also he who had a twelve-ox tripod to sell could
take in exchange three slaves reckoned at four oxen each.
To this day various objects of use or ornament pass as
currency, especially where money is scarce. Thus the
traveller in Abyssinia may have to buy what he wants
with cakes of salt, while elsewhere in Africa he has to
carry iron hoe-blades, pieces of cloth, and strings of
beads as money. Cowry-shells are still small change in
South Asia, as they have been since time immemorial.
These things do more or less clumsily what metal money
does so conveniently. The use of money arose out of
gold and silver being in old times bartered by weight for
goods, as may be seen in the pictures of the ancient
Egyptians weighing in scales heaps of rings of gold and
silver, which shows that these were not yet real money.
It is thus still with much of the gold and silver traded
with in the East, where the little ingots have to be weighed
and reckoned for what each is worth. The invention of
coin comes in when pieces of metal are made of a fixed
weight and standard, and marked with a figure or inscription to certify them, so that they may be taken
without weighing or testing. This looks a simple thing
to do, but the old Egyptians and Babylonians are not
known to have hit upon it. Perhaps the earliest money
may have been the Chinese little marked cubes of gold,
and the pieces of copper in the shapes of shirts and
knives, as though intended to represent real shirts or
knives. Coins appear in Lydia and Ægina, in their early
form, as rude dumps of precious metal stamped on one
side only with a symbol such as the tortoise, the other
side showing the mark of the anvil or tool they were
placed on to be struck, which accidental back-pattern
came to be improved in later coins into the ornamental
reverse. Art came on fast in coinage, so that among the
most beautiful coins in the world are the gold staters of

Philip of Macedon, with the laurel-crowned head on one
side and the two-horse chariot on the other.   But one
reason why coins are no longer struck in such high relief
is because they would be rubbed down by wear.   The
Roman *as* was not stamped but cast; it seems to have
been at first a pound of copper, its name meaning " one "
(as *ace* at cards still does).   From early ages the coinage
has been a government monopoly, and the practice soon
began of lowering the standard and lessening the weight
for the profit of the royal treasury.   How this debasing
the coinage was carried on in Europe by one king after
another may be seen in the fact that the *libra* or pound
of silver came down in value to the French *livre* or franc,
worth tenpence, and to the "*pound* Scots," worth
twenty pence.   Though changed in value, the coinage
of old times may be traced on to the present day, in our
still keeping accounts in the £ *s. d.* (libræ, solidi, denarii)
of the Romans.

For small trading and at home, metal money answers
well.   But there is great trouble and risk in sending coin
hundreds of miles to pay for goods bought at a distance.
An easily carried substitute for gold and silver is the
bank-note, a promise to pay so much, issued by the
treasury or some banker, and passing as money from
hand to hand.   The Emperor of China appears to have
issued such notes in exchange for treasure about the
eighth century, and in the thirteenth century Marco
Polo, the famous merchant-traveller in Tartary, describes
the Great Khan's money of stamped pieces of mulberry-
bark.   It is plain from this account that the notion of
paper-money was still strange to the mind of a European
trader, but since then bank-notes have become an
important part of the world's currency.   Even more
useful to commerce was the invention of bills of exchange.   Suppose a merchant of Genoa to have sent silks
to a merchant in London.   He does not send for his
money in return, but gives an order on a slip of paper
that his correspondent in London, who owes him so much,
is to pay it in so many days.   This slip of paper is a bill
of exchange, and is bought by another Genoese merchant
who happens to owe money in London, and pays it by
sending over the bill which claims the payment of the
money there.   Thus, instead of gold being sent backwards
and forwards to pay for shipments between London
and Genoa, one debt is set off against another.   That is
describing in its simplest form the system which is so
worked in the exchanges of mercantile cities all over the

world that the immense transactions of commerce are carried on by mutual credit, with only so much actual travelling of gold and silver as is necessary to adjust the balances between the different countries.

The main principle of modern commerce is still just what it was among the rude Indians of Brazil, where the tribes who make the deadly arrow-poison prepare more than they want for their own use, so as to exchange the rest for spears of the hard wood that grows in other districts, or the hammocks of palm-fibre netted by tribes elsewhere. Wealth is created by trade as well as by manufactures. The Canadian trapper wants for his own use but few of his plentiful furs, but all he can take are wealth to him, because the trader brings him in exchange the clothes and groceries and other things he wants. The general history of commerce in the world, which is the development of this simple principle, need not be dwelt on here by giving details of the ancient traffic of Egypt with Assyria and India, the Phœnician trading colonies on the Mediterranean, the old trade-routes across Asia and Europe, the rise of the merchant princes of Genoa and Venice, the first voyages round the Cape to the East Indies, the discovery of America, the rise of ocean steam-navigation. It is specially interesting to the student of civilization to notice that the travelling merchant had in early ages another business hardly less important than conveying ivory and incense and fine linen from where they were plentiful to where they were scarce. He was the bringer of foreign knowledge and the explorer of distant regions in days when nations were more shut up than now within their own borders, or went across them only as enemies to ravage and destroy. The merchants did much to break down the everlasting jealousy and strife between nations into peaceful and profitable intercourse. Moreover it may be plainly proved that the old hostile system of nations is kept up by every kind of restriction on trade, every protective duty imposed to force the production of commodities in countries ill-suited to them, to prevent their coming in cheap and good from where they are raised with least labour. There is no agent of civilization more beneficial than the free trader, who gives the inhabitants of every region the advantages of all other regions, and whose business is to work out the law that what serves the general profit of mankind serves also the private profit of the individual man.

CHAPTER XII

ARTS OF PLEASURE

To those who have not thought particularly about straightforward prose talk, and poetry which is set in metre artd rhyme, and song which is chanted to a tune, it may seem that these are three clearly distinct things. But on careful examination it is found that they shade into one another, and it can be made out how human speech passed into all three states. Savage tribes have some set form in their chants, which shows they feel them different from common talk. Thus Australians, to work themselves into fury before a fight, will chant, " Spear his forehead !—Spear his breast !—Spear his liver !— Spear his heart ! " and so on with the other parts of the enemy's body. Another Australian chant is sung at native funerals, the young women taking the first line, the old women the second, and all together the third and fourth.

" Kardang garro
Mammul garro
Mela nadjo
Nunga broo."

" Young-brother again
Son again
Hereafter I-shall
See never."

Here the words of the savage chant are no longer mere prose, but have passed into a rude kind of verse. All barbaric tribes hand down such songs by memory, and make new ones. The North American hunter has chants which will bring him on the bear's track next morning, or give him victory over an enemy. The following is the translation of a New Zealand song :—

" Thy body is at Waitemata,
But thy spirit came hither
And aroused me from my sleep.
Chorus—Ha-ah, ha-ah, ha-ah, ha ! "

This last shows a feature extremely common in barbaric songs, the refrain of generally meaningless syllables. We moderns are often struck with the absurdity of the nonsense-chorus in many of our own songs, but the habit is one which seems to have been kept up from the stages of culture in which the Australian savage sings " Abang ! abang ! " over and over at the end of his verse, or a Red Indian hunting-party enjoy singing in chorus ." Nyah eh wa ! nyah eh wa ! " to an accompaniment of rattles like those which children use with us.

It is among nations at a higher stage of culture that there appears regular metre, where the verses are measured accurately in syllables. The ancient hymns of the Veda are in regular metre, and this is proof how far the old Aryans had advanced beyond the savage state. Indeed the resemblances between the metre of the most ancient Indian and Persian and Greek poetry show that in the remote ages of their national connection their measured verse had already begun. Metre is best known to us from Greek and Latin verses, but there are more metres in the world than Horace knew of. For instance, when Longfellow versified a collection of American native tales in his " Song of Hiawatha," he found no metre among the Indians themselves, who were not cultured enough to have such a device; so he imitated the peculiar metre of the Kalewala, the epic poem chanted by the native bards of Finland. Our own poetry, where the verses are scanned by accent, differs in its nature from the classic metres whose syllables are measured by quantity or length. Later than the invention of metre, came other means by which the poet could please his hearers with new effects of matched and balanced sounds. Thus our early English forefathers rejoiced in alliteration, where the same consonant comes in again and again, with a frequency which would weary our modern taste, though our ear is pleased with occasional touches of it, as

" Sober he seemde, and very sagely sad."—SPENSER.

" He rushed into the field, and, foremost fighting, fell."—BYRON.

Rhyme, too, seems comparatively modern in the world's history of poetry. Its clumsy beginnings may be judged from such lines as these of an old Latin poet (perhaps Ennius) quoted by Cicero :—

" Cœlum nitescere, arbores frondescere,
Vites lætificæ pampinis pubescere,
Rami bacarum ubertate incurvescere."

Thus the Christian hymns of the Middle Ages, such as the famous " Dies Iræ," did not bring in rhyme as quite a novelty, but they used it skilfully and made it common, and it was taken up also by the Troubadours, the masters and teachers of Europe in the poetic art.

The best poetry of our own day is full of quaint fancy and delicate melody, the setting of lovely thought in harmonious language, at once pictures for the imagination and music for the ear. But besides this, it has a curious interest to the student of history, as keeping alive in our midst the ways of thought of the most ancient world. Much of poetic art lies in imitating the expressions of earlier stages of culture, when poetry was the natural utterance of any strong emotion, the natural means to convey any solemn address or ancestral tradition. The modern poet still uses for picturesqueness the metaphors which to the barbarian were real helps to express his sense. This may be seen in analyzing a poem of Shelley's :—

> " How wonderful is Death,
>   Death and his brother, Sleep !
> One, pale as yonder waning moon,
>   With lips of lurid blue;
>   The other, rosy as the morn
> When throned on ocean's wave
>   It blushes o'er the world."

Here the likeness of death and sleep is expressed by the metaphor of calling them brothers, the moon is brought in to illustrate the notion of paleness, and the dawn of redness; while to convey the idea of the dawn shining over the sea the simile of its sitting on a throne is introduced, and its reddening is compared on the one hand to a rose, and on the other to blushing. Now this is the very way in which early barbaric man, not for poetic affectation, but simply to find the plainest words to convey his thoughts, would talk in metaphors taken from nature. Even our daily prose is full of words, now come down to ordinary use, which show vestiges of this old nature-poetry, and the etymologist may, if he will, set up again the pictures of the old poetic thoughts which made the words.

To read or recite poetry as we moderns do is to alter its proper nature, for the purpose of poetry was to b⟨r⟩ chanted. But this very chanting or singing grew out of talking. On listening carefully to the talk going on around us, we may observe that it does not run in an

unchanged monotone, but that all sentences are intoned
to an imperfect tune, a rise and fall of pitch marking the
phrases, distinguishing question and answer, and touching emphatic words with a musical accent.   This half-
melody of common speech may be roughly written down
in notes; it is not the same in English and German; and
indeed one way in which a Scotchman's talking is known
from an Englishman's is the different intoning of his
phrases.   When speech becomes solemn or impassioned,
it passes more and more into natural chanting, which at
devotional meetings may be heard nearly passing into
distinct tune.   The intoning in churches arose from the
same natural utterance of religious feeling, but in course
of time it became fixed by custom, and was forced into
the regular intervals of the musical scale.   So the artificial recitative of the opera is a modern musical working
up of what has come down by tradition of the ancient
tragic declamation, which once swayed the listening
throng of the Greek theatre.

We are apt to take it as a matter of course that all
music must be made up of notes in scale, and that scale
the one we have been used to from childhood.   But the
chants of rude tribes, which perhaps best represent singing in its early stages, run in less fixed tones, so that it is
difficult to write down their airs.   The human voice is
not bound to a scale of notes, for its pitch can glide up
and down.   Nor among nations who sing and play by
musical scales are the tones of these scales always the
same.   The question how men were led to exact scales of
tones is not easy to answer fully.   But one of the simplest
scales was forced upon their attention by that early
musical instrument the trumpet, rude forms of which are
seen in the long tubes of wood or bark blown by forest
tribes in South America and Africa.   A trumpet (a six-
feet length of iron gas pipe will do) will sound the successive notes of the " common chord," which may be written
c e g c, on which the trumpeter performs the simple tunes
known so well as trumpet-calls.   This natural scale,
perfect so far as it goes, contains the most important of
musical intervals, the octave, fifth, fourth, and third.
Another scale, of more notes than this, though of fewer
than our full scale, is not less familiar to English ears.
This is the old five-tone scale, without semitones, which
can be played on the five black keys of the pianoforte,
and the best-known form of which may be written
c, d, e, g, a, c.   Old Scotch airs are on the five-tone scale,

which indeed may still be met with across the world, as where some traveller in China watching a funeral procession has been surprised to hear a melancholy dirge like what he last heard played by a piper on the shore of a Highland loch. Engel, in his *Music of Ancient Nations*, shows that music of this pentatonic or five-toned kind has belonged since early times to other Eastern nations, so that any genuine Scotch melody like " Auld Lang-syne " may give some idea of the music of antiquity. The more advanced seven-tone scale which prevails in the modern world is nearly taken from that of the musicians of classic Greece, who accompanied the singer's voice on the eight-stringed lyre. Pythagoras, who first brought musical tones under arithmetical rule, had the curious fancy that the distances of the seven planets are related as the seven tones of the octave, an idea which still dimly survives among us in the phrase " music of the spheres."

Modern music is thus plainly derived from ancient. But there has arisen in it a great new development. The music of the ancients scarcely went beyond melody. The voice might be accompanied by an instrument in unison or at an octave interval, but harmony as understood by modern musicians was as yet unknown. Its feeble beginnings may be traced in the Middle Ages, when musicians were struck by the effects got by singing two different tunes at once, when one formed a harmony to the other. It is still a joke among musicians to sing together in this old-fashioned way two absurdly incongruous tunes, for instance, " The Campbells are coming " and " The Vesper hymn," so arranged that one makes a sort of accompaniment to the other. The old rounds and catches, still popular, thus make one part of the tune serve as a harmony for the other. The Roman church part-music, and the Protestant singing by the congregation, with the organ to accompany them, had great effect in making the change by which the mere melody of the ancients grew into the harmonized melody of the moderns. This great step once understood, the student can follow in the history of music its successive stages in part-singing and orchestral composition, in the church and the concert-room, till in the hands of the great composers of the last three centuries the full resources of modern musical art were developed.

The musical instruments of the present day may all be traced back to rude and early forms. The rattle and the drum are serious instruments among savages; the rattle has come down to a child's toy with us, but the drum holds its own in peace and war. Above these monotonous instruments comes the trumpet, which, as has just been seen, brings barbaric music a long step further on. The pipe or flageolet appears in its simplest form in the common whistle, and is improved by holes, by which the player alters the length of the pipe so as to give several notes. From very remote times, and far and wide over the earth, the familiar pipe is found, played single or double, and sometimes blown with the nostril instead of the mouth. Already in the ancient world it was often provided with a skin wind-bag which made it into the bagpipe; or, held sideways and blown across the mouth-hole, it became the flute. Another way of bringing out a range of notes is seen in the Pan's pipes, the row of reeds of different lengths, in old classic days associated with the grace of rural poetry, but now come down to sound the vulgar pipings of the street showman. In the modern orchestra, the cornet is a trumpet provided with stops. The clarionet is a development of the grass-stem with a vibrating slit or tongue such as children cut in the fields in spring. The whole class of musical instruments to which the harmonium belongs work with these vibrating tongues, which by their name of " reeds " still keep up the memory of their origin. The organ carries out in the widest range and grandest proportions the principle of the simple pipe or whistle, so that there is scientific correctness in the disrespectful name of " kist o' whistles " given it by the Scotch, who disliked its use in church. Not less primitive are the rudest forms in which stringed instruments appear. It is told in the Odyssey (xxi. 410) how the avenging hero, when he has strung his mighty bow compact of wood and horn, gives the stretched string a twang that makes it sing like a swallow in a soft tone beautifully. One might well guess that the strong bow of the warrior would naturally become a musical instrument, but, what is more, it really is so used. The Damara in South Africa finds pleasure in the faint tones heard by striking the tight bowstring with a little stick. The Zulu despises the bow as a cowardly weapon, but he still uses it for music; his music-bow, shown in Fig. 75 a, has a ring slid along the string to alter the note, and is also provided with a hollow gourd acting as a resonator or sounding-box to strengthen the feeble twang. Next, looking at b in the figure, it is

seen how the ancient Egyptian harp may have been
developed from such a rude music-bow, the wooden back
being now made hollow so as to be bow and resonator in
one, while across it are strung several strings of different
lengths. All ancient harps, Assyrian, Persian, even old
Irish, were made on this plan, yet we can see at a glance
that it was defective, the bending of the wooden back
putting the strings out of tune. It was not till modern

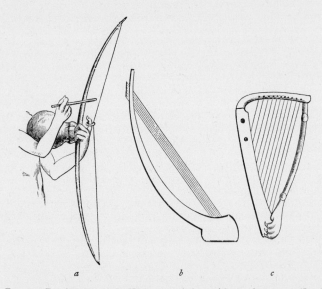

a   *b*   *c*

FIG. 75.—Development of the Harp, *a*, music-bow with gourd resonator (South
Africa); *b*, ancient harp, (Egypt); *c*, mediæval harp with front-pillar
(England).

ages that the improvement was made of completing the
harp with the front-pillar, as seen in *c*, which makes the
whole frame rigid and firm. Looking at the three
figures, it is seen how the course of invention was by
gradual growth; the harp with the pillar could not have
been first invented, for no men could have been so stupid
as to go on making harps and leave out the front-pillar
when once the idea of it had come into their minds. The
harp, though now made more perfect than of old, is losing
its ancient place in music; but the reason of this is easy

to see: it has been supplanted by modern instruments which have come from it. The very form of a grand piano shows that it is a harp laid on one side in a case, and its strings not plucked with the fingers but struck with hammers worked from a keyboard. It is the latest development from the bowstring of the præhistoric warrior.

Dancing may seem to us moderns a frivolous amusement; but in the infancy of civilization it was full of passionate and solemn meaning. Savages and barbarians dance their joy and sorrow, their love and rage, even their magic and religion. The forest Indians of Brazil, whose sluggish temper few other excitements can stir, rouse themselves at their moonlight gatherings, when, rattle in hand, they stamp in one-two-three time round the great earthen pot of intoxicating kawi-liquor; or men and women dance a rude courting dance, advancing in lines with a kind of primitive polka step; or the ferocious war-dance is performed by armed warriors in paint, marching in ranks hither and thither with a growling chant terrific to hear. We have enough of the savage left in us to feel how Australians leaping and yelling at a corrobboree by firelight in the forest can work themselves up into frenzy for next day s fight. But with our civilized notions it is not so easy to understand that barbarians' dancing may mean still more than this; it seems to them so real that they expect it to act on the world outside. Thus among the Mandan Indians, when the hunters failed to find the buffaloes on which the tribe depended for food, every man brought out of his lodge the mask made of a buffalo's head and horns, with the tail hanging down behind, which he kept for such an emergency, and they all set to dance buffalo. Ten or fifteen masked dancers at a time formed the ring, drumming and rattling, chanting and yelling; when one was tired out he went through the pantomime of being shot with bow and arrow, skinned, and cut up; while another, who stood ready with his buffalo-head on, took his place in the dance. So it would go on, without stopping day or night, sometimes for two or three weeks, till at last these persevering efforts to bring the buffalo succeeded, and a herd came in sight on the prairie. The description and sketch of the scene will be found in Catlin's *North American Indians*. Such an example shows how, in the lower levels of culture, men dance to express their feelings and wishes. All this explains how in ancient religion dancing came to be one of the chief acts of worship. Religious processions went with song and dance to the Egyptian temples, and Plato said that all dancing ought to be thus an act of religion. In fact, it was to to a great extent in Greece, as where the Cretan chorus, moving in measured pace, sang hymns to Apollo, and in Rome, where the Salian priests sang and danced, beating their shields, along the streets at the yearly festival of Mars. Modern civilization, in which sacred music flourishes more than ever, has mostly cast off the sacred dance. To see this near its old state the traveller may visit the temples of India, or among the lamas of Tibet watch the mummers in animal masks dancing the demons out, or the new year in, to wild music of drums and shell-trumpets. Remnants of such ceremonies, come down from the religion of England before Christian times, are still sometimes to be seen in the dances of boys and girls round the Midsummer bonfire, or of the mummers at Yuletide; but even these are dying out. The dances of choristers in plumed hats and the dress of pages of Philip III's time, still performed before the high altar of Seville Cathedral, are now among the quaintest relics of a rite all but vanished from Christendom. Even sportive dancing, as a graceful exercise, is falling off in the modern world. The pictures from ancient Egypt show that the professional dancers were already skilful in their art, which perhaps reached its highest artistic pitch in classic Greece and Rome. Something of the old-fashioned picturesque village-dancing may still be seen at festivals in most countries of Europe except England, but the ball-room dances of modern society have lost much of the old art and grace.

At low levels in civilization it is clear that dancing and play-acting are one. The North American dog-dance and bear-dance are mimic performances with ludicrously faithful imitations of the creatures' pawing and rolling and biting. So the scenes of hunting and war furnish barbarians with subjects for dances, as when the Gold Coast negroes have gone out to war, and their wives at home dance a fetish-dance in imitation of battle, to give their absent husbands strength and courage. Historians trace from the sacred dances of ancient Greece the dramatic art of the civilized world. Thus, in the festivals of the Dionysia, the wondrous life of the Wine-god was danced and sung, and from its solemn hymns and laughable jests arose tragedy and comedy. In the

classic ages the player's art divided into several branches.
The Pantomimes kept up the earliest form, where the
dancer acted in dumb show such pieces as the labours of
Herakles, or Kadmos sowing the dragon's teeth, while
the chorus below accompanied the play by singing the
story; the modern pantomime ballets, which keep up
remains of these ancient performances, show how
grotesque the old stage gods and heroes must have
looked in their painted masks.   In Greek tragedy and
comedy the business of the dancers and chorus was
separated from that of the actors, who recited or chanted
each his proper part in the dialogue, so that the player
could now move his audience by words of passion or wit,
delivered with such tone and gesture as laid hold on all
who listened and looked.   Greek tragedy, once begun,
soon reached its height among the fine arts, so that the
plays of Æschylos and Sophokles are read as examples of
the higher poetry, and the modern acted imitations like
the Phèdre of Racine give an idea of their power when
the genius of the actors can rise to their height of emotion.
The modern drama belongs not so much to the sacred
mystery-plays of the Middle Ages as to the classic revival
or renaissance of four centuries ago.   Those who have
seen the ruins of classic theatres at Syracuse, or on the
hill-side of Tusculum, will best understand how a modern
playhouse shows its Greek origin not only in the arrangement, but in the Greek names of its parts—the *theatre*,
or spectators' place, which still keeps its well-planned
horse-shoe shape; the *scene* with its painted background
and curtain in front; while the *orchestra* or dancing-place,
which was formerly for the *chorus*, is now given up to the
musicians.   The change in the *tragedy* and *comedy* performed in the modern theatre from those of the classic
world is partly due to their having dropped the stiff
solemn declamation which belonged to them while they
were still religious ceremonies, and their personages
divine.   In the hands of modern dramatists, of Shakspere
above all, the characters came to be more human,
though representing human nature in its most picturesque
extremes, and life in its intensest moments.   Modern
plays are not indeed bound to be strictly natural, but can
still call in the supernatural, as where now fairies or
angels may hover over the scene where in classic days the
gods used to pass in mid-air borne in their machines.   In
the modern comedy the persons dress and talk as near
as may be like daily life; yet, even here, when the

audience gravely fall in with the pretence that some of the
speeches, though spoken aloud, are " asides " not heard
by the actors close by, this shows that the modern world
has not lost the power to make-believe, on which all
dramatic art is founded.

On this same power of make-believe or imagination are
founded the two other fine arts, sculpture and painting.
Their proper purpose is not to produce exact imitations,
but what the artist strives to bring out is the idea that
strikes the beholder. Thus there is often more real art
in a caricature done with a few strokes of the pencil, or in
a rough image hacked out of a log, than in a minutely
painted portrait, or a figure at a waxwork show which is
so like life that visitors beg its pardon when they walk
up against it. The painter's and sculptor's art seems to
have arisen in the world from the same sort of rude
beginnings which are still to be seen in children's attempts
to draw and carve. The sheets of bark or skins on which
barbarous tribes have drawn men and animals, guns and
boats, remind us of the slates and barn-doors on which
English children make their early trials in outline. Many
of these children will grow up and go through their lives
without getting much beyond this childish stage. The
clergyman of a country parish some years ago set the
cottagers to amuse themselves with carving in wood such
figures as men digging or reaping. They produced figures
so curiously uncouth, and in style so like the idols of barbarous tribes, that they were kept as examples of the
infancy of sculpture, and are now to be seen in the museum
of Kew Gardens. Yet mankind, under favourable circumstances, especially with long leisure time on their
hands, began in remote antiquity to train themselves to
skill in art. Especially the sketches and carvings of
animals done by the old cave-men of Europe have so
artistic a touch that some have supposed them modern
forgeries. But they are admitted to be genuine and
found over a wide district, while forgeries which have
been really done to palm off on collectors are just wanting in the peculiar skill with which the savages who lived
among the reindeer and mammoths knew how to catch
their forms and attitude. Two of these ancient carvings
are drawn in Figs. 3 and 4, and others in Lubbock's
Prehistoric Times. The art of colouring would naturally
arise, for savages who paint their own bodies with charcoal, pipeclay, and red and yellow ochre, would daub
their carved figures and fill in their outline drawings with

the same colours. Travellers in Australia sheltering
from the storm in caves, wonder at the cleverness of the
rude frescoes on the cavern-walls of kangaroos and emus
and natives dancing, while in South Africa the Bushmen's
caves show paintings of themselves with bows and arrows,
and the bullock-waggons of the white men, 'and the
dreaded figure of the Dutch boer with his broad-brimmed
hat and pipe. Among such people as the West Africans
and Polynesians, the native sculptor's best skill has been
used on images of demons and gods, made to receive
worship and serve as bodies in which the spiritual beings
are to take up their abode. Thus the idols of barbarians,
as specimens of early stages of sculpture, have a value in
the history of art as well as of religion.

In the ancient nations of Egypt and Babylonia art had
already risen to higher levels. Indeed Egyptian sculpture reached its best in the earlier rather than the later
ages, for the stone statues of the older time stand and
step with more free life in their limbs, and the calm proud
faces of the colossal Thothmes and Rameses portraits
                show the grandest ideal of an eastern despot,
half tyrant, half deity. In the sculpture halls of the
British Museum, it is seen that the early school of
Egyptian sculptors were on their way to Greek perfection, but they stopped short. With trained mechanical
skill they wrought statues by tens of thousands, hewing
gigantic figures of the hardest granite and porphyry
which amaze the modern stone-cutter, but their art,
bound by tradition, grew not freer but more stiff and
formal. They might divide their plans into measured
squares, and set out faces and limbs by line and rule, but
their conventional forms seldom come up to the Greek
lines of beauty, and their monuments are now prized,
not as models of art, but as records of old-world history.
In the British Museum also, the alabaster bas-reliefs that
adorned the palace-courts of Nineveh give a wonderfully
clear idea of what Assyrian life was like, how the king
rode in his chariot, or let fly his arrows at the lion at bay,
or walked with the state umbrella held over his head;
how the soldiers swam the rivers on blown skins and the
storming party scaled the fortress, while the archers shot
down among them from the battlements, and the im-
paled captives hung in rows in full view outside the
walls. But in such scenes proportion did not much
matter if only the meaning were conveyed. It did not
seem artistically absurd to the Assyrians to make archers

so big that two fill a whole parapet; nor did the Egyptians feel the comic impression made on our modern minds by the gigantic figure of the king striding half across the battle-field and grasping a dozen pigmy barbarians at a grip, to slash their heads off with one sweep of his mighty falchion. It was in Greece that the rules of art were developed which reject the figures of the older nations as stiff in form and unlifelike in grouping. Greek art is sometimes written of as though it had itself begun in the rudest stage, with clumsy idols of wood and clay, till by efforts of their own surpassing genius the Greek sculptors came to hew in marble the forms which are still the wonders of the world. But great as Greek genius was, it never did this. The Greek nations had been for ages in contact with the older civilizations of the Mediterranean; their starting-point was to learn what art could do in Egypt, Phœnicia, Babylonia, and then their genius set them free from the hard old conventional forms, leading them to model life straight from nature, and even to fashion in marble shapes of ideal strength and grace. The Egyptian sculptors would not spoil polished granite with paint, but many of their statues were coloured, and there are traces of paint left on the Assyrian sculptures and on Greek statues, so that we are apt to have a wrong idea of a Greek temple, as though its marble gods and goddesses used to be of the glaring whiteness of a modern sculpture-gallery. The Greek terra-cotta statuettes in the British Museum are models of antique female grace in form and costume, only wanting the lost colour restored to make them the prettiest things in the world.

In colour-drawing, or painting, the Egyptian wall-paintings show a style half-way between the lowest and the highest. Here the scenes of old Egyptian life are caught at their characteristic moments, the shoemaker is seen drawing his thread, the fowler throwing at the ducks, the lords and ladies feasting and the flute-players and tumblers performing before them. Yet with all their clever expressiveness, the Egyptian paintings have not quite left behind the savage stage of art. In fact they are still picture-writings rather than pictures, repeating rows of figures with heads, legs, and arms drawn to pattern, and coloured in childish daubs of colour—hair all black, skin all red-brown, clothing white, and so on. The change from these to the Greek paintings is surprising; now we have no more rows of man-patterns, but grouped studies of real men. The best works of the Greek painters are only known to moderns by the admiring descriptions of the ancients, but more ordinary specimens which have been preserved give an idea what the paintings of Zeuxis and Apelles may have been. The tourist visiting for the first time the museum of Naples comes with a shock of surprise in face of Alexander of Athens' picture of the goddesses at play, the boldly drawn frescoes of scenes from the Iliad, and the groups of dancers elegant in drawing and colouring. Most of these pictures from Herculaneum and Pompeii were done by mere house decorators, but these tenth-rate Greek painters had the traditions of the great classic school, and they show plainly that from the same source we also have inherited the art of design. Modern European painting comes in two ways from ancient art. On the one hand, Greek painting spread over the Roman Empire and into the East, and for ages found its chief home in the Christian art of Constantinople, whence arose the Byzantine style, often called pre-Raffaelite, which though wanting in the older freedom of classic Athens, was expressive and rich in colour. On the other hand, when in the fifteenth century the knowledge of classic art and thought revived in Europe, the stiff pictures of saints and martyrs gave place to more natural and graceful forms, and modern painting arose under Raffaelle and Michael Angelo, Titian and Murillo, in whom the two streams from the fountain-head of Greek art, so long separated, joined again. The ancients mostly painted on walls like the present fresco-painting, or on waxed wooden panels; they did not know the use of oil to mix the ground colours with. This is just mentioned in the tenth century, so that the story of the brothers Van Eyck inventing oil-painting in the fifteenth century is not quite true. But they turned it to practical use, and from their time painters brought the substance and play of colour to a perfection which there is no reason to suppose the ancients ever approached. In modern times water-colour painting, used by the old masters for light sketches and studies, has also become an art of itself, especially in England. One branch of painting in which the moderns unquestionably surpass the ancients is landscape. Of old, however admirably the figures might be drawn, the hard conventional mountains, forests, and houses behind were still in the picture-writing stage, they rather stood as signs of the world outside than depicted it as it is. But now the artist's eyes are turned on nature, which he renders with a truthfulness unknown to the old masters who first gave living form to gods and heroes, apostles and martyrs.

Something has now to be said of games, for play is one of the arts of pleasure. It is doing for the sake of doing, not for what is done. One class of games is spontaneous everywhere, the sports in which children imitate the life they will afterwards have to act in earnest. Eskimo children play at building snow huts, and their mothers provide them with a tiny oil-lamp with a bit of wick to set burning inside. Among the savages whose custom it is to carry off their wives by force from neighbouring tribes, the children play at the game of wife-catching, just as with us children play at weddings with a clergyman and bridesmaids. All through civilization, toy weapons and implements furnish children at once play and education; the North American warrior made his boy a little bow and arrow as soon as he could draw it, and the young South Sea Islander learnt by throwing a reed at a rolling ring how in after-life to hurl his spear. It is curious to see that when growing civilization has cast aside the practical use of some ancient contrivance, it may still survive as a toy, as where Swiss children to this day play at making fire by the old-world plan of drilling one piece of wood into another; and in our country lanes the children play with bows and arrows and slings, the serious weapons of their forefathers.

It is not quite easy to say whether man in a low savage state ever goes beyond these practical sports, and invents games of mere play. But higher up in civilization, such games are known from very ancient times. A trifling game, if it exactly takes hold of the playful mind, may last on in the world almost for ever. The ancient Egyptians, as their old paintings show, used to play our childish game of hot-cockles, where the blind-man who stoops down has to guess who thumped him on the back. These Egyptians played also the game of guessing the sum of the fingers held up by the two players, which is still popular in China, and in Italy, where one hears it half the night through with shouts of " three ! " " seven ! " " five ! " " *mora !* "; it is a pity we have not this as a children's game in England, for it trains a sharp eye and a quick hand. While some of our games, such as hoops and whipping-tops, have gone on in the Old World for thousands of years, others are modern importations; thus it was only about Stuart times that English children learnt from the Chinese, or some other nation in the Far East, the art of flying kites. Or modern sports may be late improvements on old ones; the split shank-bones fastened under the shoes for going on the ice delighted the London 'prentices for centuries before they were displaced by steel skates. How a game may some-times go on for ages unchanged, and then suddenly turn into a higher form, is curiously seen in the game of ball. The ancients tossed and caught balls like children now, and a famous Greek and Roman lad's game was " com-mon ball," where there were two sides, and each tried to get the ball and throw it to the opposite goal. This is still played in a few country-places in England; its proper name is " hurling," and football with the great leather ball is a variety of it. The ancients never seem to have used a stick or bat in their ball-play. But some 1,000 or 1,500 years ago the Persians began to play ball on horseback, which of course could only be done with a long stick, mallet, or racket; in this way there came into existence the fine sport of *chaugán*, which has lasted ever since in the East, and lately established itself in England under the name of *polo*. When once the club or racket had been invented for horseback, it was easy to use it on foot, and thus in the Middle Ages there began the whole set of games in which balls are hit with bats, such as pall-mall and croquet, tennis, hockey and golf, rounders and cricket.

Indoor games, too, have their curious history. Throw-ing lots or dice is far too ancient for any record to remain of its beginning, and the very draught-boards and men which the old Egyptians used to play on are still to be seen. The Greeks and Romans were draught-players, but their games were not like our modern game of draughts. On the other hand our merells or morris belongs to an old classical group of games, and Ovid alludes to the childish game of tit-tat-to. These games are played in China as well, and it is not known at which end of the earth they were first devised. The great invention in intellectual games may have been made a thousand years or so ago, when some Hindu, whose name is lost, set to work upon the old draught-board and men, and developed out of them a war-game, where on each side a king and his general, with elephants, chariots, and cavalry, and the foot-soldiers in front, met in battle array. This was the earliest chess, which with some little change passed into the modern European chess that still holds pre-eminence among sports, taxing the mind to its utmost stretch of foresight and combination. Our modern draughts is a sort of simplified chess, where the pieces are all pawns till they get across the board and become queens. The story in the history-books that cards were invented in France to amuse Charles VI is a fiction, for they were known in the East centuries earlier. But at any rate the Europeans make with them combinations of skill and chance which excel anything contrived by their Asiatic inventors. Games which exercise either body or mind have been of high value in civilization as trainers of man's faculties. Games of pure chance played for money stand on quite a different footing; they have been from the first a delusion and a curse. In our own time, there is perhaps no more pitiable sign of the slowness with which scientific ideas spread, than to hear the well-dressed crowds round the gaming-table at Monaco talking about runs of luck, and fancying that it makes a difference whether one backs the black or the red. This goes on although schoolboys are now taught the real doctrine of chances, and how to reckon the fixed percentage of each week's stakes that will be raked in by the croupier, and not come back.

CHAPTER XIII

SCIENCE

SCIENCE is exact, regular, arranged knowledge. Of common knowledge savages and barbarians have a vast deal, indeed the struggle of life could not be carried on without it. The rude man knows much of the properties of matter, how fire burns and water soaks, the heavy sinks and the light floats, what stone will serve for the hatchet and what wood for its handle, which plants are food and which are poison, what are the habits of the animals that he hunts or that may fall upon him. He has notions how to cure, and much better notions how to kill. In a rude way he is a physicist in making fire, a chemist in cooking, a surgeon in binding up wounds, a geographer in knowing his rivers and mountains, a mathematician in counting on his fingers. All this is knowledge, and it was on these foundations that science proper began to be built up, when the art of writing had come in and society had entered on the civilized stage. We have to trace here in outline the rise and progress of science. And as it has been especially through counting and measuring that scientific methods have come into use, the first thing to do is to examine how men leant to count and measure.

Even those who cannot talk can count, as was well shown by the deaf-and-dumb lad Massieu, who wrote down among the recollections of his childhood before the Abbé Sicard educated him, " I knew the numbers before my instruction ; my fingers had taught me them." We ourselves as children began arithmetic on our fingers and now and then take to them still, so that there is no difficulty in understanding how a savage whose language has no word for a number above three will manage to reckon perhaps a list of fifteen killed and wounded, how he will check off one finger for each man, and at last hold up his hand three times to show the result. The next question is, how numeral words came to be invented. This is answered by many languages, which show in the plainest way how counting on fingers and toes led to making numerals. When a Zulu wants to express the number six, he says *tatisitupa*, which means " taking the thumb "; this signifies that the speaker has counted all the fingers of his left hand, and begun with the thumb of the right. When he comes to seven, for instance when he has to express that his master bought seven oxen, he will say *u kombile*, that is, " he pointed "; this signifies that in counting he had come to the pointing-finger or forefinger. In this way the words " hand," " foot," " man," have in various parts of the world become numerals. An example how they are worked may be taken from the language of the Tamanacs of the Orinoco; here the term for five means " whole hand," six is " one of the other hand," and so on up to ten or " both hands "; then " one to the foot " is eleven, and so on to " whole foot " or fifteen, " one to the other foot " or sixteen, and thence to " one man," which signifies twenty, " one to the hands of the next man " being twenty-one, and the counting going on in the same way to " two men " which stands for forty, &c. &c. Now this state of things teaches a truth which has sometimes been denied, that the lower races of men have, like ourselves, the faculty of progress or self-improvement. It is evident that there was a time when the ancestors of these people had in their languages no word for fifteen or sixteen, nor even for five or six, for if they had they could not have been so stupid as to change them for their present clumsy phrases about hands and feet and men. We see back to the time when, having no means of reckoning such numbers except on their fingers and toes, they found they had only to describe in words what they were doing, and such a phrase as " both hands " would serve them as a numeral for ten. Then they would keep up these as numerals after their original sense was lost, like the Vei negroes who called the number twenty *mo bande*, but had forgotten that this must have meant " a person finished." The languages of nations long civilized seldom show such plain meaning in their numerals, perhaps because they are so ancient and have undergone such change. But all through the languages of the world, savage or civilized, with exceptions too slight to notice here, there is ineffaceable proof that the numerals arose out of the primitive counting on fingers and toes. This always led men to reckon by fives, tens, and twenties, and so they reckon still. The quinary kind of counting (by fives) is that of tribes like the negroes of Senegal, who count one, two, three, four, five, five-one, five-two, &c.; we never count numbers thus in words, but we write them so in the Roman numerals. The decimal counting (by tens) is the most usual in the world, and our ordinary counting is done by it, thus eighty-three is " eight tens and three." The vigesimal counting (by twenties), which is the regular mode in many languages, has its traces left in the midst of the decimal counting of civilized Europe, as in English " fourscore and three," French " quatre-vingt trois," that is " four twenties and three." Thus it can hardly be doubted that the modern world has inherited direct from primitive man his earliest arithmetic worked on nature's counting-board—the hands and feet. This also explains (p. 14) why the civilized world uses a numeral system based on the inconvenient number ten, which will not divide either by three or four. Were we starting our arithmetic afresh, we should more likely base it on the duodecimal notation, and use dozens and grosses instead of tens and hundreds.

To have named the numbers was a great step, but words hardly serve beyond the very simplest arithmetic, as any one may satisfy himself by trying to multiply " seven thousand eight hundred and three " by " two hundred and seventeen " in words, without helping himself by turning them in thought into figures. How did men come to the use of numeral figures? To this question the beginning of an answer may be had from barbaric picture-writing, as where a North American warrior will make four little marks //// to show that he has taken four scalps. This is very well for the small numbers, but becomes clumsy for higher ones. So already when writing was in its infancy, the ancients had fallen upon the device of making special marks for their fives, tens, hundreds, &c., leaving the simple strokes to be used only for the few units over. This is well seen in Fig. 76 which shows how numeration was worked in ancient Egypt and Assyria. Nor has this old method died out in the world, for the Roman numerals I., V., X., L., still in common use among ourselves, are arranged on much the same principle. Another device, which arose out of the alphabet, was to take the letters in their order to stand for numbers. Thus the sections of Psalm cxix. are numbered by the letters of the Hebrew alphabet, and the books of the Iliad by the letters of the Greek alphabet. By these various plans the arithmetic of the ancient civilized nations made great progress. Still their numeration was very cumbrous in comparison with that of the modern world. Let us put down MMDCLXIX. and multiply by CCCXLVIII., or βχʹξʹθʹ by τʹμʹήʹ, and a few minutes' trial will not fail to convince us of the superiority of our ciphers.

To understand how the art of ciphering came to be invented, it is necessary to go back to a ruder state of things. In Africa, negro traders may be seen at market reckoning with pebbles, and when they come to five, putting them aside in a little heap. In the South Sea

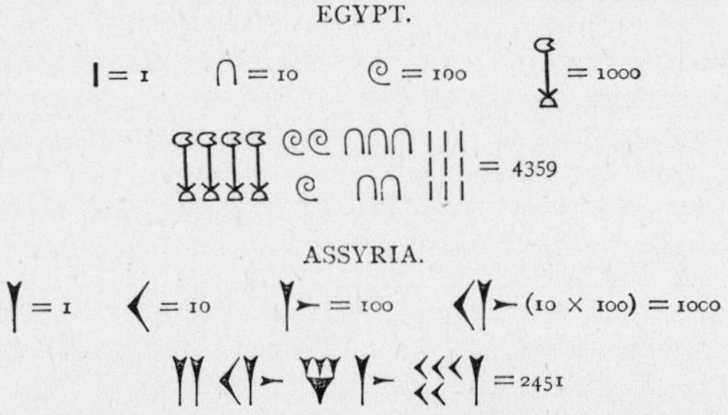

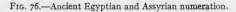

FIG. 76.—Ancient Egyptian and Assyrian numeration.

Islands it has been noticed that people reckoning, when they came to ten, would not put aside a heap of ten things, but only a single bit of coco-nut stalk to stand for ten, and then a bigger piece when they wanted to represent ten tens or a hundred. Now to us it is plain that this use of different kinds of markers is unnecessary, but all that the reckoner with little stones or beans has to do, is to keep separate his unit-heap, his ten-heap, his hundred-heap, &c. This use of such things as pebbles for "counters," which still survives in England among the ignorant, was so common in the ancient world, that the Greek word for reckoning was *psēphizein*, from *psēphos*, a pebble, and the corresponding Latin word was *calculare* from *calculus*, a pebble, so that our word *calculate* is a relic of very early arithmetic. Now to work such pebble-counting in an orderly manner, what is wanted is some kind of abacus or counting-board with divisions. These have been made in various forms, as the Roman abacus with lines of holes for knobs or pegs, or the Chinese swan-pan with balls strung on wires, on which the native calculators in the merchants' counting-houses reckon with a speed and exactness that fairly beats the European clerk with his pencil and paper. It may have been from China that the Russian traders borrowed the ball-frame on which they also do their accounts, and it is said that a Frenchman noticing it in Russia at the time of Napoleon's invasion was struck with the idea that it would serve perfectly to teach little children arithmetic; so he introduced it in France, and thence it found its way into English infants' schools. Now whatever sort of abacus is used, its principle is always the same, to divide the board or tray into columns, so that in one column the stones, beans, pegs, or balls, stand for units, in the next column they are tens, in the next hundreds, and so on, Fig. 77. Here the three stones in the right-hand column stand for 3, the nine in the next column for 90, the one in the fourth column for 1,000, and so on. The next improvement was to get rid of the troublesome stones or beans, and write down numbers in the columns, as is here shown with Greek and Roman numerals. But now the calculator could do without the clumsy board, and had only to rule lines on his paper, to make columns for units, tens, hundreds, &c. The reader should notice that it is not necessary to the principle of the abacus that each column should stand for ten times the one next it. It may be twelve or twenty or any other number of times, and in fact the columns in our account-books for £ s. d. or cwts. qrs. lbs., are surviving representatives of the old method of the abacus. Such reckoning had still the defect that the numbers could not be taken out of the columns, for even when each number from one to nine has a single figure to stand for it, there would still be here and there an empty column (as is purposely left in Fig. 77) which would throw the whole into confusion. To us now it seems a very simple thing to put a sign to show an empty column, as we have learned to do with the zero or O, so that the number expressed in the picture of the abacus can be written down without any columns, 241093. This invention of a sign for nothing was practically one of the greatest moves ever made in science. It is the use of the zero which makes the difference between the old arithmetic and our easy ciphering.   We give the credit of the invention to the Arabs by using the term Arabic numerals, while the Arabs call them Indian, and there is truth in both acknowledgments of the nations having been scholars in arithmetic one to the other.   But this does not go to the root of the matter, and it is still unsettled whether ciphering was first devised in Asia, or may be traced further back in Europe to the arithmeticians of the school of Pythagoras.   As to the main point, however, there is no doubt, that modern arithmetic comes out of ancient counting on the columns of the abacus, improved by writing a dot or a round O to show the empty column, and by this means young children now work calculations which would have been serious labour to the arithmeticians of the ancient world.

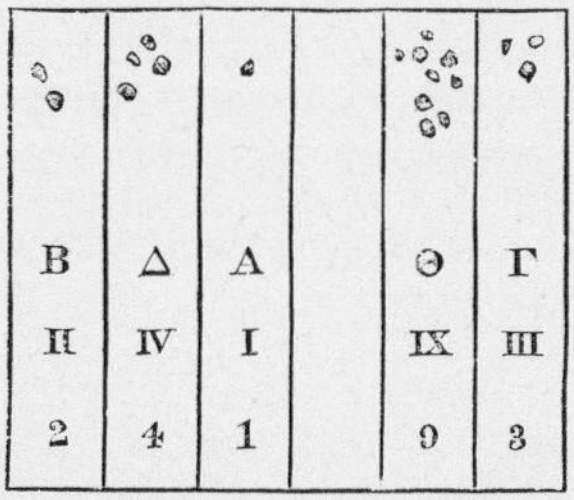

B	Δ	Λ		Θ	Γ
II	IV	I		IX	III
2	4	1		9	3

FIG. 77.—Mode of calculation by counters and by figures on Abacus.

Next as to the art of measuring.   Here it may be fairly guessed that man first measured, as he first counted, on his own body.   When barbarians tried by finger-breadths how much one spear was longer than another, or when in building huts they saw how to put one foot before the other to get the distance right between two stakes, they had brought mensuration to its first stage.   We sometimes use this method still for rough work, as in taking a horse's height by hands, or stepping out the size of a carpet.   If care is taken to choose men of average size as measurers, some approach may be made to fair measurement in this way.   That it was the primitive way can hardly be doubted, for civilized nations who have more exact means still use the names of the body-measures.   Besides the *cubit, hand, foot, span, nail*, already mentioned in p. 13, we have

in English the *ell* (of which the early meaning of arm or
forearm is seen in *el*-bow, the arm-bend), also the *fathom*
or cord stretched by the outspread arms in sailors'
fashion, and the *pace* or double step (Latin *passus*) of
which a thousand (*mille*) made the *mile*. But though
these names keep up the recollection of early measurement by men's limbs, they are now only used as convenient names for standard measures which they happen
to come tolerably near to, as for instance one may go a
long way to find a man's foot a foot long by the rule.
Our modern measurements are made by standard lengths,
which we have inherited with more or less change from
the ancients. It was a great step in civilization when
nations such as the Egyptians and Babylonians made
pieces of wood or metal of exact lengths to serve as
standards. The Egyptian cubit-rules with their divisions
may still be seen, and the King's Chamber in the Great
Pyramid measures very exactly 20 cubits by 10, the cubit
being 20·63 of our inches. Our foot has scarcely altered
for some centuries, and is not very different from the
ancient Greek and Roman feet. The French at the first
Revolution made a bold attempt to cast off the old
traditional standards and go straight to nature, so they
established the *metre*, which was to be a ten-millionth
of the distance from the pole to the equator. The
calculation however proved inexact, so that the metre is
now really a standard measure of the old sort, but so
great is the convenience of using the same measures, that
the metre and its fractions are coming more and more
into use for scientific work all over the world. The use
of scales and weights, and of wet and dry measures, had
already begun among the civilized nations in the earliest
known times. Our modern standards can even to some
extent be traced back to those of the old world, as for
instance the pound and ounce, gallon and pint, come
from the ancient Roman weights and measures.

From measuring feet in length, men would soon come
to reckoning the contents, say of an oblong floor, in
square feet. But to calculate the contents of less simple
figures required more difficult geometrical rules. The
Greeks acknowledged the Egyptians as having invented
geometry, that is, "land-measuring," and there may be
truth in the old story that the art was invented in order
to parcel out the plots of fertile mud on the banks of
the Nile. There is in the British Museum an ancient
Egyptian manual of mensuration (the Rhind papyrus),

one of the oldest books in the world, originally written
more than 1,000 years before Euklid's time, and which
shows what the Egyptians then knew and did not know
about geometry. From its figures and examples it
appears that they used square measure, but reckoned it
roughly; for instance, to get the area of the triangular
field ABC Fig. 78 (1) they multiplied half AC by AB, which
would only be correct when BAC is a right angle. When

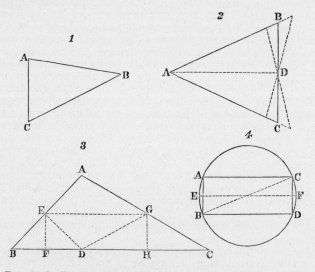

Fig. 78.—Rudimentary practical Geometry. 1, scalene triangle; 2, folded
right angle; 3, folded triangle; 4, rectangle folded in circle.

the Egyptians wanted the area of a circular field, they
subtracted one-ninth from the diameter and squared;
thus if the diameter were 9 perches, they estimated that
the circle contained 64 square perches, which the reader
will find on trial is a good approximation. All this was
admirable for the beginnings of geometry, and the record
may well be believed that Greek philosophers such
as Thales and Pythagoras, when they came to Egypt,
gained wisdom from the geometer-priests of the land.
But these Egyptian mathematicians, being a priestly
order, had come to regard their rules as sacred, and

therefore not to be improved on, while their Greek disciples, bound by no such scientific orthodoxy, were free to go on further to more perfect methods. Greek geometry thus reached results which have come down to us in the great work of Euklid, who used the theorems known to his predecessors, adding new ones and proving the whole in a logical series. It must be clearly understood that elementary geometry was not actually invented by means of definitions, axioms, and demonstrations like Euklid's. Its beginnnings really arose out of the daily practical work of land-measurers, masons, carpenters, tailors. This may be seen in the geometrical rules of the altar-builders of ancient India, which do not tell the bricklayer to draw a plan of such and such lines, but to set up poles at certain distances, and stretch cords between them. It is instructive to see that our term *straight line* still shows traces of such an early practical meaning; *line* is *linen* thread, and *straight* is the participle of the old verb to *stretch*. If we stretch a thread tight between two pegs, we see that the stretched thread must be the shortest possible; which suggests how the straight line came to be defined as the shortest distance between two points. Also, every carpenter knows the nature of a right angle, and he is accustomed to parallel lines, or such as keep the same distance from one another. To the tailor, the right angle presents itself in another way. Suppose him cutting a doubled piece of cloth to open out into the gore or wedge-shaped piece BAC in Fig. 78 (2). He must cut ADB a right angle, or his piece when he opens it will have a projection or a recess, as seen in the figure. When he has cut it right, so that BDC opens in a straight line, then he cannot but see that the sides AB, AC, and the angles ABC, ACB must exactly match, having in fact been cut out on one another. Thus he arrives, by what may be called tailor's geometry, at the result of Euklid I. 5, which now often goes by the name of the " asses' bridge." Such easy properties of figures must have been practically known very early. But it is also true that the ancients were long ignorant of some of the problems which now belong to elementary teaching. Thus it has just been mentioned how the Egyptian land-surveyors failed to make out an exact rule to measure a triangular field. Yet had it occurred to them to cut out the diagram of a triangle from a sheet of papyrus, as we may do with the triangle ABC in Fig. 78 (3), and double it up as shown in the figure, then they would

SCIENCE

have found that it folds into the rectangle EFHG, and, therefore, its area is the product of the height by half the base. It would be seen that this is no accident, but a property of all triangles, while at the same time it would appear that the three angles at A, B, C, all folding together at D, make up two right angles. Though the more ancient Egyptian geometers do not seem to have got at either of these properties of the triangle, the Greek geometers had in some way become well aware of them before Euklid's time. The old historians who tell the origin of mathematical discoveries do not always seem to have understood what they were talking of. Thus it is said of Thales that he was the first to inscribe the right-angled triangle in the circle, and thereupon sacrificed a bull. But a mathematician of such eminence could hardly have been ignorant of what any intelligent carpenter has reason to know, how an oblong board fits into a circle symmetrically; the problem of the right-angled triangle in the semicircle is involved in this, as is seen by (4) in the present figure. Perhaps the story really meant that Thales was the first to work out a stright geometrical demonstration of the problem. The tale is also told of Pythagoras, and another version is that he sacrificed a hekatomb on discovering that the square on the hypotenuse of a right-angled triangle is equal to the sum of the squares on the other two sides (Euklid I. 47). The story is not a likely one of a philosopher who forbade the sacrifice of any animal. As for the proposition, it is one which may present itself practically to masons working with square paving stones or tiles; thus, when the base is 3 tiles long, and the perpendicular 4, the hypotenuse will be 5, and the tiles which form a square on it will just be as many as together form squares on the other two sides. Whether Pythagoras got a hint from such practical rules, or whether he was led by studying arithmetical squares, at any rate he may have been the first to establish as a general law this property of the right-angled triangle, on which the whole systems of trigonometry and analytical geometry depend.

The early history of mathematics seems so far clear, that its founders were the Egyptians with their practical surveying, and the Babylonians whose skill in arithmetic is plain from the tables of square and cube numbers drawn up by them, which are still to be seen. Then the Greek philosophers, beginning as disciples of these older schools, soon left their teachers behind, and raised

mathematics to be, as its name implies, the " learning "
or " discipline " of the human mind in strict and exact
thought.   In its first stages, mathematics chiefly consisted of arithmetic and geometry, and so had to do with
known numbers and quantities.   But in ancient times
the Egyptians and Greeks had already begun methods
of dealing with a number without as yet knowing what
it was, and the Hindu mathematicians, going further in
the same direction, introduced the method now called
algebra.   It is to be noticed that the use of letters as
symbols in algebra was not reached all at once by a
happy thought, but grew out of an earlier and clumsier
device.   It appears from a Sanskrit book that the
venerable teachers began by expressing unknown
quantities by the term " so-much-as," or by the names
of colours, as " black," " blue," " yellow," and then the
first syllables of these words came to be used for shortness.   Thus if we had to express twice the square of an
unknown quantity, and called it " so much squared
twice," and then abbreviated this to *so sq* 2, this would
be very much as the Hindus did in working out the
following problem, given in Colebrooke's *Hindu Algebra* :
" The square root of half the number of a swarm of bees
is gone to a shrub of jasmin ; and so are eight-ninths of
the whole swarm : a female is buzzing to one remaining
male, that is humming within a lotus, in which he is
confined, having been allured to it by its fragrance at
night.   Say, lovely woman, the number of bees."   This
Hindu equation is worked out clumsily from the want of
the convenient set of signs $= + -$, which were invented
later in Europe, but the minus numbers are marked, and
the solution is in principle an ordinary quadratic.   The
Arab mathematicians learnt from India this admirable
method, and through them it became known in Europe
in the Middle Ages.   The Arabic name given to it is
al-jabr wa-l-mukabalah, that is, " consolidation and
opposition," this meaning what is now done by trans-
posing quantities on the two sides of an equation ; thence
comes the present word *algebra.*   It was not till about the
17th century in Europe that the higher mathematics
were thoroughly established, when Descartes worked
into a system the application of algebra to geometry, and
Galileo's researches on the path of a ball or flung stone
brought in the ideas which led up to Newton's fluxions
and Leibnitz's differential calculus, with the aid of
which mathematics have risen to their modern range and

power.   Mathematical symbols have not lost the traces
of their first beginnings as abbreviated words, as where n
still stands for *number* and r for *radius*, while $\sqrt{\,}$, which is
a running-hand r, does duty for root (*radix*), and $\int$, which
is an old-fashioned s, stands for the sum (*summa*) in
integration.

Mechanics and Physics, worked mathematically, now
form the very foundation of our knowledge of the
universe.   But in the old barbaric life, men had only
rudimentary notions of them.   The savage understands
the path of a projectile well enough to aim it, and how to
profit by momentum when he mounts his axe on a long
rather than a short handle.   But he hardly comes to
bringing these practical ideas to a principle or law.   Even
the old civilized nations of the East, though they could
lift stones with the lever, set their masonry upright with
the plumb-line, and weigh gold in the balance, are not
known to have come to scientific study of mechanical
laws.   What makes this more sure is that if they had, the
Greeks would have learnt it of them, whereas it is among
the Greek philosophers that the science is found just
coming into existence.   In Aristotle's time they were
thinking about mechanical problems, though by no
means always rightly; it was considered that a body is
drawn toward the centre of the world, but the greater
its weight the faster it will fall.   The chief founder of
mechanical science was Archimedes, who worked out
from the steelyard the law of the lever, and deduced
thence cases of all the particles of a body balancing on a
common centre, now called its centre of gravity; he even
gave the general theory of floating bodies, which mathematicians far on in the Middle Ages could hardly be
brought to understand.   Indeed, mechanical science,
after the classical period, shared the general fate of
knowledge during the long dead time when so much was
forgotten, and what was left was in bondage to the theology
of the schoolmen.   It sometimes surprises a modern
reader that the " wisdom of the ancients " should still
now and then be set up as an authority in science.   But
the scholars of the Middle Ages, who on many scientific
points knew less than the ancient Greeks, might well look
up to them.   It is curious to look at the book of Gerbert
(Pope Sylvester II), who was a leading mathematician
in the tenth century, and who bungles like an early
Egyptian over the measurement of the area of a triangle,
though the exact method as stated by Euklid had been

well known in classical times. Physical science might almost have disappeared if it had not been that while the ancient treasure of knowledge was lost to Christendom, the Mohammedan philosophers were its guardians, and even added to its store. For this they have not always had due praise. A pretty story is told of Galileo inventing the pendulum, being led to it by watching the great hanging lamp in the cathedral of Pisa swinging steadily to and fro; but as a matter of fact, it appears that six centuries earlier Ebn Yunis and other Moorish astronomers were already using the pendulum as a time-measurer in their observations. Of all the services which Galileo did for science, perhaps the greatest was his teaching clearer ideas of force and motion. People had of old times been deceived by the evidence of their senses into the belief that the force of a moving body would gradually become exhausted and it would stop of itself, but this idea of force was changed by the new principle that force is as much required to stop a moving body as to set it in motion, and that did no opposing force retard the arrow or the wheel, the one would fly and the other roll on for ever. In that age of mathematics applied to science new discoveries followed fast. If Archimedes could have come to life again, he would have seen progress going on at last, when the pressure of the air was weighed with Torricelli's barometer, and Stevin of Bruges made out the principle of the parallelogram of forces. The notion of an attractive force had come into the minds of philosophers by observing how the magnet attracts iron at a distance, and glass and other substances when rubbed become attractive. Thus the way was open for Newton to calculate the effect of gravitation as such an attractive force, and by it to explain the movements of the heavenly bodies, thus bringing the visible world within the sway of one universal law. In the present day, among the great laws which have been established in physical science, is that of the conservation of energy, that power is not created and destroyed in the processes of nature or the machines of man, but is transformed into new manifestations equivalent to those which were before. Philosophers' minds used often to be set on the invention of a perpetual moving power, that should go on creating its own force. But nowadays this idea is so discarded that, when some projector plans an absurd machine, he is sufficiently answered by being shown that if his machine could work, the perpetual

motion would be possible. The modern mechanician
has only to apply in the most desirable way the stores
of force placed at his disposal by nature, and within
this well-understood boundary his business flourishes
more and more.

Among the forms or manifestations of energy are
sound, light, heat, electricity. The classic philosophers
knew in a vague way that sound spreads like waves;
and the relation between the length of a harpstring and
its note was laid down in arithmetical rule by Pythagoras,
who measured it with the instrument we still use, the
monochord. But it was the moderns who measured
the velocity of sound, explained musical pitch by the rate
of vibration, and made the science of tone. About light
the ancients knew more. Their polished metal mirrors,
flat and curved, had taught them the first principles of
reflexion. Nor were they ignorant of refraction; they
already knew the familiar experiment of putting a ring
in a basin and pouring in water till it becomes visible.
A rock-crystal lens has been dug up at Nineveh, and the
Greeks and Romans were well acquainted with glass
lenses. One is surprised that neither the Arab astronomers, who knew a good deal of optics, nor Roger Bacon,
who in the thirteenth century gave an intelligent account
of their science, ever seem to have combined two lenses
into a telescope. It was not till the seventeenth century
that a telescope is plainly mentioned in Holland, and
Galileo, hearing of it, made the famous instrument with
which he saw Jupiter's moons, and revolutionized men's
ideas of the universe. The microscope and telescope
may be called inverted forms of one another, and their
inventions came nearly together. By these two instruments the range of man's vision has been so vastly
extended beyond his unaided eyesight, that animalcules
under a ten-thousandth of an inch long can now be
watched through all the stages of their life, while stars
whose distance from the earth is hundreds of thousands
of billions of miles, are within the maps of the universe.
The rainbow led to the problem of the decomposition of
light and the theory of colour. The doctrine that light
was as it were bright particles emitted in straight lines
from the luminous body failed to explain effects such as
light extinguishing light by interference, and it has
yielded to the undulatory theory, of ethereal light-waves
of extreme smallness and speed. In our own day the
lines of the spectrum have become the means of recogniz-

ing a glowing substance, so that the astronomer whose telescope reveals the faint shine of a nebula in the depths of the heavens, may test its composition with the spectroscope, as if it were a gas-jet on the laboratory table. Closely connected with the science of light is the science of heat. Not only do heat and light proceed together from the sun or fire, but the two were seen to be subject to the same laws when it was noticed that the mirror or lens which concentrated a bright spot of light, also brought to the same focus heat that would set wood on fire. The great step in the study of heat was the invention of the heat-measurer or thermometer. Who first made it is not known, but it was about three centuries ago, and its earliest form may have been the air-flask with its tube in which coloured water rises and falls, which is still the most striking way of showing a class the principle of thermometers. The doctrine of heat as due to vibration explains how heat is transformed force, so that the steam-hammer worked by the heat used in the furnace can be set to beat cold iron till it is white-hot; thus part of the force which came from heat has gone back into heat, and with the heat re-appears the other form of radiant energy, light. Lastly, the history of electricity comes from the time when the ancients wondered to see amber when rubbed pick up morsels of straw, and the loadstone draw bits of iron. The pointing of the loadstone south and north seems to have been earliest noticed by the Chinese, whence in the Middle Ages came its world-wide use in navigation. The electrical machine is only an enlarged form of the old experiment of rubbing the bit of amber. But the discoveries associated with the names of Volta and Galvani brought in a new method of generating electricity by chemical action in the battery. Franklin's kite proved the lightning-flash to be but a great electric spark. Oersted's current-wire deflecting a magnetic needle showed the relation between electricity and magnetism, and set on foot the line of invention to which the world owes the electric telegraph and much besides.

Next, as to chemistry. Its beginnings lie in practical processes such as smelting metal from the ore, fusing sand and soda into glass, and tanning leather with astringent pods or bark. The oldest civilized nations knew these and many other chemical arts, which not only were learnt by the artificers of Greece and Rome, but from time to time new processes were added to the store of knowledge, as when we hear of their distilling mercury from cinnabar, or treating copper with vinegar to make verdigris. In early civilized ages also there arose beside these practical recipes the first dim outlines of scientific chemistry. The Greek philosophers expressed their ideas of the states of matter by the four elements, fire, air, water, earth; and they also had learnt or invented the doctrine of matter being made up of atoms—a principle now more influential than ever in modern lecture-rooms. The successors of the Greeks were the Arabic alchemists, and their disciples in mediæval Christendom. Their belief that matter might be transmuted or transformed led many of them to spend their lives among their furnaces and alembics in the attempt to turn baser metals into gold. To modern chemists, who would not be surprised to find all the many so-called elements proved to be forms of one matter, the alchemists' idea does not seem quite unreasonable in itself, and practically it led them to the pursuit of truth by experiment, so that though they found no philosophers' stone, they were repaid by discoveries such as alcohol, ammonia, sulphuric acid. Their method, being founded on trials of real fact, cleared itself more and more from the magical folly it had grown up with, and the alchemist prepared the way for the later chemist. What of all things brought on the new chemical knowledge was the explanation of what takes place in burning, rusting, and breathing. How is it that the air in a receiver is spoilt by a burning candle or a mouse within, so that it no longer allows flame or life? How is it that while some substances, like charcoal, seem to be dissipated by fire, others, like lead or iron, turn into matter heavier than before? The answers to such questions led the way to clearer notions of chemical combination, but it was long before it was understood by what fixed laws of affinity and proportion this combination takes place. The advanced student of chemistry may spend an instructive hour in looking over old chemistry books, where the catalogue of substances is a confused chaos, not as yet brought into form and order on the lines of Dalton's atomic theory.

From the chemical nature of matter we pass to the nature of living things. The more evident parts of biology or the science of life, have come under man's attentive observation from the first. So far as zoology and botany consist in noticing the forms and habits of

animals and plants, savages and barbarians are skilled in
them.   Such people, for instance, as the natives of the
South American forests, have names for each bird and
beast, whose voices, resorts, and migrations they know
with an accuracy that astonishes the European naturalist
whom they guide through the jungle.   The catalogue of
the Brazilian native names of animals and plants, often
curiously descriptive of their natures, would make a
small book.   Thus the *jaguara pimina* or painted jaguar
is distinguished from the *jaguarete* or great jaguar; the
capybara signifies the creature " living in the grass," the
ipe-caa-goene, or " little wayside-plant-emetic," is our
ipecacuanha.   Mankind everywhere possesses this sort
of popular Natural History.   So it is with anatomy.
When the savage kills a deer, cuts it up, cooks the joints,
heart, and liver, makes clothes and straps of the hide,
cuts harpoon-heads and awls out of the long bones, and
uses the sinews for thread, it stands to reason that he
must have a good rough knowledge of the anatomy of an
animal.   The barbaric warrior and doctor have beyond
such butchers' anatomy an acquaintance with the
structure of man's body, as may be seen in the description
of the wounds of the heroes in the Iliad, where the spear
takes one in the diaphragm below the heart, and another
has the shoulder-tendon broken which makes his arm
drop helpless.   Among the Greeks such rough knowledge passed into the scientific stage when Aristotle
wrote his book on animals, and Hippokrates took
medicine away from the priests and sorcerers to make it a
method of treatment by diet and drugs.   The action of
the body came to be better understood during this
classical period, as, for instance, is seen in the nerves
leading to and from the brain being no longer con-
founded with the sinews which pull the limbs, although
the same Greek word *neuron* (*nerve*) still continued to be
used for both.   It is curious how long it took the ancients
to get at the notion of what muscle is, and how it acts.
They never understood the circulation of the blood,
though they had ideas about it, as in Plato's celebrated
passage in the Timaios which compares the heart to a
fountain sending the blood round to nourish the body,
which is like a garden laid out with irrigating channels.
Imperfect as ancient knowledge was, it may be plainly
seen how modern science is based upon it.   Thus the
medical terms of Galen's system, such as the *diagnosis*
of disease, are still used; and indeed many old physician's

SCIENCE 194

words have passed into common talk, as when one is said
to be in a *sanguine humour*, which carries us back to the
time when the humours or fluids of the body were thought
to cause the state of mind, the humour which is sanguine,
or " of the blood," being lively and impetuous. But in
knowledge of the body the moderns have left the ancients
quite behind, now that the microscope shows its minute
vessels and tissues, and there have been made out the
circulation of the blood, the process of respiration, the
chemistry of digestion, and the travelling of currents
along the nerves. Natural History still goes on the
principles of Aristotle, when he traces life on from lifeless
matter through the series of plants and animals. Modern
naturalists like Linnæus so improved the old classification, that it became possible to take a plant or animal
one had never seen before and did not know the name of,
and make out by examination that it must belong to such
and such a genus and species. Moreover, naturalists
have long been seeking to understand why the thousands
of species should arrange themselves in groups or genera,
the species in each genus being connected by a common
likeness, and the genera themselves falling into higher
groups, or orders. The thought that the likeness among
the species forming a genus is a family likeness, due to
these species being in fact the varied descendants of one
race or stock, is the foundation of that theory of development or evolution which for many ages has been in the
minds of naturalists, and now so largely prevails. This
is not the place to discuss the doctrine of descent or
development   but it is worth while to
remember that the very word *genus* meant originally
birth or race, so that the naturalist who sets down the
horse, ass, zebra, quagga, as all belonging to one genus
Equus, is really suggesting that they are all descended
from one kind of animal, and are in fact distant cousins,
which is the first principle of the development-theory.

The world we live in is the subject of astronomy, geography, geology. It seems plain how the rudiments of
these sciences began from the evidence of men's senses.
Children living unschooled in some wild woodland would
take it as a matter of course that the earth is a circular
floor, more or less uneven, arched over with a dome or
firmament springing from the horizon. Thus the natural
and primitive notion of the world is that it is like a round
dish with a 'cover. Rude tribes in many countries are
found thinking so, and working out the idea so as to

account for such phenomena as rain, which is water from above dripping in through holes in the sky-roof. This firmament is studded with stars, and is a few miles off. There is nothing to suggest to the savage that the sun should be enormously more distant than the cloud it seems to plunge into. The sun seems to go down in the west into the sea, or through an opening in the horizon, and to rise in like manner in the east, so that sunset and sunrise force on the minds of the first rude astronomers the belief in an under-world or infernal region, through which the sun travels in the night, and which to many a nation has seemed also the abode of departed souls, when after their bright day of life they sink like the sun into the night of death. The sun and moon move as living gods in the heaven, or at least are drawn or driven by such celestial powers, while the presence of living beings in the sky seems peculiarly manifest in eclipses, when invisible monsters seize or swallow the sun and moon. All this is very natural, so natural indeed that more correct astronomy has not yet rooted it out of Europe. Not many years ago a schoolmaster who ventured to lecture on astronomy in the west of England roused the displeasure of the country folk, that this young man should tell them the world was round and went about, when they had lived on it all their lives and knew it was flat and stood still. One part of the earliest astronomy, which was so sound as to have held its own ever since, was the measurement of time by the sun, moon, and stars. The day and the month fix themselves at once. In a less exact way the seasons of the year, such as the rainy season, or the icy season, or the growing season, furnish a means of reckoning, as where a savage tells of his father's death having been three rains or three winters ago. Rude tribes, who observe the stars to find their way by, notice also that the rising and setting of particular stars or constellations mark the seasons. Thus the natives of South Australia call the constellation Lyra the Loan-bird, for they notice that when it sets with the sun, the season for getting loan-birds' eggs has begun. It stands to reason that the great facts of the year's course, the change of the sun's height at noon, and the lengthening and shortening of the days, would be noticed, so that, even among people who have not as yet measured them with any accuracy, there exists in a loose way the notion of the year. Within the year, too, the successive moons or months come to be arranged with some regularity, as

where the Ojibwas reckoned in order the wild-rice moon,
the leaves-falling moon, the ice-moon, the snow-shoes
moon, and so forth. But such lunar months have to be
got into the year as they best may. Indeed what
distinguishes the uncivilized calendar is that, though
days, months, and years are known, the days are not yet
fitted regularly into the months, nor is it settled how
many months, much less how many days, the year is to
consist of.

When we look from this to the astronomy of the
ancient cultured nations, we find great progress made in
observing and calculating. Yet the astronomer-priests
who for ages watched and recorded the aspect of the
heavens, had not yet cut themselves free from the ideas
of their barbarian forefathers as to what the world as a
whole was like. In the Egyptian Book of the Dead, the
departed souls descend with the sun-god through the
western gate, and travel with him among the fields and
rivers of the under-world, and the Assyrian records also
tell of the regions below, where Ishtar descends into the
dark abode of fluttering ghosts, the house men enter but
cannot depart from. Yet the Egyptians who held to this
primitive astronomy had set the Great Pyramid by the
cardinal points with remarkable exactness. In reckoning the year, they not only added to the 12 solar months
of 30 days 5 intercalary days to make 365, but becoming
aware that even this was not accurate, they recorded its
variation till it should come round in a cycle of 1,461
years, as determined by the rising of Sirius. Even more
advanced was the astronomy of the Chaldæans, with its
records of eclipses extending over 2,000 years. In the
astronomy of barbarians the five planets Mercury,
Venus, Mars, Jupiter, and Saturn, are not thought much
of in comparison with the Sun and Moon. But among
the Chaldæans all the seven planets were classed together
as objects of worship and observation, starting the ideas
of the sacred number seven, which thence pervaded the
mystical philosophy of the ancients. It may have been
among the Babylonian astronomers that the study of the
motions of the planets led to the theory that they were
carried round on seven crystal spheres; to this day
people talk of being " in the seventh heaven." The next
and great step in astronomy was when the long-treasured
knowledge of Babylon and Egypt was taken up by the
Greeks, to be carried on by the exact methods of the
geometer. The Greek astronomers were familiar with

the idea of the earth being a sphere; they calculated its circumference, and, usually taking it as the centre of the universe, they measured the apparent movements of the heavenly bodies. This system in its most perfect form, known as the Ptolemaic, held its place into the middle ages, when it came into rivalry with the Copernican system of a central sun round which revolve the earth and other planets. How this became in the hands of Kepler and Newton a mechanical theory of the universe, and how man was at last stripped of the fond conceit that his little planet was the centre of all things, need not be re-told here.

Geography is a practical kind of knowledge in which the rudest tribes are well skilled, so far as it consists in the lie of their own land, the course of the streams, the passes over the mountains, how many days' marches through forest and desert to reach some distant hunting-ground, or the hillside where hard stone for hatchets is to be found. However uncivilized a people may be, they name their mountains and rivers in such terms as " red hill " or " beaver brook." Indeed the atlas contains hundreds of names of places that once had meanings in tongues which no man any longer speaks. Scientific geography begins when men come to drawing maps, an art which perhaps no savage takes to untaught, but which was known to the early civilized nations; the oldest known map is an Egyptian plan of the gold-mines of Æthiopia. The earliest known mention of a geographer attempting a map of the world is by Herodotus, who tells of Aristagoras's bronze tablet inscribed with the circuit of the whole earth, the sea and all rivers. But to the ancients the known world was a very limited district round their own countries. It brings the growth of geography well before our minds to look at the map in Gladstone's *Juventus Mundi*, representing the world according to the Homeric poems, with its group of nations round the Mediterranean, and the great Ocean River encircling the whole. Later, in the world as known to geographers such as Strabo, the lands of men form a vast oval, reaching from the pillars of Herakles across to far India, and from tropical Africa up to polar Europe. How land and sea came to lie as they do, it is the business of geology to explain. This is among the most modern of sciences, yet its problems had long set rude men thinking. Even the Greenlanders and the South Sea Islanders have noticed the fossils inland and high on the mountains, and account for them by declaring that the earth was once tilted over, or that the sea rose in a great flood and covered the mountains, leaving at their very tops the remains of fishes. In the infancy of Greek science, Herodotus speculated more rightly as to how the valley of Egypt had been formed by deposits of mud from the Nile, while the shells on the mountains proved to him that the sea had once been where dry land now is. But two thousand years had to pass before these lines of thought were followed up by the modern geologists, to whom the earth is now revealing the long history of the deposit and removal, rising and sinking of its beds, and the succession of plants and animals which from remote ages have lived upon it.

From this survey of the various branches of science, it is clear that their progress has been made in age after age by facts being more fully observed and more carefully reasoned on. Reasoning or logic is itself a science, but like other sciences, it began as an art which man practised without stopping to ask himself why or how. He worked out his conclusions by thinking and talking, untold ages before it occurred to him to lay down rules how to argue. Indeed, speech and reason work together. A language which distinguishes substantive, adjective, and verb, is already a powerful reasoning-apparatus. Men had made no mean advance toward scientific method when their language enabled them to class wood as heavy or light, and to form such propositions as, light wood floats, heavy wood sinks. The rise of reasoning into the scientific stage was chiefly due to the Greek philosophers, and Aristotle brought argument into a regular system by the method of syllogisms. Of course the simpler forms of these had always belonged to practical reasoning, and a savage, aware that red-hot coals burn flesh, would not thank a logician for explaining to him that in consequence of this principle a particular red-hot coal will burn his fingers. It must not be supposed that the introduction of logic as a science had the effect of at once stopping bad argument, and it was rather by setting practically to work on exact reasoning, especially in mathematics, that the Greeks brought on a general advance in knowledge. The importance of science was recognized when the famous Museum of Alexandria flourished, the type of later universities, with its great libraries, its laboratories, its zoological and botanical gardens. Hither students came by thousands to follow mathematics, chemistry, anatomy, under professors who resorted there at once to teach others and to learn themselves. Looking at the history of science for eighteen hundred years after this flourishing time, though some progress was made, it was not what might have been expected, and on the whole things went wrong. The so-called scholastic period which prevailed in Europe was unfavourable, partly because excessive reverence for the authority of the past fettered men's minds, and partly because the learned successors of Aristotle had come to believe so utterly in argumentation as to fancy that the problems of the world could be dealt with by arguing about them, without increasing the stock of real knowledge. The great movement of modern philosophy, with which the name of Bacon is associated as a chief expounder, brought men back to the sound old method of working experience and thought together, only now the experience was more carefully sought and observed, and thought arranged it more systematically. We who live in an age when every week shows new riches of nature's facts, and new shapeliness in the laws that connect them, have the best of practical proof that science is now moving on a right track.

The student who wishes to compare the mental habits of rude and ancient peoples with our own, may look into a subject which has now fallen into contempt from its practical uselessness, but which is most instructive in showing how the unscientific mind works. This is Magic. In the earlier days of knowledge men relied far more than we moderns do on reasoning by analogy or mere association of ideas. In getting on from what is known already to something new, analogy or reasoning by resemblance always was, as it still is, the mind's natural guide in the quest of truth. Only its results must be put under the control of experience. When the Australians picked up the bits of broken bottles left by the European sailors, the likeness of the new material to their own stone flakes at once led them to try it for teeth to their spears; experience proved that in this case the argument from analogy held good, for the broken glass answered perfectly. So the North American Indian, in default of tobacco, finds some more or less similar plant to serve instead, such as willow-bark. The practical knowledge of nature possessed by savages is so great that it cannot have been gained by mere chance observations; they must have been for ages constantly

noticing and trying new things, to see how far their
behaviour corresponded with that of things partly like
them.   And where the matter can be brought to practical
trial by experiment, this is a thoroughly scientific
method.   But the rude man wants to learn and do far
more difficult things—how to find where there is plenty
of game, or whether his enemies are coming, how to save
himself from the lightning, or how to hurt some one he
hates, but cannot safely throw a spear at.   In such
matters beyond his limited knowledge, he contents
himself with working on resemblances or analogies of
thought, which thus become the foundation of magic.
On looking into the " occult sciences," it is easy to make
out in them principles which are intelligible if one can
only bring one's mind down to the childish state they
belong to.   Nothing shows this better than the rules of
astrology, although this is far from the rudest kind of
magic.   According to the astrologers, a man born under
the sign Taurus is likely to have a broad brow and thick
lips, and to be brutal and unfeeling, but, when enraged,
violent and furious.   If he had been born under the sign
Libra, he would have had a just and well-balanced mind.
All this is because two particular groups of stars happen
to have been called the bull and the balance; the child
whose hour of birth has some sort of astronomical relation
to these constellations is imagined to have a character
resembling that of a real bull or a real pair of scales.   So
with the planets.   He over whom Mars presides in his
better aspect will be bold and fearless, but where the
planet is " ill-dignified," then he will be a boastful
shameless bully, ready to rob and murder.   Had he but
been born when Venus was in the ascendant, how
different would he have been, with dimpled cheek and
soft voice apt to speak of love.   Practically foolish as all
this is, it is not unintelligible.   There is in it a train of
thought which can be followed quite easily, though it is
a train of thought hardly strong enough for a joke, much
less for a serious argument.   Yet such is the magic
which still pervades the barbaric world.   The North
American Indian, eager to kill a bear to-morrow, will
hang up a rude grass image of one and shoot it, reckoning
that this symbolic act will make the real one happen.
The Australians at a burial, to know in what direction
they may find the wicked sorcerer who has killed their
friend, will take as their omen the direction of the flames
of the grave-fire.   The Zulu who has to buy cattle may

be seen chewing a bit of wood, in order to soften the hard heart of the seller he is dealing with. The accounts of such practices would fill a volume, and they do not seem broken-down remains of old ideas, for there is no reason to suppose they ever had more sense in them than is to be plainly seen now. They may be derived from some such loose savage logic as this :—Things which are like one another behave in the same way—shooting this image of a bear is like shooting a real bear—therefore, if I shoot the image I shall shoot a real bear. It is true that such magical proceedings, if tested by facts, prove to be worthless. But if we wonder that nevertheless they should so prevail among mankind, it may be answered that they last on even in our own country among those who are too ignorant to test them by facts—the rustics who believe a neighbour's ill-wishing had killed their cow, and who, on true savage principles, try to punish the evil-doer by putting a heart spitefully stuck full of pins up the chimney to shrivel in the smoke, that in like manner sharp pangs may pierce him and he may waste away.

In another and very different way the student of science is interested in magic. Loose and illogical as man's early reasonings may be, and slow as he may be to improve them under the check of experience, it is a law of human progress that thought tends to work itself clear. Thus even the fancies of magic have been sources of real knowledge. Few magical superstitions are more troublesome than the Chinese geomancy or rules of " wind and water," by which a lucky site has to be chosen for building a house. Absurd as this ancient art is, its professors appear to have been the earliest to use the magnetic compass to determine the aspects of the heavens, so that it seems the magician gave the navigator his guide in exploring the world. What exact science owes to astrology is well known, how in Chaldæa the places of the stars were systematically observed and recorded for portents of battle and pestilence, and registers of lucky and unlucky days. The old magical character hung to astronomy even into modern ages, when astrologers like Tycho Brahe and Kepler, who believed that the destinies of men were foretold by the planets, helped by their observation and calculation to foretell the motions of the planets themselves. Thus man has but to go on observing and thinking, secure that in time his errors will fall away, while the truth he attains to will abide and grow.

CHAPTER XIV

THE SPIRIT-WORLD

It does not belong to the plan of this book to give a general account of the many faiths of mankind. The anthropologist, who has to look at the religions of nations as a main part of their life, may best become acquainted with their general principles by beginning with the simple notions of the lower races as to the spirit-world. That is, he has to examine how and why they believe in the soul and its existence after death, the spirits who do good and evil in the world, and the greater gods who pervade, actuate, and rule the universe. Anyone who learns from savages and barbarians what their belief in spiritual beings means to them, will come into view of that stage of culture where the religion of rude tribes is at the same time their philosophy, containing such explanation of themselves and the world they live in as their uneducated minds are able to receive.

The idea of the soul which is held by uncultured races, and is the foundation of their religion, is not difficult to us to understand, if we can fancy ourselves in their place, ignorant of the very rudiments of science, and trying to get at the meaning of life by what the senses seem to tell. The great question that forces itself on their minds is one that we with all our knowledge cannot half answer, what the life is which is sometimes in us, but not always. A person who a few minutes ago was walking and talking, with all his senses active, goes off motionless and unconscious in a deep sleep, to wake after a while with renewed vigour. In other conditions the life ceases more entirely, when one is stunned or falls into a swoon or trance, where the beating of the heart and breathing seem to stop, and the body, lying deadly pale and insensible, cannot be awakened; this may last for minutes or hours, or even days, and yet after all the patient revives. Barbarians are apt to say that such a one died for a while, but his soul came back again. They have great difficulty in distinguishing real death from such trances. They will talk to a corpse, try to rouse it and even feed it, and only when it becomes noisome and must be got rid of from among the living, they are at last certain that the life has gone never to return. What, then, is this soul or life which thus goes and comes in sleep, trance, and death? To the rude philosopher, the question seems to be answered by the very evidence of his senses. When the sleeper awakens from a dream, he believes he has really somehow been away, or that other people have come to him. As it is well known by experience that men's bodies do not go on these excursions, the natural explanation is that every man's living self or soul is his phantom or image, which can go out of his body and see and be seen itself in dreams. Even waking men in broad daylight sometimes see these human phantoms, in what are called visions or hallucinations. They are further led to believe that the soul does not die with the body, but lives on after quitting it, for although a man may be dead and buried, his phantom-figure continues to appear to the survivors in dreams and visions. That men have such unsubstantial images belonging to them is familiar in other ways to the savage philosopher, who has watched their reflexions in still water, or their shadows following them about, fading out of sight to reappear presently somewhere else, while sometimes for a moment he has seen their living breath as a faint cloud, vanishing though one can feel that it is still there. Here then in few words is the savage and barbaric theory of souls, where life, mind, breath, shadow, reflexion, dream, vision, come together and account for one another in some such vague confused way as satisfies the untaught reasoner. The Zulu will say that at death a man's shadow departs from his body and becomes an ancestral ghost, and the widow will relate how her husband has come in her sleep and threatened to kill her for not taking care of his children; or the son will describe how his father's ghost stood before him in a dream, and the souls of the two, the living and the dead, went off together to visit some far-off kraal of their people. The Malays do not like to wake a sleeper, lest they should hurt him by disturbing his body while his soul is out. The Ojibwas describe how one of their chiefs died, but while they were watching the body, on the third night his shadow came back into it, and he sat up and told them how he had travelled to the River of Death, but was stopped there and sent back to his people. The Nicaraguans, when questioned by the Spaniards as to their religion, said that, when a man or woman dies, there comes out of their mouth something that resembles a person and does not die, but the body remains here—it is not precisely the heart that goes above, but the breath that comes from their mouth and is called the life. The lower races sometimes avoid such confusion of thoughts as this, by treating the breath, the dream-ghost, and other appearances, as being separate souls. Thus, some Greenlanders reckoned man as having two souls, his shadow and his breath; and the Fijians said that the "dark spirit" or shadow goes down to the world below, but the "light spirit" or reflexion seen in water stays near where he dies. The reader may call to mind examples how such notions of the soul lasted on hardly changed in the classic world; how in the Iliad the dead Patroklos comes to the sleeping Achilles, who tries in vain to grasp him with loving hands, but the soul like smoke flits away below the earth; or how Hermotimos, the seer, used to go out from his body, till at last his soul, coming back from a spirit-journey, found that his wife had burnt his corpse on the funeral pile, and that he had become a bodiless ghost. At this stage the idea of the soul was taken up by the Greek philosophers and refined into more metaphysical forms; the life and mind were separated by dividing the soul into two, the animal and the rational soul, and the conception of the soul as of thin ethereal substance gave place to the definition of the immaterial soul, which is mind without matter. To follow the discussion of these transcendental problems in ancient and modern philosophy will occupy the student of metaphysics, but the best proof how the earlier and grosser soul-theory satisfied the uncultured mind is that to this day it remains substantially the belief of the majority of the human race. Even among the most civilized nations language still plainly shows its traces, as when we speak of a person being in an *ecstasy* or "out of himself" and "coming back to himself," or when the souls of the dead are called *shades* (that is, "shadows") or *spirits* or *ghosts* (that is, "breaths"), terms which are relics of men's earliest theories of life.

It may have occurred to some readers that the savage philosopher ought, on precisely the same grounds, to

believe his horse or dog to have a soul, a phantom-likeness
of its body.   This is in fact what the lower races always
have thought and think still, and they follow the reasoning out in a way that surprises the modern mind, though
it is quite consistent from the barbarian's point of view.
If a human soul seen in a dream is a real object, then the
spear and shield it carries and the mantle over its shoulders are real objects too, and all lifeless things must have
their thin flitting shadow-souls.   Such are the souls of
canoes and weapons and earthen pots that the Fijians
fancy they see swimming down the stream pellmell into
the life to come, and the ghostly funeral gifts with which
the Ojibwas imagine the souls of the dead laden on their
journey to the spirit-land—the men carrying their
shadowy guns and pipes, the women their baskets and
paddles, the little boys their toy bows and arrows.   The
funeral sacrifices, which in one shape or other are remembered or carried on still in every part of the globe, give us
the clearest idea how barbaric religion takes in together
the souls of men, animals, and things.   In Peru, where a
dead prince's wives would hang themselves in order to
continue in his service, and many of his attendants would
be buried for him to take their souls with him, people
declared that they had seen those who had long been dead
walking about with their sacrificed wives, and adorned
with the things that were put in the grave for them.   So
only a few years since in Madagascar it was said that the
ghost of King Radama had been seen dressed in a uniform
buried with him, and mounted on one of the horses that
were killed at his tomb.   With such modern instances
before us, we understand the ancient funeral rites of
which the traces remain in the burial-mounds on our own
hills, with their skeletons of attendants lying round the
chief, and the bronze weapons and golden arm-rings.
Classic literature abounds in passages which show how
truly the modern barbarian represents the ancient; such
are the burning of Patroklos with the Trojan captives and
the horses and hounds, the account of the Scythian
funerals by Herodotus, and his story of Melissa's ghost
coming back shivering because the clothes had not been
burnt for her at her burial.   There are " native " districts
in India where the *suttee* or " goodwife " is still burnt on
her husband's funeral pile.   In Europe, long after the
wives and slaves ceased thus to follow their master, the
warrior's horse was still solemnly killed at his grave and
buried with him.   There is a description of this barbaric

rite being performed as lately as 1781 at Treves, at the funeral of Friedrich Kasimir, Count Boos von Waldeck, a Knight of the Teutonic Order. In England the pathetic ceremony of leading the horse in the soldier's funeral is the last remnant of the ancient sacrifice. Other quaint relics of the old funeral customs are to be met with. There are German villages where the peasants put shoes on the feet of the corpse (the " hell-shoon " with which the old Northmen were provided for the dread journey to the next world), and elsewhere a needle and thread is put in for them to mend their torn clothes, and the dead has a piece of money put in his hand or mouth (like the obol of Charon) to pay his way with, or for the ferry across the river of death.

Mention has just been made of ancient burial-mounds. Seeing how barbarians reverence and fear the souls of the dead, we may understand the care they take of their bodies, leaving the hut as a dwelling for the dead, or drying the corpse and setting it up on a scaffold, or burying it in a canoe or coffin, or building up a strong tomb over it, or for the ashes, if the people have taken to cremation. Prehistoric burial-places in our own country are still wonders to us for the labour they must have cost their barbaric builders. Most conspicuous are the great burial-mounds of earth or cairns of stones. Some of the largest of these appear to date from the stone-age. But their use lasted on through the bronze-age into the iron-age; and to this day in the Highlands of Scotland the memory of the old custom is so strong that the mourners, as they may not build a cairn over the grave in the church-yard, will sometimes set up a little one where the funeral procession stops on the way. Within the old burial-mounds or barrows, there may be a cist or rude chest of stone slabs for the interment, or a chamber of rude stones, sometimes with galleries. Many such stone structures are to be seen above ground, especially the *dolmens*, *i.e.* stone tables, formed of three or four great upright stones, with a top-stone resting on them, such as Kit's Coty House, not far from Rochester. The remains dug up show that the dolmens were tombs. Another kind of early stone monuments are the *menhirs*, *i.e.* long stones set up singly. It happens that the Khasias of north-east India have gone on to modern times setting up such rude pillars as memorials of the dead, so that it may be reasonably guessed that those in Brittany, for instance, had the same purpose. Another kind of rude stone structures

well known in Europe are the *cromlechs*, or stone circles,
formed of upright stones in a ring, such as Stanton Drew,
not far from Bristol.   There is proof that the stone circles
have often to do with burials, for they may surround a
burial-mound, or have a dolmen in the middle.   But
considering how tombs are apt to become temples where
the ghost of the buried chief or prophet is worshipped,
it is likely that such stone circles should also serve as
temples, as in the case of South India at the present time,
where cocks are actually sacrificed to the village deity,
who is represented by the large stone in the centre of a
cromlech.   Rude stone monuments may be traced in a
remarkable line on the map, from India across to North
Africa, and up to the west side of Europe (*see* Fergusson's
map).   The purpose of them all is not fully understood,
especially the lines of great stones at Carnac and Abury,
and Stonehenge with its great hewn upright and cross
stones.   But, as has been here shown, there are facts
which go far to explain the meaning of dolmens, menhirs,
and cromlechs.   The fanciful speculations of the old-
fashioned antiquaries, such as that the dolmens were
" Druid's altars," are giving place to sober examination
such as the reader may find in Lubbock's *Prehistoric
Times.*
   In the barbaric religion, which has left such clear traces
in our midst, what is supposed to become of the soul after
death ?   The answers are many, but they agree in this,
that the ghosts must be somewhere whence they can
come to visit the living, especially at night time.   Some
tribes say that the soul continues to haunt the hut where
it died, which is accordingly deserted for it; or it hovers
near the burial-ground, which is sometimes the place of
village resort, so that the souls of ancestors can look on
kindly, like the old people sitting round the village green
watching the youngsters at their sports; or the ghosts flit
away to some region of the dead in the deep forests or on
mountain-tops or far-away islands over the sea, or up on
the plains above the sky, or down in the depths below the
ground where the sun descends at night.   Such people as
the Zulus can show the holes where one can descend by a
cavern into the under-world of the dead, an idea well
known in the classic lake Avernus, and which has lasted
on to our own day in St. Patrick's Purgatory in Lough
Dearg.   By a train of fancy easy to follow, it is often held
that the home of the dead has to do with that far-west
region where the sun dies at night.   Islanders like

the Maoris imagine the souls speeding away from the westernmost cape of New Zealand, just as on the coast of Brittany, where Cape Raz stands out westward into the ocean, there is the " bay of souls," the launching-place where the departed spirits sail off across the sea. Many rude tribes think the spirit-world to be the pleasant land they see in dreams, where the dead live in their spirit-villages, and there is game and fish in plenty, and the sun always shines; but others fancy it the dim land of shadows, the cavernous under-world of night. Both ideas are familiar to us in poetry—one in the earthly paradise of the legends, the other in such passages as describe Odysseus' visit to the bloodless ghosts in the dreary dusk of Hades, or the shadows of the dead in Purgatory wondering to see Dante there, whose fleshly body, unlike their own phantom forms, stops the sunlight and casts a shadow.

Hitherto we have been speaking of the bodiless souls or ghosts of the dead, but it also agrees with their nature that they may enter into new bodies and live again on earth. In fact one of the most usual beliefs of the lower races is that the souls of dead ancestors are re-born in children, an idea which explains the fact of children having a likeness to the father's or mother's family. For instance, the Yoruba negroes greet a new-born child with the salute, " Thou art come ! " and then set themselves to decide what ancestral soul has returned. It does not, however, follow that the body in which the soul takes up its new abode should be human : it may enter into a bear or jackal, or fly away in a bird, or, as the Zulus think, it may pass into one of those harmless snakes which creep about in the huts, liking the warmth of the family hearth, as they did while they were old people, and still kindly taking the food given by their grandchildren. In such simple forms there appears among the lower races the notion of transmigration which in Brahmanism and Buddhism becomes a great religious doctrine.

To return to the souls of the dead which flit to and fro as ghosts. These, wherever they dwell, are naturally believed to keep up their interest in the living, and their families hold kindly intercourse with them. Thus, in North America a Mandan woman will talk by the hour to her dead husband or child; and a Chinese is bound to announce any family event, such as a wedding, to the spirits of his ancestors, present in their memorial tablets. The ghosts of dead kinsfolk are not only talked to but fed ; the family offer them morsels of food at their own meals, and hold once a year a feast of the dead, when the souls of ancestors for generations back are fancied present and invisibly partaking of the food. Such offerings to the dead not only go on through the savage and barbaric world, but last on into higher civilization, their traces still remaining in Europe. The Russian peasant, who fancies the souls of his forefathers creeping in and out behind the saints' pictures on the little icon-shelf, puts crumbs of cake there for them. One has only to cross the Channel to see how the ancient feast of the dead still keeps its primitive character in the festival of All Souls, which is its modern representative; even at the cemetery of Père-Lachaise they still put cakes and sweetmeats on the graves, and in Brittany the peasants that night do not forget to make up the fire and leave the fragments of the supper on the table, for the souls of the dead of the family who will come to visit their home. All this belongs to the ancestor-worship or religion of the divine dead, which from remote antiquity has been, as it is even now, the main faith of the larger half of mankind. But this worship does not come only from family affection, for the ghosts of the dead are looked upon as divine beings, powerful both for good and harm. The North American Indian, who prays to the spirits of his fore-fathers to give him good weather or luck in hunting, if he happens to fall into the fire will believe he has neglected to make some offering to the spirits, and they have pushed him in to punish him. In Guinea the negroes who regularly bring food and drink to the images of their dead relatives look to them for help in the trials of life, and in times of peril or distress crowds of men and women may be seen on the hill-tops or the skirts of the forest, calling in the most piteous and touching tones on the spirits of their ancestors. Such accounts help us to understand what real meaning there is in the ancestor-worship which to a Chinese or Hindu is the first business of life, and how the pious rites for the dead ancestors or lares formed the very bond which held a Roman family together. Our modern minds have rather lost the sense of this, and people often think the apotheosis of a dead Roman emperor to have been a mere act of insane pride, whereas in fact it was an idea understood by any barbarian, that at death the great chief should pass into as great a deity.

That barbarians should imagine the manes or ghosts of their dead to be such active powerful beings, arises naturally from their notions of the soul; but this requires a word of explanation. As during life the soul exercises power over the body, so after death when become a ghost it is believed to keep its activity and power. Such ghosts interfering in the affairs of the living are usually called good and evil spirits, or demons. There is no clear distinction made between ghosts and demons; in fact, savages generally consider the demons who help or plague them to be souls of dead men. Good or evil, the man keeps after death the temper he had in mortal life. Not long ago, in South India, where the natives are demon-worshippers, it was found that they had lately built a shrine of which the deity was the ghost of a British officer, a mighty hunter, whose votaries, mindful of his tastes in life, were laying on his altar offerings of cheroots and brandy. The same man will be a good spirit to his friends and an evil spirit to his enemies, and even to his own people he may be sometimes kind and sometimes cruel, as when the Zulus believe that the shades of dead warriors of their tribe are among them in battle and lead them to victory; but if these ghostly allies are angry and turn their backs, the fight will go against them. When people like the American Indians or the African negroes believe that the air around them is swarming with invisible spirits, this is not nonsense. They mean that life is full of accidents which do not happen of themselves; and when in their rude philosophy they say the spirits make them happen, this is finding the most distinct causes which their minds can understand. This is most plainly seen in what uncivilized men believe about disease. We have noticed already that they account for fainting or trance by supposing the soul to leave the body for a time, and here it may be added that weakness or failure of health is in the same way thought to be caused by the soul or part of it going out. In these cases, to bring the soul back is the ordinary method of cure, as where the North American medicine-man will pretend to catch his patient's truant soul and put it back into his head, or in Fiji a sick native has been seen lying on his back, bawling to his own soul to come back to him. But in other conditions of disease the patient's behaviour seems rather that of a man who has got a soul in him that is not his proper soul. In any painful illness, especially when the sick man is tossing and shaking in fever, or writhing in convulsions on the ground, or when in delirium or delusion he no longer thinks his own thoughts or speaks

with his own voice, but with distorted features and
strange, unearthly tones breaks into wild raving, then
the explanation which naturally suggests itself is that
another spirit has entered into or possessed him. Any
one who watches the symptoms of a hysterical-epileptic
patient, or a maniac, will see how naturally in the infancy
of medical science demoniacal possession came to be
the accepted theory of disease, and the exorcism or
expulsion of these demons the ordinary method of treatment. It is so among savages, as when a sick Australian
will believe that the angry ghost of a dead man has got
into him and is gnawing his liver; or when in a Patagonian
skin hut the wizards may be seen dancing, shouting, and
drumming to drive out the evil demon from a man down
with fever. Such ideas were at home in ancient history,
as in the well-known Egyptian tablet referring to the time
of Rameses XII (12th century B.C.) to be seen in the Paris
Library, and translated in *Records of the Past*, where the
Egyptian god Khons was sent in his ark to cure the little
princess Bentaresh of the evil movement in her limbs.
When he came, the demon said, " Great god who chasest
demons, I am thy slave, I will go to the place whence I
came." Then they made a sacrifice for that spirit, and
he went in peace, leaving the patient cured. As far back
as the history of medicine reaches, we find the contest
between this old spirit-theory of disease and the newer
ideas of the physicians, with their diet and drugs; and
though the doctors have now taken the upper hand, yet
in any nation short of the most civilized the earlier
notions may still be found unchanged. When Prof.
Bastian, the anthropologist, was travelling in Burma, his
cook had an apoplectic fit, and the wife was doing her
best to appease the offended demon who had brought it
on, by putting little heaps of coloured rice for him, and
prayers, " Oh, ride him not ! Ah, let him go ! Grip him
not so hard ! Thou shalt have rice ! Ah, how good that
tastes ! " In countries where this theory of disease prevails, the patients' own delusions work in with and confirm it in most striking ways. As fully persuaded as the
bystanders of the reality of their demons, they will recognize them in the figures they dream or see in their
delirium, and, what is more, under delusion or diseased
imagination they so lose their sense of being themselves,
as to talk with what they believe to be the voice of the
demon within them, answering in its name, just as the
sick princess does in Syria three thousand years ago.

Englishmen in India and the Far East often have the opportunity of being present at these strange old-world scenes, and hearing the demon-voice whisper, or squeak, or roar, out of the patient's mouth, that he is the spirit so-and-so, and tell what he is come for; at last, when satisfied with what he wants, or subdued by the exorcist's charms and threats, the demon consents to go, and then the patient leaves off his frantic screams and raving, his convulsive writhing quiets down, and he sinks into an exhausted sleep, often relieved for a time when the malady is one where mental treatment is effective. Nor is it necessary to go to India or China for illustrations of this early theory of disease. In Spain the priests still go on exorcising devils out of the mouths and feet of epileptic patients, though this will probably cease in a few years, when it is known how successfully that hitherto intractable disease may be treated with potassium bromide.

In other ways the notion of spirits serves to account for whatever happens. That certain unusually fierce wolves or tigers are "man-eaters" is explained by the belief that the souls of wicked men go out at night and enter into wild-beast bodies to prey on their fellow-men; these are the man-tigers and were-wolves—that is, " man-wolves " —which still live in the popular superstition of India and Russia. Again, we all know that many living people grow pale and bloodless and pine away; in Slavonic countries this is thought to be caused by blood-sucking nightmares, whose dreadful visits the patient is conscious of in his sleep, and these creatures are ingeniously accounted for as demon-souls dwelling in corpses, whose blood accordingly keeps fluid long after death; they call them vampires. It has been suggested that primitive men gained from their ideas of souls and spirits their first clear notions of a cause of anything, and this is at any rate so far true that rude tribes do find in the doings of spirits around them a reason for every stumble over a stone, every odd sound or feeling, every time they lose their way in the woods. Thus, in the scores of good and evil chances which meet the barbarian from hour to hour, he finds work for many friendly or unfriendly spirits. Especially his own luck or fortune takes shape in a guardian spirit who belongs to him and goes about with him. This may be, as the rude Tasmanians have thought, a dead father's soul looking after his son, or such a patron-spirit as the North American warrior fasts for till he sees it in a dream; or it may be, like the *genius* of the ancient Roman, a spirit born with him for a companion and guardian through life. The genius of Augustus was a divine being to be prayed and sacrificed to, but how we moderns have left behind the thoughts of the ancients, while still using their words, is curiously seen in the changed meaning with which we now talk of the genius of Handel or Turner. Not less striking is the change which has come in our thoughts about the world around us, the sky and the sea, the mountains and the forests. We have learnt to watch the operation of physical laws of gravity and heat, of growth and decomposition, and it is only with an effort that we can get our imagination back to the remote days when men looked to an infinite multitude of spiritual beings as the causes of nature. Yet this belief arises plainly from the theory of the soul, for these spirits are looked upon as souls working nature much as human souls work human bodies. It is they who cast up the fire in the volcano, tear up the forest in the hurricane, spin the canoe round in the whirlpool, inhabit the trees and make them grow. The lower races not only talk of such nature-spirits, but deal with them in a thoroughly personal way which shows how they are modelled on human souls. Modern travellers have seen North Americans paddling their canoes past a dangerous place on the river and throwing in a bit of tobacco with a prayer to the river-spirit to let them pass. An African woodcutter who has made the first cut at a great tree has been known to take the precaution of pouring some palm-oil on the ground, that the angry tree-spirit coming out may stop to lick it up, while the man runs for his life. The state of mind to which these nature-spirits belong must have been almost as clearly remembered by the Greeks, when they could still fancy the nymphs of the lovely groves, and springs, and grassy meadows, coming up to the council of the Olympian gods and sitting around on the polished seats, or the dryads growing with the leafy pines and oaks, and uttering screams of pain when the woodman's axe strikes the trunk. The Anglo-Saxon dictionary preserves the curious word *woodmare* for an echo (*wudu-mær* = wood-nymph), a record of the time when Englishmen believed, as barbarians do still, that the echo is the voice of an answering spirit; the word *mare*, for spirit or demon, appears also in *nightmare*, the throttling dream-demon who was as real to our forefathers as he is to the natives of Australia now. Super-

seded by physical science, the old nature-spirits still find
a home in poetry and folk-lore; the Loreley is only a
modernized version of the river-demon who drowns the
swimmer in the whirlpool; the healing water-spirits of
the old sacred wells have only taken saints' names, the
little elves and fairies of the woods are only dim recollections of the old forest-spirits. It may surprise the
readers of Huxley's *Physiography* to recognise in fairy-
tales the nature-spirits in whose personal shape prehistoric man imagined the forces of nature.

Above the commonalty of souls, demons, and nature-
spirits, the religions of all tribes recognize higher spirits,
or gods. Where ancestor-worship prevails, the souls of
great chiefs and warriors or any celebrated persons may
take this divine rank. Thus, the Mongols worship as
good deities the great Genghis Khan and his princely
family. The Chinese declare that Pang, who is worshipped by carpenters and builders as their patron
divinity, was a famous artificer who lived long ago in the
province of Shangtung, while Kwang-tae, the War-god,
was a distinguished soldier who lived under the Han
dynasty. The idea of the divine ancestor may even be
carried far enough to reach supreme deity, as where the
Zulus, working back from ghostly ancestor to ancestor,
talk of Unkulunkulu, the Old-Old-one, as the creator
of the world; or the Brazilian tribes say that Tamoi
the Grandfather, the first man, dwelt among them and
taught them to till the soil, at last rising to the sky,
where he will receive their souls after death. Among the
nature-spirits also the barbarian plainly perceives great
gods who rule the universe. The highest deity of the
African negroes is the Sky, who gives the rain and makes
the grass grow, and when they wake in the morning they
thank him for opening the door to let the sun in. Thus
they are at the same stage of thought as our Aryan
ancestors, whose great deity *Dyaus*, sung of in the hymns
of the Veda, was at once the solid personal Sky that rains
and thunders, and the Heaven-god who animates it.
This deity remains even in name in the Greek *Zeus*, and
Latin *Jupiter*, the Heaven-father, both religions keeping
up its double sense of sky and sky-god, belonging to the
barbaric theology which could see massive life in the
over-arching firmament, and could explain that life by an
indwelling deity, modelled on the human soul. We may
best understand what was meant by the Heaven-god, if
we think of him as the soul of the sky. Among all the

relics of barbaric religion which surround us, few are more striking than the phrases which still recognize as a deity the living sky, as "Heaven forgive me!" "The vengeance of Heaven will overtake him." The rain and thunder are mostly taken as acts of the Heaven-god, as where Zeus hurls the thunderbolt and sends the showers. But some peoples have a special Rain-god, like the Khonds of Orissa, who pray to Pidzu Pennu that he will pour down the waters through his sieve upon their fields. Others have a special Thunder-god, like the Yorubas, who say it is Shango who casts down with the lightning-flash and the thunder-clap his thunder-axes, which are the stone celts they dig up in the ground; we English keep up the memory of the god Thunder or Thor in our word *Thursday*, which is a translation of *Dies Jovis*. In barbaric theology, Earth, the mother of all things, takes her place, as when the pious Ojibwa Indian digging up his medicine-plants is careful to leave an offering for great-grandmother Earth. No fancy of nature can be plainer than that the Heaven-father and the Earth-mother are the universal parents, nor could any ceremony acknowledge them more naturally than the Chinese marriage when bride and bridegroom prostrate themselves before Heaven and Earth. The Earth-goddess is clear in classic religion, Dēmētēr, Terra Mater, and perhaps the last trace of her worship among ourselves may be the leaving of the last handful of corn-ears standing in the field or the carrying it in triumph in the harvest-home. In modern times it is among the negroes of the Guinea coast that the clearest idea of the Sea-god is to be found, when the native kings, praying him not to be boisterous, would have rice and cloth and bottles of rum, and even slaves, cast into the sea as sacrifices. So a Greek or Roman general, before embarking on the dangerous waves, would sacrifice a bull to Poseidōn or Neptune. To men who could thus look on the sky, earth, and sea as animated, intelligent beings, the Sun, giver of light and life to the world, rising and crossing the sky and descending at night into the under-world whence he arose, has the clearest divine personality. There is a quaint simplicity in the account which not many years ago a Samoyed woman gave of her daily prayers; at sunrise, bowing to the sun, she said, "When thou, God, risest, I too rise from my bed!" and in the evening, "When thou, God, goest down, I too get me to rest." As far back as ancient history reaches, the Sun-god appears, as where, in the pictures on Egyptian mummy-cases, Ra, the Sun, is seen travelling in his boat through the upper and lower regions of the universe. Every morning those modern ancients, the Brahmans, may be seen standing on one foot with their hands held out before them and their faces turned to the east, adoring the Sun : among the oldest prayers which have come down unchanged from the old Aryan world is that which they daily repeat, " Let us meditate on the desirable light of the divine Sun; may he rouse our minds ! " The Moon-god or goddess marks the festivals of rude forest tribes who dance by the light of the full moon. It is not uncommon for the Moon to rank above the Sun, as perhaps for astronomical reasons was the case in ancient Babylonia; but more usually the Sun stands first, as seems to us more natural; and commonly Sun and Moon are looked on as a pair, brother and sister, or husband and wife. It is easy to understand why at the famous temple in Syria, Sun and Moon had no images like the other gods, because they themselves were to be seen by all men. No doubt this is why of all the old nature-gods they alone still have personal obeisance done to them among us to this day; in Germany or France one may still see the peasant take off his hat to the rising sun, and in England the new moon is saluted with a bow or curtsey, as well as the curious practice of " turning one's silver," which seems a relic of the offering of the moon's proper metal. Fire, though hardly a deity of the first order, is looked upon as a personal being, and worshipped both for the good and harm it does to man, and as minister of the greater gods. Among the Aryan nations, the first word of the Veda is the name of *Agni*, the Fire-god (Latin *Ignis*), the divine priest of sacrifice; the Parsis, representatives of the religion of ancient Persia, whose most sacred place is the temple at the burning wells of Baku (p.   ), are typical fire-worshippers; among the old Greeks Hestia, the sacred hearth, was fed with fat and libations of sweet wine, and in Rome the ancient fire-cult was kept up in the temple of Vesta, with the eternal fire in her sanctuary. The Wind-gods are as well known to the North American Indians and the South Sea Islanders as they were to the Greeks, from whose religion they have come down to us so that every ploughman's child hears of rude Boreas and gentle Zephyr. To conclude the list, the Rivers have seemed beings so far greater than the little spirits of the brooks that they often, like Skamandros and Spercheios, had temples and priests of their own; men swore by them, for they could seize and drown the perjurer in their floods, and to the Hindus still the most awful of oaths is by a divine river, above all the Ganges.

Such a list of gods, the vast souls of the sky, earth and sea, of the sun and moon, and the rest of the great powers of nature, each with his own divine personality, his own rational purpose and work in the world, goes far to explain polytheism, as it is found in all quarters of the globe. The explanation cannot, however, be complete, because both the names and natures of many gods have become confused. A deity worshipped in several temples is apt to split up into several deities, and men go on worshipping these by different names after their first sense is forgotten. Among nations who have become blended by alliance or conquest, the religions also mix, and the various gods lose their distinct personality. The classical dictionary is full of examples of all this. The thundering sky and the rainy sky, Jupiter Tonans and Jupiter Pluvius, came to be adored like two distinct beings. The Latin Neptunus and the Greek Poseidōn, put together into one because both were sea-gods, form a curious divine compound. Under the name of Mercurius, god of trade, comes in another ancient deity, the Greek Hermes, messenger of the gods, leader of the dead into the land of Hades, god of thieves and merchants, of writing and science, who himself bears traces of having been pieced together out of yet older deities, among them the writing-god of ancient Egypt, the ibis-headed Thoth. This will give a notion of the confusion which begins in religion as soon as the worshippers cease to think of a deity by his first meaning and purpose, and only know of him as the god so-and-so, whose image stands in such-and-such a temple. The wonder is not that the origin of so many ancient gods is now hard to make out, but that so many show so clearly as they do what they were at first, a divine ancestor, or a sun, or sky, or river. The gods of barbaric religion also show plainly at work, in the minds of the rude theologians, a thought destined to vast importance in higher stages of civilization. Regarding the world as the battle-ground of good and evil spirits, some religions see these ranged in two contending armies with higher good and evil gods over them, and above all the sovereign good deity and evil deity. This system of dualism, as it is called, is worked out in the contest between the powers of light and dark-

ness, under Ormuzd and Ahriman, the good and evil
spirits, in the religion of ancient Persia. In barbaric
stages of religion there appears also in rude forms the
system of divine government, so well known in the faiths
of more cultured nations. As among the worshippers
themselves there are common men, and chiefs above
them, and great rulers or kings above all, with high and
low officers to do their bidding; so among their gods
they frame schemes of lower and higher ranks of deities,
with above all the majesty of a supreme deity. It is not
agreed everywhere which god is to have this supremacy.
As has been already said, men who look to the souls of the
dead as their gods may hold even the highest divinity to
be such a soul, an ancestor expanded into creator and
ruler of the world. Often, and naturally, the heaven-god
is looked upon as supreme creator and controller of the
universe. Among the nations of West Africa, some say
Heaven does his will through his servants, the lesser
spirits of the air, but others think him too high above to
trouble himself much with earthly things. The doctrine
of the Congo negroes shows a thoughtful, if not a happy,
philosophy of life. They say it is the crowd of good and
evil spirits, souls of the departed, who are still active in
the concerns of life, and mostly the evil spirits have the
best of it; but now and then, when they have made the
world unbearable, the great Heaven rouses himself,
terrifies the bad demons with his thunder, and lets fly his
thunderbolts at the most obstinate; then he goes back to
rest, and lets the spirits rule as before. A more cheerful
view of nature-spirits working beneath heaven is familiar
to us in the Homeric court of the gods on Olympus, where
Zeus, the personal sky, sits enthroned above, holding
sway over the lower gods of earth, air, and sea. In other
countries the Sun may be looked upon as supreme, as he
is among many hill-tribes of India, where he rules over
the gods of the forest and the plain, the tribe-gods, and
the ancestral ghosts. But the "Great Spirit," creator and
controller of the universe, of whom we read in modern
descriptions of the North American Indians, came from
the teaching of the Jesuits in the seventeenth century;
and similar divine beings elsewhere seem as little genuine.
When the reader goes on to study the religion and philosophy of the ancient civilized world, he will find men's
thoughts working in these same two ways towards
pantheism or monotheism, according as they conceive the
whole universe as one vast body animated by one divine

soul, or raise to the same divine height the one deity who reigns supreme over the rest. It lies beyond our range to follow this argument further here.

Let us now look at the chief acts of barbaric worship, which are not hard to understand when it is borne in mind that the deities they are paid to are actual human souls, or transformed human souls, or beings modelled on human souls. Even among savages, prayer is already found; indeed, nothing could be more natural than the worshipper should address with respectful words and entreaties for help a divine being who is perhaps his own grandfather. The prayers of barbarians have often been listened to and written down. Thus among the Zulus, the sacrificer says: " There is your bullock, ye spirits of our people. I pray for a healthy body that I may live comfortably, and thou so-and-so, treat me with mercy, and thou so-and-so " (mentioning by name the dead of the family). The following is part of a prayer of the Khonds, when offering a human sacrifice to the Earth-goddess: " By our cattle, our flocks, our pigs, and our grain we procured a victim and offered a sacrifice. Do you now enrich us. Let our herds be so numerous that they cannot be housed; let children so abound that the care of them shall be too much for the parents, as shall be seen by their burnt hands; let our heads ever strike against brass pots innumerable hanging from our roofs; let the rats form their nests of shreds of scarlet cloth and silk; let all the kites in the country be seen in the trees of our village, from beasts being killed there every day. We are ignorant of what it is good to ask for. You know what is good for us. Give it to us." These two specimens of prayers are chosen because they show how closely prayer is connected with sacrifice, how the offering is brought and the favour asked with it, just as would be done to a living chief. Barbaric sacrifices are not mere formal tokens of respect; they are mostly food, and will be consumed by the divinity, though he, being a spirit, is apt to take only the spirit, flavour, or essence, of the viands; or he snuffs up the stream or smoke as it ascends from the altar fire, a spiritual food of much the same thin ethereal substance which the spirit or god himself is thought to be of. It is in the higher religions that the sacrificial rite loses its grosser sense of feeding the deity, so that, although the drink-offering is still poured out and the bullock burnt on the altar, the act has passed into the giving up of something prized by the worshipper, and a sign of adoration acceptable to the god.

There are several ways in which the worshipper can hold personal intercourse with his deities. These, being souls or spirits, are of course to be seen at times in dreams and visions, especially by their own priests or seers, who thus get (or pretend to get) divine answers or oracles from them. Being a soul, the god can also enter a human body, and act and speak through it, and thus hysterical and epileptic symptoms, which we have seen to be ascribed to an evil demon possessing the patient, are looked on more favourably when the spirit is considered to be a deity come to inspire his minister and talk by his voice. The convulsions, the unearthly voice in which the possessed priest answers in the name of the deity within, and his falling into stupor when his god departs, all fit together, and in all quarters of the world the oracle-priests and diviners by familiar spirits seem really diseased in body and mind, and deluded by their own feelings, as well as skilled in cheating their votaries with sham symptoms and cunning answers. The inspiration or breathing-in of a spirit into the body of a priest or seer appears to such people a mechanical action, like pouring water into a jug. Also, as in the ordinary transmigration of souls, a deity is considered able to enter into the body of an animal, as when he flies from place to place in the form of a sacred bird, or lives in the divine snake fed and worshipped among the negroes of the Slave coast. This leads on to a belief which seems still stranger to our minds. The modern Englishman wonders that a human being, however ignorant, should prostrate himself before a stake stuck in the ground or a stone picked up by the wayside, and even talk to it and offer it food; but when the African or Hindu explains that he believes this stock or stone to be a receptacle in which a divine spirit has for a time embodied itself, this shows that there is a rational meaning in the act. Images of gods, from the rudely carved figures of ancestors which the Ostyaks set up in their huts, to the Greek statues shaped by Phidias or Praxiteles to represent the heaven-god or the sun-god, are mostly formed in the likeness of man—an additional proof of how these nature-gods are modelled on human beings. When such images stand to represent gods, the worshipper may look on them as mere signs or portraits, but commonly he is led by his spirit-philosophy to treat them as temporary bodies for the deities. A Tahitian priest, when asked about his carved wooden idol, would explain that his god was not always in the image, but only now and then flew to it in the body of a sacred bird, and at times would come out of the idol and enter his own (the priest's) body, to give divine oracles by his voice. This takes us back to the times when, fifteen hundred years ago, Minucius Felix describes the heathen gods entering into their idols and fattening on the steam of the altars, or creeping as thin spirits into the bodies of men, to distort their limbs and drive them mad, or making their own priests rave and whirl about. Lastly, rude tribes may believe in and worship spirits without having come to build houses for them and set up tables for their food. Yet such temples and altars appear far back in barbaric religion, and remain still with the thoroughly human character of the worship as plain as ever in them; as when in India the image of Vishnu is washed and dressed by his attendants, and set up in the place of honour in his temple with a choice feast before him, and musicians and dancing girls to divert him. This is the more instructive to us, because we know Vishnu before his original meaning was so spoilt, when he was a sun-god, an animating principle or soul of the sun in personal human shape, and thus a remnant of prehistoric natural philosophy.

We have hitherto only looked at barbaric religion as such an early system of natural philosophy, and have said nothing of the moral teaching which now seems so essential to any religion. The philosophical side of religion has been kept apart from the moral side, not only because a clearer view may be had by looking at them separately, but because many religions of the lower races have in fact little to do with moral conduct. A native American or African may have a distinct belief in souls and other spirits as the causes of his own life and of the events of the surrounding world, and he may worship these ghostly or divine beings, gaining their favour or appeasing their anger by prayers and offerings. But though these gods may require him to do his duty towards them, it does not follow that they should concern themselves with his doing his duty to his neighbour. Among such peoples, if a man robs or murders, that is for the party wronged or his friends to

avenge; if he is stingy, treacherous, brutal, then punishment may fall on him or he may be scouted by all good
people; but he is not necessarily looked upon as hateful
to the gods, and in fact such a man is often a great
medicine-man or priest.   While they hold also that the
soul will continue to exist after death, flitting as a ghost
or demon among the living or passing to the gloomy
under-world or the shining spirit-land, they often think
its condition will be rather a keeping-up of earthly
character and rank than a reward or punishment for
the earthly life.   If some readers find it difficult to
understand such theology separate from morals, they
may be reminded how, among more civilized nations,
religions may drop into the same state by losing the use
of the moral laws they profess; as when a Hindu may
lead the wickedest of lives, while the priests for gifts
make his peace with the gods, or as in Europe brigands
are notoriously devout church goers.   As a rule, the
faiths of the higher nations have more and better moral
influence than the faiths of the ruder tribes.   Yet even
among savages the practical effect of religion on men's
lives begins to show itself.   The worship of the dead
naturally encourages good morals; for the ancestor
who, when living, took care that his family should do
right by one another, does not cease this kindly rule
when he becomes a divine ghost powerful to favour or
punish.   This manes-worship does not bring in new
doctrines or reforms; indeed it is felt that nothing dis-
pleases the ancestral deity like changing the old customs
he was used to.   But for keeping up old-fashioned family
goodness, the worship of ancestors has an influence
over the many nations among whom it still prevails,
from the Zulu, who believes that he must not ill-treat
his brothers lest the father should come in a dream and
make him ill, to the Chinese, who lives ever in presence
of the family spirits, and fears to do wrong lest they
should leave him to fall into distress and die.   In the
great old-world religions, where a powerful priesthood
are the intellectual class, the educators and controllers
of society, we find moral teaching fully recognized among
the great duties of religion.   The gods take on themselves the punishment of the wicked; the Heaven-god
smites the perjurer with his thunderbolt, and the Nation-
god brings sickness and death on the murderer.   The
doctrine of the transmigration of souls is brought to
bear as a moral power; as where the Hindu books

threaten evil-doers with being reborn in other bodies in punishment for their sins done in this, when the wicked shall be born again blind or deformed, the scandal-monger shall have foul breath and the horse-stealer shall go lame, the cruel man shall be born as a beast of prey, the grain-stealer as a rat; and thus, eating the fruits of past actions, men shall work out the consequences of their deeds, souls sunk in darkness being degraded to brutes, while the good rise in successive births to become gods. Even more widely spread is the doctrine that man's life is followed by judgment after death, when evil-doers are doomed to misery, and only those who have lived righteously on earth will enter into bliss. How this doctrine prevailed in ancient Egypt, the papyrus strips of the Book of the Dead, and its pictures and hieroglyphic formulas on the mummy-cases, remain to show. Thus in any museum we may still see the scene of the weighing of the soul of the deceased, and his trial by Osiris, the judge of the dead, and the forty-two assessors, while Thoth, the writing-god, stands by to enter the dread record on his tablets. In the columns of hieroglyphics are set down the crimes of which the soul must clear itself, a curious mingling of what we should call ceremonial and moral sins, among them the following : " I have not privily done evil against man-kind. I have not told falsehoods in the tribunal of Truth. I have not done any wicked thing. I have not made the labouring man do more than his task daily. I have not calumniated the slave to his master. I have not murdered. I have not done fraud to men. I have not changed the measures of the country. I have not injured the images of the gods. I have not taken scraps of the bandages of the dead. I have not committed adultery. I have not withheld milk from the mouths of sucklings. I have not hunted wild animals in the pasturage. I have not netted sacred birds. I am pure, I am pure, I am pure ! " Thus, among the cultured old-world nations, already in the earliest historical ages theology had joined with ethics, and religion as a moral power was holding sway over society.

Animism, or the theory of souls, has thus been shown as the principle out of which arose the various systems of spirits and deities, in barbaric and ancient religions, and it has been noticed also, how already among rude races such beliefs begin to act on moral conduct. We here see under their simplest aspects the two sides of religion, its philosophical and its moral side, which the reader should keep steadily in view in further study of the faiths of the world. In looking at the history of a religion, he will have to judge how far it has served these two great purposes—on the one hand that of teaching man how to think of himself, the world around him, the awful boundless power pervading all—on the other hand that of practically guiding and strengthening him in the duties of life. One question the student will often ask himself—how it is that faiths once mighty and earnest fall into decay and others take their place. Of course to no small extent such changes have come by conquest, as where in Persia the religion of Mohammed well nigh stamped out the old Zoroastrian faith of Darius and Xerxes. But the sword of the conqueror is only a means by which religions have been set up and put down in the world by main force, and there are causes lying deeper in men's minds. It needs but a glance through history at the wrecks of old religions to see how they failed from within. The priests of Egypt, who once represented the most advanced knowledge of their time, came to fancy that mankind had no more to learn, and upheld their tradition against all newer wisdom, till the world passed them by and left them grovelling in super-stition. The priests of Greece ministered in splendid temples and had their fill of wealth and honours, but men who sought the secret of a good life found that this was not the business of the sanctuary, and turned away to the philosophers. Unless a religion can hold its place in the front of science and of morals, it may only gradually, in the course of ages, lose its place in the nation, but all the power of statecraft and all the wealth of the temples will not save it from eventually yielding to a belief that takes in higher knowledge and teaches better life.

CHAPTER XV

HISTORY AND MYTHOLOGY

HISTORY is no longer looked to for a record of the earliest ages of man. As the first chapter of this work shows, we moderns know what was hidden from the ancients themselves about the still more ancient ancients. Yet it does not at all follow that ancient history has lost its value. On the contrary, there are better means than ever of confirming what is really sound in it by such evidence as that of antiquities and language, while masses of very early writings are now newly opened to the historian. It was never more necessary to have clear ideas of what tradition, poetry, and written records can teach as to the times when history begins.

The early history of nations consists more or less of traditions handed down by memory from ages before writing. Our own experience does not tell us much as to what such oral tradition may be worth, for it has so fallen out of use in the civilized world that now one knows little of what happened beyond one's great-grandfather's time, unless it has been written down. But writing has not yet quite overspread the globe, and there are still peoples left whose whole history is the tradition of their ancestors. Thus the South Sea Islanders, who till quite lately had no writing, were intelligent barbarians, much given to handing down recollections of bygone days, and, in one or two cases which it has been possible to test among them, it seems as though memory may really keep a historical record long and correctly. It is related by Mr. Whitmee the missionary that in the island of Rotuma there was a very old tree, under which according to tradition, the stone seat of a famous chief had been buried; this tree was lately blown down, and, sure enough, there was a stone seat under its roots, which must have been out of sight for centuries.

In the Ellice group, the natives declared that their ancestors came from a valley in the distant island of Samoa generations before, and they preserved an old worm-eaten staff, pieced to hold it together, which in their assemblies the orator held in his hand as the sign of having the right to speak; this staff was lately taken to Samoa, and proved to be made of wood that grew there, while the people of the valley in question had a tradition of a great party going out to sea exploring, who never came back. Among these Polynesian traditions the best known are those handed down by the Maoris as to the peopling of New Zealand by their ancestors. They tell how, after a civil war, their forefathers migrated in canoes from Hawaiki in the far north-east; they give the names of the builders and crews of these vessels and show the places where they landed; they repeat, generation by generation, the names of the chiefs descended from those who came in the canoes, by which they reckon about eighteen generations, or 400 to 500 years, since their taking possession of the islands. Notwithstanding that, as might be expected, the traditions of various districts disagree a good deal, they are admitted as the title-deeds by which the natives hold land in the right of their ancestors who landed in the canoes Shark (*Arawa*) and God's-Eye (*Mata-atua*), and it can hardly be doubted that such genealogies, constantly repeated among people whose lands depended on them, are founded on fact. Yet these Maori traditions are about half made up of the wildest wonder-tales; when the builder of one of the canoes cuts down a great tree to make the hull, on coming back to the forest next morning he finds that the tree has got up again in the night; and when the canoe is finished and puts to sea, a certain magician is left behind, but on getting to New Zealand there he is before them on the shore, having come across the ocean on the back of a sea-monster, like Arion on his dolphin. These traditions of a modern barbarous people may give us not an unfair idea of the mixture of real memory and mythic fancy in the early history of Egypt or Greece, where it has come down by tradition from the distant past when there was as yet no scribe to engrave on a stone tablet even the names of kings.

Traditions are yet more lasting when handed down in fixed words, which is especially when the poets have set them in vėrse. Even now in England some notable event may be made into a ballad and sung through the

length and breadth of the land.   In days before printing,
the importance of the poet as historian was far greater,
and many an old European chant has touches of true
chronicle. The old songs of Brittany are often very
true to history, as where in one there is mention of
Bertrand du Guesclin's hair being like a lion's mane,
and in another, Jeanne de Montfort (Jeanne-la-Flamme),
going forth from Hennebont with sword and burning
brand to fire the French camp, is described as putting
on her suit of armour, which history elsewhere records
that she really wore. But though the poet or minstrel
preserves many picturesque incidents like these, he has
not the historian's conscience about facts. Eager to
rouse and delight his audience, to flatter the national
pride of his people and the family pride of the chieftain
in whose halls he sang, the singer brought in real names
and events, but he shifted them as would best suit his
dramatic scenery, or he even made his own history outright. The great German epic, the Nibelungen Lied,
begins in Burgundy, where the three kings hold court
at Worms on the Rhine, their sister is the lovely Kriem-
hilt, whose husband Sîfrit is treacherously slain at the
well by Hagen's spear; afterwards she marries Attila
the Hun-king, and the tale of blood, ending with her
vengeance and death, leaves Attila and Theodoric of
Verona (Etzel and Dietrich von Bern) weeping together
over the slaughter of their men. Here are places and
personages historical enough to make a poem history, if
history could be made by such means; but the reader
of Gibbon knows that Attila really died two years before
Theodoric was born. In fact the poem is a late version
of a story preserved in an earlier shape in Scandinavia
as the saga of the Volsungs; the court at Worms, and
the tournament, and the rest of the historic names and
local circumstances, are worked in to give poetic substance and colour. If poets ventured thus to falsify
history in the Middle Ages, when the chronicles were
there to convict them, how are we to tell fact from
fiction in the poems of ages where the check of history is
wanting?   The Iliad and the Odyssey may contain many
memories of real men and their deeds, an Agamemnon
may have reigned in Mykēnai, there may have been a
real siege of Troy, perhaps round the very mound where
Schliemann has dug out the golden cups and necklace.
But it is too hard a task to sift out historic truth in
Homer, where natural events are as hopelessly mixed

up with miracles as in the Maori legends. It is too hard
to judge how far chronicles of old nations are impartially
preserved by a bard whose rule it is (as Mr. Gladstone
points out in his *Primer of Homer*) that no considerable
Greek chieftain is ever slain in fair fight by a Trojan.
Were nothing to be had out of ancient poetry except distorted memories of historical events, the anthropologist
might be wise to set it aside altogether. Yet, looked
at from another point of view, it is one of his most
perfect and exact sources of knowledge.

Although what the poet relates may be fiction, what
he mentions is apt to be history. In the names of
nations and countries and cities, he is unconsciously
portraying for us the world and its inhabitants as they
were in his time. The catalogue of ships and men in
the second book of the Iliad is a chart and census of the
Mediterranean. Homer knows of the Egyptians, their
irrigated fields and their skill in medicine, and of the
ship-famed Phœnicians and their purple stuffs. The
names of Kadmos belongs to the Phœnician tongue, and
signifies the " Eastern," while the " seven-gated " Thebes
built by his people shows that they had that reverence
for the mystic number seven, which has its origin in the
worship of the seven planets in Babylon. The poet
can hardly have thought, when he told his wonder-tales
with the circumstances of the actual world around him,
how future ages would prize for itself that record of
real life. Odysseus, clinging under the belly of the
great ram, or sailing to the land of Hades to the weak
shades of the dead, is mere myth. Yet the description
of Polyphēmos is one of the few ancient pictures of the
manners of low barbarians, and the visit to Hades is a
chapter of old Greek religion, recording what men thought
of the dull ghost-life beyond the tomb. So it is with the
descriptions of life and manners. Nausikaa, the king's
daughter, drives the wain with the pair of mules down
to the river's mouth to carry the clothes to be washed.
Odysseus walks through the streets of the seafaring
Phaiakians, wondering at the haven and the mighty
walls and bastions, till he crosses the bronze threshold
of the palace of Alkinoos, and, entering, clasps the knees
of Queen Arētē; then he crouches on the hearthstone in
the ashes, till the king, mindful of Zeus the Thunderer
standing near to care for the suppliant, takes the guest
by the hand, and makes him sit by him on his own
son's glittering seat. Thus, following the romantic

fortunes of the many-wiled Odysseus, we see as in the
scenes of a dissolving-view how the heroes of old days
went spear in hand with their swift dogs at their heel,
how at the house-door they threw aside their garments to
go into the bath-chamber, and came forth anointed with
oil to the feast where with no such refinements as plates
or knives they ate their fill of roast meat and cakes of
bread; how they diverted themselves with throwing
quoits on the smooth turf, or lounged on outspread hides
in the sunshine playing merells; how in solemn rites
they poured the libations of dark wine and burned the
meat in sacrifice, with prayers for what their hearts
desired, yet knowing all the while that the gods would,
as they listed, this grant and that deny. All this is not
only history, but history of the finest kind. Looked at
by the student of culture, even the wild mixture of the
natural and supernatural, so bewildering to the modern
mind, is the record of an early stage of religious thought.
The gods meet in council in the halls of cloud-gathering
Zeus, to settle what shall be done with their contending
armies of worshippers on the plains below. In the very
fray of mortal warriors divine beings take part;
Poseidōn plucks out the bronze-tipped spear from the
shield of Aineias, lifts up the Trojan hero and bears
him away unharmed over the heads of the warriors;
even the goddesses set on one another like mortal shrews,
when Hērē tears away the bow and quiver of Artemis,
and with scornful laughter boxes her ears with them till
the virgin huntress goes off in tears, leaving her bow
behind. It would be wrong to think that all this seemed
mere make-believe and poetic ornament to the men who
first listened to the wondrous rhapsodies. They were
in the changing state of religion described in the last
chapter (see p. 217) when the spiritual beings, which to
their ruder forefathers had served as personal causes of
nature and events, were passing away from their first
clearness, yet were still regarded as divinities presiding
over nature and interfering with men's lives. Contrast-
ing such a state of thought with that of the present day
will help us to realize one of the greatest events in all
history, the change of men's minds from the mythological
temper to the historical temper. This change did not
happen all at once, but has for many ages been gradually
coming about. There is hardly a more instructive
chapter in Grote's *History of Greece* than that in which
he describes the philosophic age, when the Greeks were

beginning to notice with perplexity and pain that the
Homeric poems, become to them a sacred book, agreed
but ill with their own experience of life, so that they
asked themselves, can the world have really so changed
since the days when men sat at table with the gods ?

Much of what is called ancient history has to be looked
at in this way.   Historical criticism, that is, judgment,
is practised not for the purpose of disbelieving but of
believing.   Its object is not to find fault with the author,
but to ascertain how much of what he says may be
reasonably taken as true.   Thus a modern reader may
have a sounder opinion about early Roman history than
the Romans themselves had in the time of Livy and
Cicero.   We see more plainly than they that the name
of Rome is less likely to have been given from a man
called Romulus, than that the name of Romulus was
invented to account for the city being called Rome.
To modern minds, the whole famous story of the wolf-
fostermother of Romulus and Remus collapses when it
is known to be only a version of the same old wonder-
tale told by Herodotus as the story of the birth of Cyrus.
Yet here again may be seen the indirect value of history
even where its events are most questionable.   Though
there may never have been any such person as Romulus,
the legend of the tracing of the city walls by his bronze
plough-share is a true record of the ceremony with which
cities were anciently founded.   Even later history, where
the historian had written records to go upon, must often
be sifted in this way.   Suppose a class reading the 35th
book of Livy.   Such matters as Hannibal's oath, and
the preparations for war with Antiochus, are taken
without question as good history.   But when it comes
to the story that about this time an ox belonging to
one of the consuls uttered the awful words " Roma,
cave tibi ! " there is a laugh.   Here it is not enough for
the form-master simply to pass the story by as Livy's
nonsense.   He has to admit that the historian probably
took it from the official record of prodigies, so that at
any rate it is good historical evidence that in ancient
Rome men not only believed that an ox might speak,
but that its so doing would be a divine portent, and
notions of this kind had so become part of the national
religion and government that the augurs took care a
regular supply of such omens should be forthcoming to
guide the rulers of the state, or at least to enable them
to impose upon the multitude.   Thus the passages of

history which seem at first sight most silly and false
may be solid facts in the history of civilization.

It is plain that the compositions which serve as records
of old-world life need not have been intended as history.
If only the genuine words and thoughts of the ancients
about anything have been handed down, it is for the
moderns to extract history from them.   Thus the Sanskrit hymns collected in the Veda serve as a record of the
daily life of the early Aryans who chanted them.   For
when a hymn to the wind gods brings them in as driving
in chariots with strong felloes and well-fashioned reins
and cracking whips, then it is plain to the modern reader
that the Aryan people among whom the hymn was
made drove themselves in such chariots.   Where the
bright gods have gold chains on their breasts for beauty,
carry spears on their shoulders and daggers at their
sides, this mythical fancy gives a real picture of the
accoutrement of the Aryan warrior.   Thus, piece by
piece, this præhistoric hymn-book shows the old patriarchal Aryan life, with the herds of cattle roaming over
wide pastures or shut in the winter cow-stall, the ploughing of the fields and the reaping of the corn, the family
ties and legal rights, the worship of the great nature-gods
of sky and earth, sun and dawn, fire and water and
winds, the intense belief in the shining regions of the
immortal dead, the honour to the almsgiver and praise
to the just man.   In the sacred books of the old Persians,
collected in the Avesta, have come down the long-
remembered traditions of another branch of the Aryan
race, who, dividing off from their Brahman kinsfolk,
followed the faith of Zarathustra.   The deep schism
between the two religions is seen in the Zarathustrians
having degraded the bright gods (*deva*) of the Brahmans into evil demons (*daeva*)   Their horror of defiling
the sacred fire by burning corpses as the Brahmans
do had already led them to expose the dead to be
devoured by wild beasts and carrion birds, as the Parsis
still do in their " towers of silence."   In the beginning
of the Avesta, there is mentioned as first and best of the
good regions created by the good deity, the country
called *Airyana vaejo*, the " Aryan power," which afterwards the evil deity cursed with ten months' winter;
this description of the climate looks as though the old
Persians believed their early Aryan home was on the
bleak slopes of Central Asia toward the sources of the
Oxus and Yaxartes.   Here and there among the sacred

verses comes a touch of the life of these proud fierce
herdsmen and tillers of the soil, little like the corrupt
Persian and the thrifty Parsi of modern times. Their
enthusiasm for the rough work of making the earth fit for
man's abode is quaintly shown where they sing of the
delight the earth feels when the husbandman drains the
wet soil and waters the dry, how she brings wealth to
him who tills her with the right arm and the left, with
the left arm and the right :

> " When the corn grows, then the demons hiss;
> When the shoots sprout, then the demons cough;
> When the stalks rise, then the demons weep;
> When the thick ears come, then the demons fly."

So necessary were the fierce dogs which kept the wolf
from the fold and the thief from the village, that there
are solemn ordinances about them, how the dog who
does not bark and is not right in his mind is to be muzzled
and tied up, and what punishment is to be inflicted on
the man who gives a dog bad food; it is as sinful (they
say) as if he had done it to a well-to-do householder.
One forms a lifelike picture of the sturdy farmers who
made these laws to be repeated to their children's children
and carried on to future ages.

While these rough Aryans were handing on memories
of the past by word of mouth in their sacred verses, more
cultured nations had long since begun to write down
memorials of their own times. The best way to bring to
our minds what this earliest contemporary history was
like is to look at the translations of Egyptian and
Assyrian documents in *Records of the Past*, published
under the directions of the *Society of Biblical Archæology*.
Here is to be found, for instance, Dr. Birch's translation
of the inscription recording the expeditions of Una, crown-
bearer to king Teta, before 3000 B.C. (see   p. 3),
and of the account on the sanctuary walls of Karnak,
of the battle of Megiddo, where Thothmes III, about
1500 B.C., overcame the armies of Syria and Mesopotamia and opened the way into the interior of Asia.
It is related how the king, marching from Gaza, reached
the south of Megiddo on the shore of the waters of
Kaner, where he pitched his tent and made a speech
before his whole army : " Hasten ye, put on your
helmets, for I shall rush to fight with the vile enemy in
the morning ! " The watchword was passed, " Firm,
firm, watch, watch, watch actively at the king's pavi-
lion ! " It was on the morning of the festival of the

new moon that the king went forth in his golden deco-
rated chariot in the midst of his army, the god Amun
being the protection in his active limbs, and he prevailed over his enemies; they fell prostrate before him,
left their horses and chariots, and fled to the fort, where
the garrison shut up inside pulled off their clothes to
haul them up over the walls.   The Egyptians slaughtered
their enemies till they lay in rows like fish, and, conquering, entered the fort of Megiddo, where the chiefs of
the land came bearing tribute, silver and gold, lapis
lazuli and alabaster, vessels of wine and flocks.   The
lists of spoil, made with curious minuteness, include
living captives 240, hands (cut off the dead) 83, mares
2,041, fillies 191, an ark of gold of the enemy, 892 chariots
of the vile army, and so on.   A later part of the inscription commemorates the liberal endowments bestowed
by the victorious king on the god Amen Ra, the fields
and gardens to supply his temple, the pairs of geese to
fill his lakes, to supply him with the two trussed geese
daily at sunset, a charge to remain for ever, and so
on with the loaves of bread and pots of beer for daily
rations.   As the king says in his inscription, he does
not boast of what he has done, saying that he has done
more when he has not, and so causing men to contradict
him.   Here we see the check of public opinion beginning
to act in history.   It does not really compel exact
truth, it allows national victories to be exaggerated and
defeats kept out of sight, but even the vainglorious
scribes of Egypt would hardly venture to record events
without a foundation of fact.   Turning now to the
inscriptions of the Babylonian-Assyrian district, we may
take as an example a temple-brick of the famous city
Ur of the Chaldees, now called Mugheir, which bears
these words in cuneiform writing :

> " To the Moon-god, the eldest son of Mul-lil his king,
> Ur-bagas, the powerful prince, the fierce warrior,
> The king of Ur, the king of Sumir and Akkad,
> Has built E-Tem-ili the temple of his choice."

Sumir and Akkad, here mentioned, were the seats of the
old Chaldæan civilization.   As early as the 16th century
B.C., Hammurabi overcame these nations, a great event
in the change that absorbed their ancient culture and
religion into the conquering Assyrian empire.   In an
inscription of this king of Babylon, he says, " the favour
of Bel gave into my government the people of Sumir

and Akkad, for them I dug out afresh the canal called by my name, the joy of men, a stream of abundant waters for the people, all its banks I restored to newness, new supporting walls I heaped up, perennial waters I provided for the people of Sumir and Akkad."

By the aid of such contemporary writings, historians are now able to check the recorded lists of ancient kings, and to piece together something like a continuous line of dynasties in Egypt and Babylonia since the foundation of the great cities Memphis and Ur. We may notice where the records and traditions of the Israelites, written down in later ages in the historical books of the Old Testament, come in contact with ancient history from the monuments. Israelite tradition records (Gen. xi., xii.) that their ancestors had been in the Chaldæan district of Ur, and in Egypt, which is evidence of their intercourse with the two great nations of the ancient world. The mention in Exodus (i. 11) of the Israelites being set to build for Pharaoh a city called Rameses, points to their oppression in Egypt having been under the Great Rameses II. of the XIX. dynasty, apparently about 1400 B.C., which makes a point of contact between Egyptian and Hebrew chronology. In the Books of Kings there come into view later persons and events, well known in the contemporary records of other countries, as in the mention of Shishak, king of Egypt, who fought against Rehoboam and plundered the temple (1 K. xiv. 25). It seems likely, when Herodotus (ii. 141) describes the army of Sennacherib, king of Assyria, being put to flight from the mice gnawing the soldiers' bows, that this is a version of the great disaster of Sennacherib, of which the Bible gives a different account (2 K. xix.).

With Herodotus the student comes in view of the Old World as it was known to a Greek traveller and geographer of the 5th century B.C. The Father of History, as he has been called, wrote not as a chronicler of his own nation, but with the larger view of an anthropologist to whom all knowledge of mankind was interesting. The way in which modern discoveries have come in to confirm his statements justifies us in relying on ancient historians when, like him, they are careful to distinguish mere legend or hearsay from what they have themselves enquired into. Thus Herodotus tells the strange story of the impostor who passed himself off as Smerdis, and sat on the throne of Persia till he was detected by his cropped ears, and Darius slew him. When, a few years ago, the cuneiform characters of the inscription sculptured in a high wall of rock near Behistan in Persia were deciphered, it proved to be the very record set up by Darius the king in the three languages of the land, and it matches the account given by Herodotus closely enough to show what a real grasp he had of the course of events in Persia a century before his time. Yet more remarkable is the test which can be put to what Herodotus says he learnt from the priests in Egypt about their kings who reigned 2000 years before. From their dictation he wrote down the names of the pyramid-kings Cheops, Chephren, Mykerinos. In later ages critics had sometimes come to doubt whether these kings belonged to fact or fable, but when the lost meaning of the Egyptian hieroglyphics was anew interpreted by modern scholars, there stood the names recognizable as the Greek historian heard them. The best ancient history is apt to receive such confirmation from long-lost monuments. Thucydides relates (vi. 54) that Peisistratos (the younger) dedicated two altars, from one of which the Athenians erased the inscription, but the other (the historian says) may still be read, though in faint letters : " this monument of his archonship Peisistratos son of Hippias set up in the enclosure of Pythian Apollo." Part of this very stone with its inscription was found in 1878 in a courtyard near the Ilissos, and is now in a museum in Athens. How lively a sense of reality such monuments give to history may be understood by the student who, fresh from his books, goes to the British Museum and sees among the ancient coins the grand head of Alexander the Great with the ram's horns, commemorating that curious episode of his life when he was declared to be son of Zeus Ammon; or who notices with surprise the gold coins that prove Cymbeline, now best known in Shakspere, to have been a real British king who coined money with his name.

Having thus looked at the sources of early history as belonging to the study of mankind, we need not go over the well-trodden ground of later history. It remains to notice myth, the stumbling-block which historians have so often fallen over. Myth is not to be looked on as mere error and folly, but as an interesting product of the human mind. It is sham history, the fictitious narrative of events that never happened. Historians, especially in writing of early ages, have copied down the

traditions of real events so mixed up with myths that
it is one of the hardest tasks of the student to judge
what to believe and what to reject. He is fortunate
when he can apply the test of possibility, and declare
an event did not happen because he knows enough of
the course of nature to be sure it could not. For instance,
cultured nations have learnt from science that what
appears to be a blue dome or firmament above our heads,
the sky or heaven, is not really the solid vault the
ancients thought it was, but only thin air and watery
vapour. The consequence of knowing this is that
people have had to strike out of their history the old
myths of gods dwelling in palaces and holding courts in
the skies, of men climbing or flying up from earth into
heaven, of giants heaping mountain Ossa on Pelion, to
scale the cloudy heights and wage battle with the gods
above. Besides this way of detecting myth by its relat-
ing what could not have taken place, there are other
means of judging it. It is often possible to satisfy oneself that some story is not really history, by knowing
the causes which led to its being invented.

We know how strong our own desire is to account for
everything. This desire is as strong among barbarians,
and accordingly they devise such explanations as satisfy
their minds. But they are apt to go a stage further,
and their explanations turn into the form of stories
with names of places and persons, thus becoming full-
made myths. Educated men do not now consider it
honest to make fictitious history in this way, but people
of untrained mind, in what is called the myth-making
stage, which has lasted on from the savage period and
has not quite disappeared among ourselves, have no
such scruples about converting their guesses at what
may have happened into the most life-like stories of
what they say did happen. Thus, when comparative
anatomy was hardly known, the finding of huge fossil
bones in the ground led people to think they were the
remains of huge beasts, and enormous men, or giants,
who formerly lived on the earth. Modern science
decides that they were right as to the beasts, which
were ancient species of elephant, rhinoceros, &c., but
wrong as to the giants, none of the great bones really
belonging to any creature like man. But while the
belief lasted that they were bones of giants, men's
imagination worked in making stories about these giants
and their terrific doings, stories which are told still in

all quarters of the globe as though they were traditions of real events. Thus the Sioux of the western prairies of North America say their land was once inhabited by great animals, bits of whose bones they still keep for magic, and also they tell of the giant Ha-o-kah, who could stride over the largest rivers and the tallest pines, and to whom they sing and dance at their festivals. It appears that fossil bones, very likely of the mastodon, had to do with this native belief in old monstrous beasts, nor need we be surprised at the giants coming into the story, considering that so lately as the last century Dr. Cotton Mather, the Puritan divine, sent to our Royal Society an account of the discovery of such bones in New England, which he argued were remains of antediluvian giants.

Another thing which in all parts of the world has set the imagination of myth-makers to work, is the fact that people live in tribes or nations, each known by a particular name, such as Ojibwa, Afghan, Frank. The easiest and favourite way of accounting for this is to suppose each tribe or nation to have had an ancestor or chief of the like name, so that his descendants or followers inherited their tribe-name from him. It really happens so sometimes, but in most cases a pretended tradition of such an eponymic or name-ancestor arises from the makers of genealogies first inventing him out of the name of the tribe, and then treating him as a historical personage. They may now and then be caught in the act of doing this. Thus among the native race of Brazil and Paraguay, some tribes are called *Tupi* and others *Guarani*, so to account for this division, a tradition is related that two brothers named *Tupi* and *Guarani* came over the sea to Brazil, and with their children peopled the country, but a talking parrot made strife between the wives of the two brothers, and this grew into a quarrel and separation, Tupi staying in the land, and Guarani going off with his family into the region of La Plata. Now there happens to be a means of checking this story, for Martius says that the name guarani (meaning warrior) was first given by the Jesuits to the southern Indians whom they collected in their missions, so that the tale of the two ancestor-brothers must be a myth of modern manufacture. Such eponymic myths of national ancestors were not only made in ancient times, but are mixed up in the chronicles of Old World nations as though they were real history. The classical student

knows the legends of the twin brothers *Danaos* and
Aigyptos, ancestors of the *Danaoi* (Greeks) and *Ægyptians*;
and of *Hellēn*, father of the *Hellēnes*, whose three sons
Aiolos, *Dōros*, *Xouthos* (father of *Achaios* and *Iōn*), were
fathers of the *Æolians*, *Dorians*, &c.

Having looked at these two frequent kinds of myths
derived from fossil bones and national names, it is worth
while to notice how both come together in our own
country. The History of the Britons, compiled in the
12th century by Geoffrey of Monmouth, relates that our
island was in old time called Albion, and was only
inhabited by a few giants; but *Brutus*, a banished Trojan
prince, landed with his followers and called the land
Britain, after his own name, and his companions *Britons*.
With him came a leader called *Corineus*, and he called
the part of the country which fell to him *Corinea* and
his people *Corineans*, that is, *Cornish*. In that part the
giants were most numerous, and one especially, named
Goemagot (elsewhere called *Gogmagog*) was twelve cubits
high, and could pull up an oak like a hazel wand. On a
certain day, when there had been a battle and the
Britons had overcome a party of giants and slain all
except this hugest monster, he and Corineus had a
wrestling-match, when Corineus caught the giant up in
his arms, and running with him to the top of the cliff
now called the Hoe at Plymouth, cast him over, where-
fore (says the chronicler) the place is called " Goemagot's
leap " to this day. Quaint as this legend is, it is not
hard to find the sense of it. It was the fashion to trace
the origin of nations from Troy; *Brutus* and *Corineus*
were invented to account for the names of *Britain* and
Cornwall; *Goemagot* or *Gogmagog* is the Biblical *Gog*
and *Magog* rolled into one, these personages being recognised in tradition as giants. But why the story of his
having been thrown over the Hoe at Plymouth?· The
answer seems to be that this is a place where the bones
of fossil animals are actually dug up, such as were
looked upon as remains of giants. Even in modern
times, when excavations were being made on the Hoe
for the fortifications, huge jaws and teeth were found,
which were at once settled by public opinion to be the
remains of Gogmagog.

These are examples of the myths easiest for modern
civilised minds to enter into, for they are little more
than inferences or guesses as to what may have actually
happened, worked up with picturesque details which

give them an air of reality. But to understand another
kind of myths we must get our minds into a mood which
is not that of scientific reasoning in the class-room, but
of telling nursery tales in the twilight, or reading poetry
in the woods on a summer afternoon. Former chapters
have shown how, in old times and among uncultured
people, notions of the kind which still remain among us
as poetic fancy were seriously believed. When to the
rude philosopher the action of the world around him was
best explained by supposing in it nature-life like human
life, and divine nature-souls like human souls, then the
sun seemed a personal lord climbing proudly up the sky,
and descending dim and weary into the under-world at
night; the stormy sea was a fearful god ready to swallow
up the rash sailor; the beasts of the forest were half-
human in thought and speech; even the forest-trees were
the bodily habitations of spirits, and the woodman, to
whom the rustling of their leaves seemed voices, and
their waving branches beckoning arms, hewed at their
trunks with a half-guilty sense of doing murder. The
world then seemed to be " such stuff as dreams are made
on "; transformation of body and transmigration of
spirit were ever going on; a man or god might turn
into a beast, a river, or a tree; rocks might be people
transformed into stones, and sticks transformed snakes.
Such a state of thought is fast disappearing, but there
are still tribes living in it, and they show what the
men's minds are like who make nature-myths. When a
story-teller lives in this dreamland, any poetic fancy
becomes a hint for a wonder-tale, and though (one would
think) he must be aware that he is romancing, and that
the adventures he relates are not quite history, yet
when he is dead, and his story has been repeated by
bards and priests for a few generations, then it would
be disrespectful, or even sacrilegious, to question its
truth. This has happened all over the world, and the
Greek myths of the great nature-gods which Xenophanes
and Anaxagoras ventured to disbelieve with such ill
consequences to themselves were of much the same
fabric as those of modern barbarians like the South Sea
Islanders. Let us look at a few nature-myths, choosing
such as most transparently show how they came to be
made.

The Tahitians tell tales of their sea-god Hiro, whose
followers were sailing on the ocean while he was lulled
to sleep in a cavern in the depths below; then the wind-

god raised a furious storm to destroy the canoe, but the sailors cried to Hiro, till, rising to the surface, he quelled the storm, and his votaries came safe to port. So in Homer, Poseidōn the sea-god, dweller in caves of ocean, sets on the winds to toss the frail bark of Odysseus among the thundering waves, till Ino comes to his rescue and bids him strip and swim for the Phaiakian shore. Both tales are word-pictures of the stormy sea told in the language of nature-myth, only with different turns. The New Zealanders have a story of Maui imprisoning the winds, all but the wild west-wind, whom he cannot catch to shut into its cavern by a grest stone rolled against its mouth; all he can do is to chase it home sometimes, and then it hides in the cavern, and for a while dies away. All this is a mythic description of the weather, meaning that other winds are occasional, but the west wind prevalent and strong. These New Zea-landers had never heard of the classic myth of Æolus and the cave of the winds, yet how nearly they had come to the same mythic fancy, that it is from such blow-holes in the hill-sides that the winds come forth. The negroes of the West Indies tell a tale of the great quarrel between Fire and Water, how the Fire came on slowly, stopped by the stream, till he called the Wind to his aid, who carried him across everything, and the great fight came off, the Bon Dieu looking on from behind a curtain of clouds. It is not likely that these negro slaves had ever heard of the twenty-first Iliad, to know how the same world-old contest of the elements is told in the great battle between the Fire-god and the Rivers, when the Winds were sent to help, and carried the fierce flames onward, and the eels and fish scuttled hither and thither as the hot breath of the blast came upon them.

The beams of light darting down from the sun through openings in the clouds seem to have struck people's fancy in Europe as being like the rope over the pulley of an old-fashioned draw-well, for this appearance is called in popular phrase, "the sun drawing water." The Polynesians also see the resemblance of the rays to cords, which they say are the ropes the sun is fastened by, and they tell a myth how the sun once used to go faster, till a god set a noose at the horizon and caught him as he rose, so that he now travels bound and slowly along his daily appointed path. In English such an expression as that the sun is "swallowed up by night" is now a mere metaphor, but the idea is one which in ancient and barbaric times people took more seriously. The Maoris have made out of it the story of the death of their divine hero Maui. You may see, they say, Maui's ancestress, Great-Woman-Night, flashing and as it were opening and shutting out on the horizon where sea and sky come together; Maui crept into her body and would have got through unharmed, but just at that moment the little flycatcher, the *tiwakawaka*, broke out with its merry note and awoke the Night, and she crushed Maui. That at least one bird which sings at sunset figures in a version of this story suggests its being a nature-myth of the setting sun dying as he plunges into the darkness. Of all the nature-myths of the world, few are so widely spread as those on this theme of night and day, where with mythic truth the devoured victims were afterwards disgorged or set free. The Zulu story-tellers describe the maw of the monster as a country where there are hills and houses and cattle and people living, and when the monster is cut open, all the creatures come out from the darkness; with a neat touch of nature which shows that the story-teller is thinking of the dawn, the cock comes out first, crying, " *kukuluku!* I see the world ! " Our English version of the old myth is the nursery tale of Little Red Riding-hood, but it is spoilt by leaving out the proper end (which German nurses have kept up with better memory), that when the hunter ripped up the sleeping wolf, out came the little damsel in her red satin cloak, safe and sound.

Such stories are fanciful, but the fancy of the myth-maker can take yet further flights. The mythic persons as yet described have been visible objects like the sun, or at least what can be perceived by the senses and made real objects of, such as wind, or day. But when the poet is in the vein of myth-making, whatever he can express by a noun and put a verb to becomes capable of being treated as a person. If he can say, summer comes, sleep falls on men, hope rises, justice demands, then he can set up summer and sleep, hope and justice, in human figures, dress them, and make them walk and talk. Thus the formation of myth is helped by what Professor Max Muller has called a " disease of language." This, however, is not the whole matter. We saw in the last chapter how the notion of soul or spirit helped men on to the notion of cause. When the cause of anything presents itself to the ancient mind as a kind of soul or spirit, then the cause or spirit of summer, sleep, hope, justice, comes easily to look like a person. No one can really understand old poetry without knowing this. Homer could fancy on the field of battle the awful *Kēr*, whose figure was shown on the shield of Achilles with blood-stained garment flung over her shoulders, as she seized some warrior wounded to the death, or dragged a corpse by the feet out of the fighting throng. This being is not merely a word turned into a reality, she is a personal cause, a spirit-reason, why one warrior is slain and not another. So far is the idea of her spread in Aryan mythology, that it appears again among the Northmen, when Odin sends to every battle the maidens who in Walhalla serve the feast and fill the bowls with ale for the spirits of the heroes; these maidens are the Valkyriur, who guide the event of victory, and choose the warriors who shall fall. Another well-known mythic group shows again how what to us moderns are but ideas expressed in words took personal form in the minds of the ancients. In the classic books of Greece and Rome we read of the three fate-spinners, the Moirai or Parcæ, and their Scandinavian counterparts appear in the Edda as the three wise women whose dwelling is near the spring under the world-ash Yggdrasil, the Norns who fix the lives of men. The explanation of these three mythic beings is that they are in personal shape the Past, Present, and Future, as is shown by the names they bear, *Was, Is, Shall (Urdhr, Verdhandi, Skuld)*.

Stories are always changing and losing their meanings, and from age to age new bards and tale-tellers shape the old myths into new forms to suit new hearers. Considering how stories thus grow and change, one must expect their origins to be as often as not lost beyond recovery. While, as we have seen, it may be often possible to make out what they came from, this must be done cautiously. Clever writers are too apt to sit down and settle the mythic origin of any tale, as if this could be done by ingenious guessing. Even if it is nonsense and never was intended for anything else, the myth-interpreter can find a serious origin for it all the same. Thus a learned but rash mythologist declares that in our English nursery rhyme, "the cow jumped over the moon," is a remnant of an old nature-myth, describing as a cow a cloud passing over the moon. What is really wanted in interpreting myths is something beyond simple guessing; there must be reasons why one particular guess is more probable than the other. Con-

stellation-myths, combining name and nature, are models
of plain meaning. Among the Pleiad sisters, Meropē
is hard to see, and myth says she hides for shame of her
mortal husband; these Pleiads are chased down to
Ocean by the hunter Orion, who himself disappears in
the light of Dawn, carried off, as Homer has it, by rosy-
fingered Eōs. We may choose another example from
the mythology of India, in the story of Vâmana, the tiny
Brahman, who, to humble the pride of King Bali, begs
of him as much land as he can measure in three steps,
but when the boon is granted, the little dwarf expands
into the gigantic form of Vishnu, and, striding with one
step across the earth, another across the air, and a third
across the sky, drives Bali down into the infernal regions,
where he still reigns. This most remarkable of all the
Tom Thumb stories seems really a myth of the sun,
rising tiny above the horizon, then swelling into majestic
power and crossing the universe. For Vâmana, the
"dwarf," is one of the incarnations of Vishnu, and
Vishnu was originally the Sun. In the hymns of the
Veda the idea of his three steps is to be found before it
had become a story, when it was as yet only a poetic
metaphor of the Sun crossing the airy regions in his three
strides. "Vishnu traversed (the earth), thrice he put
down his foot; it was crushed under his dusty step.
Three steps hence made Vishnu, unharmed preserver,
upholding sacred things."

It remains to see how myths spread. Whenever a
good story is told, whether real or made-up does not
matter, it becomes part of the story-teller's stock, who
puts to it any new name that will suit, and often succeeds
in planting it not only in popular legend, but even in
history. There is a fragment by Demaratus preserved
in the collection of Stobæus, where there is related with
Greek names, as an episode of the history of Arkadia,
the grand story which we were taught as an event of
Roman history, the legend of the Horatii and Curiatii.
Roman history, it seems, only borrowed it from an
earlier tale, much as modern Swiss history borrowed
from older folklore the tale of the archer and the apple,
to adorn their national hero, Tell. To show how legend
is put together from many sources, historical and
mythical, let us take to pieces one of the famous children's
tales of Europe. Blue Beard was a historical person.
He was Gilles de Retz, Sieur de Laval, Marshal of
France, nicknamed Barbe Bleue from having a beard of

blue-black shade. Persuaded by an Italian alchemist that his strength could be restored by bathing in the blood of infants, he had many children entrapped for this hideous purpose into his castle of Champtocé on the Loire, the ruins of which are still to be seen. At last the horrible suspicions of the country folk as to what was going on were brought to proof, and the monster was burnt at the stake at Nantes in 1440. In all this, however, there is not a word about murdered wives. Indeed the historical Blue Beard, in his character of murderous monster, seems to have inherited an older tale belonging to the wife-murderer of Breton legend, Comor the Cursed, Count of Poher, whose name and deeds are set down to near a thousand years earlier, in the legendary chronicles which tell of him as a usurper and tyrant who married and murdered one wife after another, till at last when he had wedded and killed the beautiful Trifine, vengeance overtook him, and he was defeated and slain by the rightful prince. It is not easy to say whether this is a version of a yet older story, or whether there is a historical foundation for it; if Henry VIII of England had lived in those times, such a legend might have gathered round his name. Other points of the modern Blue Beard appear already in the story of Trifine, her sending for aid to her kinsmen when she knows her danger, and her discovery of the murder of the former wives. This last, however, does not come to pass in the modern way; in the legend, Trifine goes down into the chapel to pray in the hour of need, and there the tombs of the four murdered wives open and their corpses stand upright, each with the knife or cord or whatever she was murdered with in her hand. Instead of this powerful and ghastly scene, the modern version brings in the hackneyed episode of the forbidden chamber, which had long been the property of story-tellers for use on suitable occasions, and is to be found in the *Arabian Nights*. The old Trifine legend has a characteristic ending. Her wicked husband pursues her into the forest and cuts her head off, but St. Gildas makes her body carry it back to Comor's castle, which he over-throws by flinging a handful of dust at it, then he puts Trifine's head on for her again, and she retires into a convent for the rest of her life. The story-tellers of later times prefer a more cheerful if more commonplace finish.

The miracle-legend just quoted brings us back to the

historical use of myth, which was spoken of earlier in this chapter. The story of St. Gildas bringing the fair Trifine back to her castle with her head in her hand, and his afterwards putting it back on her shoulders, is history. It records the intellectual state of the age when it was held edifying to tell such wonders of holy men, for holy men were believed able to do them. Old tales which seem extravagant to our minds are apt thus to have historical value by pointing back to the times when, seeming possible, they were made. This is true even of Æsop's fables. In the stage of thought when human souls are thought able to live in animals' bodies, when a wolf may have one's enemy's soul in him, or one's grandfather may be crawling on the hearth in the body of a snake, stories of rational beasts themselves seem rational. Among the Buddhists, where beast-tales early became moral apologues, they are told as incidents of the many births or transmigrations of the great founder of the religion. It was Buddha himself who, as a bird, took the bone out of the lion's throat, and was repaid by being told that he was lucky to be so well out of it. It was Buddha who, born in the body of a peasant, listened to the ass in the lion's skin, and said he was an ass. That millions of people should have this as part of their sacred literature is a fact of interest in the study of civilization, warning us not to cast aside a story as worthless, because it is mythical. For understanding the thoughts of old-world nations, their myths tell us much we should hardly learn from their history.

CHAPTER XVI

SOCIETY

In the reports of crimes which appear daily in the news-papers of our civilized land, such phrases often occur as *savage* fury, *barbarous* cruelty. These two words have come to mean in common talk such behaviour as is most wild, rough, and cruel. Now no doubt the life of the less civilized people of the world, the *savages* and *bar-barians*, is more wild, rough, and cruel than ours is on the whole, but the difference between us and them does not lie altogether in this. As the foregoing chapters have proved, savage and barbarous tribes often more or less fairly represent stages of culture through which our own ancestors passed long ago, and their customs and laws often explain to us, in ways we should otherwise have hardly guessed, the sense and reason of our own. It should be understood that it is out of the question to give here even a summary of the complicated systems of society : all that can be done is to put before the reader some of its leading principles in ancient and modern life.

Mankind can never have lived as a mere struggling crowd each for himself. Society is always made up of families or households bound together by kindly ties, controlled by rules of marriage and the duties of parent and child. Yet the forms of these rules and duties have been very various. Marriages may be shifting and temporary pairing, or unions where the husband may have several wives, and the wife several husbands. It is often hard to understand the family group and its ties in the rude and ancient world. Thus it seems to us a matter of course to reckon family descent in the male line, and this is now put in the clearest way by the son taking the father's surname. But in lower stages of civilization, on both sides of the globe, many tribes take the contrary idea as a matter of course. In most Australian tribes the children belong to the mother's clan, not the father's; so that in native wars father and son constantly meet as natural enemies. Chiefship often goes down in the royal mother's line, as among the Natchez, who had their sun-temples in what is now Louisiana. Yet this widespread law of female descent, deep as it lies in the history of society, had been so lost sight of among the ancient civilized nations, that when Herodotus noticed it among the Lykians, who took their names from their mothers and traced their pedigrees through the female branches only, the historian fancied this was a peculiar custom, in which they were unlike all other people. In the savage and barbaric world there prevails widely the rule called by McLennan exogamy or marrying-out, which forbids a man to take a wife of his own clan—an act which is considered criminal, and may even be punished with death. It is a strange contrast to the popular idea that savage life has no rules, when we find Australian tribes where every man is bound to marry into the particular clan which is, so to speak, the wife-clan to his own. Among the Iroquois of North America the children took the clan-name or totem of the mother; so if she were of the Bear clan, her son would be a Bear, and accordingly he might not marry a Bear girl, but might take a Deer or Heron. Such laws appear also among higher nations who reckon descent in the male line. Thus in India a Brahman is not to marry a wife whose clan-name (her " cow-stall," as they say) is the same as his; nor may a Chinese take a wife of his own surname. Though the family and tribe rules of the savage and barbaric world are too intricate to be fully discussed here, there are some instructive points to which attention should be called. Marriage is in early stages of society a civil contract. Thus, among the wild hunting-tribes of Nicaragua, the lad who wishes a girl for a wife kills a deer and lays it with a heap of firewood at the door of her parents' hut, which symbolic act is his offer to hunt and do man's work; if the gift is accepted, it is a marriage, without further ceremony. Among peoples of higher culture more formal promises and ceremonies come in, with feasts and gatherings of kinsfolk; and then, as in other important matters of life, the priest is called in to give divine blessing and sanction to the union. Where this is done, a wedding has come to be very different from what it was in the rough times of marriage by capture, such as might be seen in our own day among fierce forest tribes in Brazil, where the warriors would make forays on distant villages and by main force bring home wives. Ancient tradition knows this practice well, as where the men of Benjamin carry off the daughters of Shiloh dancing at the feast, and in the famous Roman tale of the rape of the Sabines, a legend putting in historical form the wife-capture which in Roman custom remained as a ceremony. What most clearly shows what a recognized old-world custom it was, is its being thus kept up as a formality where milder manners really prevail. It had passed into this state among the Spartans, when Plutarch says that, though the marriage was really by friendly settlement between the families, the bridegroom's friends went through the pretence of carrying off the bride by violence. Within a few generations the same old habit was kept up in Wales, where the bridegroom and his friends, mounted and armed as for war, carried off the bride; and in Ireland they used even to hurl spears at the bride's people, though at such a distance that no one was hurt, except now and then by accident, as happened when one Lord Hoath lost an eye, which mischance seems to have put an end to this curious relic of antiquity. It was one of the consequences of increase of property in the world that the practice of buying wives came in, as where a Zulu bargains with a girl's people to let him have her perhaps for five oxen or ten. This was the custom in England among our barbaric forefathers, as appears in the West-Saxon law of Ine—" If a man buy a wife," &c. Cnut somewhat later forbade the wife to be sold, but the husband might give something of his own will. It is an interesting problem in the history of law how the money once paid as the bride's price passed into a gift or dower for her; some provision of this kind became necessary when the widow was no longer provided for by being taken, as she would have been in a ruder state of society, as a wife by her husband's brother.

Marriage has been here spoken of first, because upon it depends the family, on which the whole framework of society is founded. What has been said of the ruder kinds of family union among savages and barbarians shows that there cannot be expected from them the

excellence of those well-ordered households to which
civilized society owes so much of its goodness and
prosperity. Yet even among the rudest clans of men,
unless depraved by vice or misery and falling to pieces,
a standard of family morals is known and lived by.
Their habits, judged by our notions, are hard and coarse,
yet the family tie of sympathy and common interest is
already formed, and the foundations of moral duty
already laid, in the mother's patient tenderness, the
father's desperate valour in defence of home, their daily
care for the little ones, the affection of brothers and
sisters, and the mutual forbearance, helpfulness, and
trust of all. From the family this extends to a wider
circle. The natural way in which a tribe is formed is
from a family or group, which in time increases and
divides into many households, still recognizing one
another as kindred, and this kinship is so thoroughly
felt to be the tie of the whole tribe, that, even when
there has been a mixture of tribes, a common ancestor is
often invented to make an imaginary bond of union.
Thus *kindred* and *kindness* go together—two words
whose common derivation expresses in the happiest
way one of the main principles of social life.

Among the lessons to be learnt from the life of rude
tribes is how society can go on without the policeman
to keep order. It is plain that even the lowest men
cannot live quite by what the Germans call " faust-
recht," or " fist-right," and we call " club-law." The
strong savage does not rush into his weaker neighbour's
hut and take possession, driving the owner out into the
forest with a stone-headed javelin sent flying after him.
Without some control beyond the mere right of the
stronger, the tribe would break up in a week, whereas
in fact savage tribes last on for ages. Under favourable
circumstances, where food is not too scarce nor war too
wasting, the life of low barbaric races may be in its
rude way good and happy. In the West Indian islands
where Columbus first landed lived tribes who have been
called the most gentle and benevolent of the human
race. Schomburgk, the traveller, who knew the warlike Caribs well in their home life, draws a paradise-like
picture of their ways, where they have not been corrupted
by the vices of the white men; he saw among them
peace and cheerfulness and simple family affection, un-
varnished friendship, and gratitude not less true for not
being spoken in sounding words; the civilized world, he

says, has not to teach them morality, for though they
do not talk about it, they live in it. At the other side
of the world in New Guinea, Kops, the Dutch explorer,
gives much the same account of the Papuans of Dory,
who live in houses built on piles in the water, like the
old lake-men of Switzerland; he speaks of their mild
disposition, their inclination to right and justice, their
strong moral principles, their respect for the aged and
love for their children, their living without fastenings
to their houses—for theft is considered by them a grave
offence, and rarely occurs. Among the rude non-Hindu
tribes of India, English officials have often recorded with
wonder the kindliness and cheerfulness of the rude men
of the mountains and the jungle, and their utter honesty
in word and deed. Thus Sir Walter Elliot mentions a
low poor tribe of South India, whom the farmers employ
to guard their fields, well knowing that they would
starve rather than steal the grain in their charge; and
they are so truthful that their word is taken at once in
disputes even with their richer neighbours, for people
say " a Kurubar always speaks the truth." Of course
these accounts of Caribs and Papuans show them on the
friendly side, while those who have fought with them
call them monsters of ferocity and treachery. But
cruelty and cunning in war seem to them right and
praiseworthy; and what we are here looking at is their
home peace-life. It is clear that low barbarians may
live among themselves under a fairly high moral standard,
and this is the more instructive because it shows what
may be called natural morality. Among them religion,
mostly concerned with propitiating souls of ancestors
and spirits of nature, has not the strong moral influence
it exerts among higher nations; indeed their behaviour
to their fellows is little affected by divine command or
fear of divine punishment. It has more to do with their
life being prosperous or miserable. When want or the
miseries of war upset their well-being, they (like their
betters) become more brutal and selfish in their ways,
and moral habits are at all times low among the comfortless hordes of savages whose daily struggle for existence is too harsh for the gentler feelings to thrive.
Moreover, there is this plain difference between low and
high races of men, that the dull-minded barbarian has
not power of thought enough to come up to the civilized
man's best moral standard. The wild man of the forest,
forgetful of yesterday and careless of to-morrow, lolling

in his hammock when his wants are satisfied, has little of the play of memory and foresight which is ever unrolling before our minds the panorama of our own past and future life, and even sets us in thought in the places of our fellows, to partake of their lives and enter into their joys and sorrows. Much of the wrong-doing of the world comes from want of imagination. If the drunkard could see before him the misery of next year with something of the vividness of the present craving, it would overbalance it. Ofttimes in the hottest fury of anger, the sword has been sheathed by him across whose mind has flashed the prophetic picture of the women weeping round the blood-stained corpse. The lower races of men are so wanting in foresight to resist passion and temptation that the moral balance of a tribe easily goes wrong, while they are rough and wantonly cruel through want of intelligent sympathy with the sufferings of others, much as children are cruel to animals through not being able to imagine what the creatures feel. What we now know of savage life will prevent our falling into the fancies of the philosophers of the last century, who set up the " noble savage " as an actual model of virtue to be imitated by civilized nations. But the reality is quite as instructive, that the laws of virtue and happiness may be found at work in simple forms among tribes who make hatchets of sharpened stones and rub sticks together to kindle fire. Their life, seen at its best, shows with unusual clearness the great principle of moral science, that morality and happiness belong together—in fact that morality is the method of happiness.

It must not be supposed that in any state of civilization a man's conduct depends altogether on his own moral sense of right and wrong. Controlling forces of society are at work even among savages, only in more rudimentary ways than among ourselves. Public opinion is already a great power, and the way in which it acts is particularly to be noticed. Whereas the individual man is too apt to look to his own personal interest and the benefit of his near friends, these private motives fall away when many minds come together, and public opinion with a larger selfishness takes up the public good, encouraging the individual to set aside his private wishes and give up his property or even his life for the commonwealth. The assembled tribe can crush the mean and cowardly with their scorn, or give that reward of glory for which the high-spirited will risk goods and life. Travellers have remarked that the women, however down-trodden, know how to make their influence felt in this way, and many a warrior whose heart was failing him in face of the enemy has turned from flight when he thought of the girls' mockery when he should slink home to the village, safe but disgraced. This pressure of public opinion compels men to act according to custom, which gives the rule as to what is to be done or not done in most affairs of life. Explorers of wild countries, not finding the machinery of police they are accustomed to at home, have sometimes rashly concluded that the savages lived unrestrained at their own free will. We have here already noticed that this is a mistake, for life in the uncivilized world is fettered at every turn by chains of custom. To a great extent it is evident that customs have come into existence for the benefit of society, or what was considered so. For instance, it is generally held right in wild countries that hospitality shall be freely given to all comers, for everyone knows he may want it any day himself. But whether a custom is plainly useful or not, and even when its purpose is no longer known, once established as a custom it must be conformed to. Savages may have finger-joints cut off, or undergo such long and severe fasts that many die; but often the only reason they can give for inflicting such suffering on themselves is that it was the custom of their ancestors. In some parts of Australia custom forbade to the young hunters, and reserved for the old men, much of the wild fowl and the best joints of the large game. No doubt this was in some measure for the public benefit, as the experienced elders, who were past the fatigue of hunting, were able to stay in camp, make nets and weapons, teach the lads, and be the repositories of wisdom and the honoured counsellors of the tribe. Nothing could prove more plainly how far society is, even among such wild men of the desert, from being under the mere sway of brute force.

Thus communities, however ancient and rude, always have their rules of right and wrong. But as to what acts have been held right and wrong, the student of history must avoid that error which the proverb calls measuring other people's corn by one's own bushel. Not judging the customs of nations at other stages of culture by his own modern standard, he has to bring his knowledge to the help of his imagination, so as to see institutions where they belong and as they work. Only thus

can it be made clear that the rules of good and bad,
right and wrong, are not fixed alike for all men at all
times. For an example of this principle, let us observe
how people at different stages of civilization deal with
the aged. Some of the lower races take much care of
their old folks even after they are fallen into imbecility,
treating them with almost gentle considerateness and
very commonly tending them till death, when respect to
the living ancestor passes into his worship as an ancestral
spirit. But among other tribes filial kindness breaks
down earlier, as among those fierce Brazilians who knock
on the head with clubs the sick and aged, and even eat
them, whether they find their care too burdensome, or
whether they really think, as they say, that it is kind
to end a life no longer gladdened with fight and feast
and dance. We realize the situation among roving
tribes. The horde must move in quest of game, the
poor failing creature cannot keep up in the march, the
hunters and the heavily laden women cannot carry him;
he must be left behind. Many a traveller has beheld
in the desert such heartrending scenes as Catlin saw
when he said farewell to the white-haired old Puncah
chief, all but blind and shrunk to skin and bone, crouched
shivering by a few burning sticks, for his shelter a
buffalo-hide set up on crutches, for his food a dish of
water and a few half-picked bones. This old warrior
was abandoned at his own wish when his tribe started
for new hunting-grounds, even as years before, he said,
he had left his own father to die when he was no longer
good for anything. When a nation settled in the agricultural state has reached something of wealth and comfort, there is no longer the excuse of necessity for killing
or abandoning the aged. Yet history shows how long
the practice was kept up even in Europe, partly with the
humane intent of putting an end to lingering misery,
but more through the survival of a custom inherited
from harder and ruder times. The Wends in what is
now Germany practised the hideous rite of putting the
aged and infirm to death, cooking and eating them, much
as Herodotus describes the old Massagetæ as doing. In
Sweden there used to be kept in the churches certain
clumsy wooden clubs, called " family-clubs," of which
some are still preserved, and with which in ancient times
the aged and hopelessly sick were solemnly put to death
by their kinsfolk. It is interesting to trace in the old
German records the change from such hard ancient

barbarism to gentler manners, when the infirm old house-father, dividing his substance among his children, is to sit henceforth well cared for in the " cat's place " by the hearth. One of the marks of advancing civilization was the growing sense of the sacredness of human life, even apart from its use and pleasure, and under this feeling the cutting short of even a burdensome and suffering existence, which our ancestors resorted to without reproach, has come to be looked upon with horror.

It must be clearly understood also that the old-world rules of moral conduct were not the same towards all men. A man knew his duty to his neighbour, but all men were not his neighbours. This is very clearly seen in the history of men's ideas of manslaughter and theft. The slaying of a man is scarcely held by the law of any people to be of itself a crime, but on the contrary it has been regarded as an allowable or praiseworthy act under certain conditions, especially in self-defence, war, revenge, punishment, and sacrifice. Yet no known tribe, however low and ferocious, has ever held that men may kill one another indiscriminately, for even the savage society of the desert or the jungle would collapse under such lawlessness. Thus all men acknowledge some law " thou shalt not kill," but the question is how this law applies. It is instructive to see how it works among those fierce tribes who approve the killing of men simply as a proof of valour. Thus the young Sioux Indian, till he had killed his man, was not allowed to stick the feather in his head-dress and have the title of brave or warrior; he could scarcely get a girl to marry him till he had " got the feather." So the young Dayak of Borneo could not get a wife till he had taken a head, and it was thus with the skull or scalp which the Naga warrior of Asam had to bring home, thereby qualifying himself to be tattooed and to marry a wife, who had perhaps been waiting years for this ugly marriage-licence. The trophy need not have been taken from an enemy, and might have been got by the blackest treachery, provided only that the victim were not of the slayer's own tribe. Yet these Sioux among themselves hold manslaughter to be a crime unless in blood-revenge; and the Dayaks punish murder. This state of things is not really contradictory; in fact its explanation lies in the one word " tribe." The tribe makes its law, not on an abstract principle that manslaughter is right or wrong, but for its own preservation. Their existence depends on holding their own in deadly strife with neighbouring tribes, and thus they put a social premium on the warrior's proof of valour in fight against the enemy, though in these degenerate days they allow the form to be meanly fulfilled by bringing in as a warrior's trophy the head of some old woman or wretched waylaid stranger. In this simple contrast between one's own people and strangers, the student will find a clue to the thought of right and wrong running through ancient history, and slowly passing into a larger and nobler view. The old state of things is well illustrated in the Latin word *hostis*, which, meaning originally stranger, passed quite naturally into the sense of enemy. Not only is slaying an enemy in open war looked on as righteous, but ancient law goes on the doctrine that slaying one's own tribesman and slaying a foreigner are crimes of quite different order, while killing a slave is but a destruction of property. Nor even now does the colonist practically admit that killing a brown or black man is an act of quite the same nature as killing a white countryman. Yet the idea of the sacredness of human life is ever spreading more widely in the world, as a principle applying to mankind at large.

The history of the notion of theft and plunder follows partly the same lines. In the lower civilization the law, " thou shalt not steal," is not unknown, but it applies to tribesmen and friends, not to strangers and enemies. Among the Ahts of British Columbia, Sproat remarks that an article placed in an Indian's charge on his good faith is perfectly safe, yet thieving is a common vice where the property of other tribes or of white men is concerned. But, he says, it would be unfair to regard thieving among these savages as culpable in the same degree as among ourselves, for they have no moral or social law forbidding thieving between tribe and tribe, which has been commonly practised for generations. Thus, although the Africans within their own tribe-limits have strict rules of property, travellers describe how a Zulu war-party, who have stealthily crept upon a distant village and massacred men, women, and children, will leave behind them the ransacked kraal flaring on the horizon and return with exulting hearts and loads of plunder. The old-world law of a warlike people is well seen among the ancient Germans in Cæsar's famous sentence, " Robberies beyond the bounds of each community have no infamy, but are commended as a means of exercising youth and diminishing sloth.'' Even in the midst of modern civilization, a declaration of war may still carry society back to the earlier stages of plunder and prize-money. But in peace the safety of property as well as life is becoming more settled in the world. The extradition treaties by which criminals, deprived of their old refuge over the border, are now given up to justice in the country where they offended, mark the modern tendency to unite nations in one community, which recognises among all its members mutual right and duty.

Hitherto we have been looking at right and wrong chiefly as worked by men's own moral feelings and by public opinion. But stronger means have at all times been necessary. It is now reckoned one of the regular duties of civilization to have a criminal law to punish wrong-doers with fine, imprisonment, blows, and even death. This system, however, only gradually arose in the world, and history can show plain traces of how it grew up from the early state of things when there were as yet no professional judges or executioners, but it was every man's right and duty to take the law into his own hands, and that law was what we now call vengeance. When in barbaric life fierce passion breaks loose and a man is slain, this rule of vengeance comes into action. How it works as one of the great forces of society may well be seen among the Australians. As Sir George Grey says in his account of it, the holiest duty a native is called on to perform is to avenge the death of his nearest relation. If he left this duty unfulfilled, the old women would taunt him; if he were unmarried, no girl would speak to him; if he had wives, they would leave him; his mother would cry and lament that she had given birth to so degenerate a son, his father would treat him with contempt, and he would be a mark for public scorn. But what is to be done if the murderer escapes, as must in so wild and thinly peopled a country be easy? Native custom goes on the ancient doctrine that the criminal's whole family are responsible; so that when it is known that a man has been slain, and especially when the actual culprit has escaped, his kinsfolk run for their lives; the very children of seven years old know whether they are of kin to the manslayer, and, if so, they are off at once into hiding. Here then we come in view of two principles which every student of law should have clearly in his mind in tracing its history up from its lowest stages. In the primitive law of vengeance of blood, he sees society using for the public benefit the instinct of revenge which man has in common with the lower animals; and by holding the whole family answerable for the deed of one of its members, the public brings the full pressure of family influence to bear on each individual as a means of keeping the peace. No one who sees the working of blood-vengeance can deny its practical reasonableness, and its use in restraining men from violence while there are as yet no judges and executioners. Indeed among all savages and barbarians the avenger of blood, little as he thinks it himself in his wild fury, is doing his part toward saving his people from perishing by deeds of blood. Unhappily his usefulness is often marred through ignorance and delusion turning his vengeance against the innocent. These Australians are among the many savages who do not see why anybody should ever die unless he is killed, so they account for what we call natural death by settling it that some enemy killed the sufferer by magic art, wounding him with an invisible weapon, or sending a disease-demon to gnaw his vitals. Therefore, when a man dies, his kinsmen set themselves to find out by divination what malignant sorcerer did him to death, and when they have fixed on some one as the secret enemy the avenger sets out to find and slay him; then of course there is retaliation from the other side, and an hereditary feud sets in. This is one great cause of the rancorous hatred between neighbouring tribes which keeps savages in ceaseless fear and trouble.

Passing to higher levels of civilization, among the nations of the ancient world we still find the law of blood-vengeance, but it is being gradually modified by the civilization which in time ousts it altogether. Thus the law of the Israelites, while still authorizing the avenger of blood, provides that there shall be cities of refuge, and that the morally innocent manslayer shall not be as the wilful murderer. Among nations where wealth has been gathered together, and especially where it has come to be measured by money, the old fierce cry for vengeance sinks into a claim for compensation. In Arabia to this day the earlier and later stages may be seen side by side; while the roaming Beduin tribes of the desert carry on blood-feuds from generation to generation with savage ferocity, the townsfolk feel that life can hardly go on with an assassin round every street-corner, so they take the blood-money and loose the feud. This state of things is instructive as being like that of our own early ancestors when the Teutonic law was still that a man took vengeance for hurt done to him or his, unless he compounded it. The Anglo-Saxon word for such composition was *wér-gild*, probably meaning " man-money," 200 shillings for a free man, less for lower folk, and less for a Welshman than an Englishman. Again, where the rule of vengeance is a life for a life, lesser hurts are also repaid in kind, which is the Roman *lex talionis*, or " law of the like "—*retaliation*. This is plainly set forth in the Jewish law, life for life, eye for eye, tooth for tooth, wound for wound, stripe for stripe. It is still law in Abyssinia, where not long since a mother prosecuted a lad who had accidentally fallen from a fruit-tree on her little son and killed him; the judges decided that she had a right to send another son up into the tree to drop on the boy who had un-intentionally caused the first one's death, which remedy however she did not care to avail herself of. Of course retaliation came to be commuted into money, as when old English laws provide that, if any one happen to cut off the fist or foot of a person, let him render to him the half of a man's price, for a thumb half the price of a hand, and so on down to 5s. for a little finger and 4d. for a little-finger nail. In the times we live in, justice has passed into a higher stage, where the State takes the duty of punishing any serious wilful hurt done to its citizens. Reading some murderous tale of a Corsican " vendetta," we hardly stop to think of it as a relic of ancient law lingering in a wild mountain island. Yet our criminal law grew out of such private vengeance, as is still plain to those who attend to traces of the past, when they hear such phrases as " the vengeance of the law," or think what is meant by the legal form by which a private person is bound over to prosecute, as though he must still be suing, as he would have done in long-past ages, for his own revenge or compensation. It is now really the State that is seeking to punish the criminal for the ends of public justice. The avenger of blood, once the guardian of public safety, would now be him-self punished as a criminal for taking the law into his own hands, while the moralists, now that the conditions of society are changed, lay it down that vengeance is sinful.

Law, however, though it has so beneficially taken the

place of private vengeance, has not fully extended its
sway over the larger quarrels between State and State.
The relation of private vengeance to public war is well
seen among rude tribes, such as inhabit the forests of
Brazil. When a murder is done within the tribe, then
of course vengeance lies between the two families concerned; but if the murderer is of another clan or tribe,
then it becomes a public wrong. The injured community hold council, and mostly decide for war if they
dare; then a war-party sets forth, in which the near
kinsmen of the murdered man, their bodies painted with
black daubs to show their deadly office, rush foremost
into the fight. Among neighbouring tribes the ordinary
way in which war begins is by some quarrel or trespass,
then a man is killed on one side or the other, and the
vengeance for his death spreads into blood-feud and
tribal war ever ready to break out from generation to
generation. This barbaric state of things lasted far on
into the history of Europe. It was old German law that
any freeman who had been injured in body, honour, or
estate might, with the help of his own people, avenge
himself if he would not take the legal commutation;
that is to say, he had the right of private war. It was
a turning-point in English history when King Edmund
made a law to restrain this "unrighteous fighting,"
but it was not stopped at once, especially in North-
umberland, and we know how it went on into modern
times between clan and clan in the wild Scotch Highlands. Long after the mere freeman ceased to go to war
with his neighbours, there were nobles who stood to
their old right. As late as the time of Edward IV
Lord Berkeley and his followers fought a battle with
Lord Lisle at Nibley Green in Gloucestershire. Lord
Lisle was slain, and in the end Lord Berkeley compounded by a money payment to the widow. Freeman,
who in his *Comparative Politics* mentions this curious
incident of fifteenth-century history, thinks it the last
English example either of private war or the payment
of the wér-gild. The law of England which forbids the
levying of private war represents one of the greatest
steps in national progress. The State now replaces, by
the justice of legal tribunals, the barbaric expedients of
private vengeance and private war. But State and
State still fight out their quarrels in public war, which
then becomes on a larger scale much what deadly feud
used to be between clan and clan.

The civil law of property may, like the criminal law, be traced from the ideas of old times. A fair notion may be had of what early rules of property were like, by noticing what they are in the uncivilized world still. Among the lower races, the distinction which our lawyers make between real and personal property appears in a very intelligible way. Of the land all have the use, but no man can be its absolute owner. The simplest land-law, which is also a game-law, is found among tribes who live chiefly by hunting and fishing. Thus in Brazil each tribe had its boundaries marked by rocks, trees, streams, or even artificial landmarks, and trespass in pursuit of game was held so serious that the offender might be slain on the spot. At this stage of society in any part of the world, every man has the right to hunt within the bounds of his own tribe, and the game only becomes private property when struck. Thus there is a distinct legal idea of common property in land belonging to the clan or tribe. There is also a clear idea of family property : the hut belongs to the family or group of families who built it; and when they fenced in and tilled the plot of ground hard by, this also ceased to be common land, and became the property of the families, at least while they occupied it. To each family belonged also the hut-furniture, such as hammocks, mealing-stones, and earthen pots. At the same time personal ownership appears, though still under the power of the family, through the father or head. Personal or individual property was chiefly what each wore or carried—the man's weapons, the ornaments and scanty clothing of both sexes, things which they had some power to do as they liked with during life, and at death very commonly took away with them to the world beyond the grave (see p. 205). Here then we find barbarians already acquainted with the ideas of common land, family freehold, family and personal property in movables, which run through the systems of old-world law. Not that they are worked out in the same way everywhere. Thus in the village communities which had so great a part in settling Asia and Europe, and whose traces still remain in modern England, not only the hunting-grounds and meadows were held in common, but the families did not even own the ploughed fields, which were tilled by common labour or re-allotted from time to time among the households, so that the family freehold did not reach beyond its house and garden-plot.

At various times in history, the rise of military nations revolutionized the earlier ways of land-holding. In invaded countries, lands of the conquered were distributed by the king or leader to be held by his captains or soldiers doing military service in return; the greatest and best-known example is the feudal system of Europe in the Middle Ages. It is instructive to notice how in England, before the Norman Conquest, the folk-land, the common property of the state, was already passing into the hands of the king to grant at his pleasure. Or in a military state the sovereign may become the universal landlord, allowing his subjects to hold lands on payment of an annual tribute or tax—a system well known in ancient Egypt and modern India. In Roman history we find the state or families owning large lands letting portions of them as farms to tenants who paid part of the produce in return. This shows the beginning of rent, a thing unknown to primitive law. While these changes were coming on as to the land, movable property was becoming more and more important. War-captives kept as slaves to till the soil became part of the wealth of the family, and the pastoral life brought in cattle, not only for food, but to plough the fields. The manufacture of valuable goods, the growth of commerce, the accumulation of treasure, and the use of money, added other possessions. If now we look at our modern ways of dealing with property, it is seen what great changes we have made by taking it out of the hands of the family and allowing an individual owner to hold and dispose of it—an arrangement suited to our age of shifting trading enterprise. Even land is bought and sold by individuals, though the law, by making a field and cottage transferable by a different process and with greater formality and cost than a diamond necklace or a hundred chests of tea, keeps up traces of the old system under which it could only have changed hands, if at all, with difficulty and by the consent of many parties. Through all changes it is instructive to notice how far the old family system of property holds its place. This is well seen by considering what becomes of a man's property when he dies. The two most usual arrangements made in early times are the simplest, namely, either that the family shall go on living on the undivided property, or that it shall be divided among the children, or sons. When the eldest son is patriarchal head of the family, to keep up this dignity he may have an extra or double portion for his " birth-right "; this is a well-known ancient rule, common to the Aryan and Semitic nations, for it is both in the Hindu laws of Manu and in Deuteronomy. In France at this day the ancient principle of division is legally enforced, and the family take their shares as a matter of right. In England the power of wills has become so great that in theory a man may leave his property to whom he pleases; but practically this is kept within bounds by moral feeling and public opinion, which condemn it as an unnatural act for a man to strip his own children to endow a stranger or a hospital. If the Englishman dies without leaving a will, the law recognises the rights of his family by fairly dividing among them his personal property. It is otherwise with the land or real estate, which in most cases will pass to the eldest son. Why the law should thus allow the claims of the rest of the family to the money, but not to the land, is an interesting point of history. The reader of Maine's *Ancient Law* will find how, in Europe about a thousand years ago, lands held as fiefs came to pass to the eldest son, not by any means for the purpose of enriching him by disinheriting the others, but that the united kinsfolk might live upon the land and defend it under him as chief of the little clan. If in modern times the head of the family has become possessed of the family estate for his own use, this is because old laws working under new circumstances are apt to produce results which those who framed them never foresaw. Primogeniture did not prevail over the whole of England, but older rules of family inheritance have in some parts lasted on from times before feudalism. The best known of these is where at the father's death the land is divided among the sons, as Domesday Book shows was usual in Edward the Confessor's time. This is now known as gavelkind, or the custom of Kent, but it appears elsewhere; for instance, Kentish Town in the north of London is supposed to have its name from lands so held there. There even exists in England a rule of inheritance which seems to belong to a yet earlier state of society. This is the custom of borough-english, by which, for instance at Hackney or Edmonton, if a man die intestate the land passes to his youngest son. This right of the youngest, strange as it seems to us, is still found here and there in Europe and Asia. It is a reasonable law of inheritance of the settlers in a new country, where there is yet plenty of land to be had for the taking, and the sons as they grow up and marry go out and found new homesteads of their own. But the youngest stays at home and takes care of the old father and mother; he is, as the Mongols say, the "fire-keeper," and at their death he naturally succeeds to the family home. This is one of the hundreds of cases of customs which seem arbitrary and unreasonable, because they have lost their sense by lasting on from the state of life to which they properly belonged.

In the old days before there were lawyers and law books, solemn acts and rights were made plain to all men by picturesque ceremonies suited to lay hold of unlettered minds. Many of these old ceremonies are still kept up and show their meaning as plainly as ever. For example, when two parties wish to make firm peace or friendship, they will go through the ceremony of mixing their blood, so as to make themselves blood-relations. Travellers often now ally themselves in such blood-brotherhood with barbarous tribes; an account of East Africans performing the rite describes the two sitting together on a hide so as to become "of one skin," and then they made little cuts in one another's breasts, tasted the mixed blood, and rubbed it into one another's wounds. Thus we find still going on in the world a compact which Herodotus describes among the ancient Lydians and Skythians, and which is also mentioned in the Sagas of the old Northmen and the ancient Irish legends. It would be impossible to put more clearly the great principle of old-world morals, that a man owes friendship not to mankind at large but only to his own kin, so that to entitle a stranger to kindness and good faith he must become a kinsman by blood. With much the same thought even rude tribes hold that eating and drinking together is a covenant of friendship, for the guest becomes in some sort one of the household, and has to be treated as morally one of the family. This helps to explain the vast importance people everywhere give to the act of dining together. Among the millions of India at this day the very constitution of society turns on the caste rules whom a man may or may not eat with. Among the marriage ceremonies of the world, one well known in the Far East is that the couple by eating together out of one dish become man and wife. How ceremony expresses meaning in still more striking meta-phor is seen in the Hindu marriage, where the skirts of the bridegroom and bride's garments are tied together as a sign of union, and the bride steps on a stone to show she will be as firm as stone. A custom is described among English vagrants of the last century, where a man and woman would join hands across the body of a dead beast, thus promising that they would be joined till death should part them. Among the dramatic ceremonies known to European law is the scene in an ancient Roman law-court, where a man put in his claim to a slave by stepping forward and touching him with a rod which represented a spear; or when in old Germany a piece of land was transferred by the owner handing over a sod of the turf with a green twig stuck up in it; or when in feudal times the vassal placed his hands between the lord's, and so " putting himself in his hands " became his man.

There were ceremonies in old-world law which were more than such gesture-language. Barbaric law early began to call on magical and divine powers to help in the difficult tasks of discovering the guilty, getting the truth out of witnesses, and making a promise binding. This led to the widespread system of ordeals and oaths. Some ordeals have really served to discover truth by their effect on the conscience of the evil-doer. It is thus with the mouthful of rice taken by all of a suspected household in India, which the thief's nervous fear often prevents him from swallowing. This used to be done in England with the corsnæd or trial-slice of consecrated bread or cheese; even now peasants have not forgotten the old formula, " May this bit choke me if I lie ! " Another of the few ordeals that linger in popular memory may be seen when, in some out-of-the-way farm-house, all suspected of a theft are made to hold a bible hanging to a key, which is to turn in the hands of the thief; this keeps up a form of divination practised in the classic world with a sieve hanging by the points of an open pair of shears. Ordeals have had their day, and are now discarded from the laws of the most civilised nations. Nowadays one has to go to such countries as Arabia to find the ordeal by hot iron recognised by law, as it was in England in the days when the legend was told of Queen Emma walking over the red-hot ploughshares; the conjurors now go through this ancient performance as a circus-show. Yet even of late years, English rustics have been known to duck some wretched old woman supposed to be a witch, little knowing that they were keeping up the ancient water-ordeal, where the sacred element rejects the wrong and accepts the right, so that the guilty floats and the innocent sinks—a judicial rite which forms part of the old Hindu law-book of Manu, and which in English law, till the beginning of the 13th century, was a legal means of trying those accused of murder and robbery.   Ordeals by which the taker brings down present harm on himself if he is guilty are of much the same nature as oaths.   It is usual, however, for oaths to call down future punishment, in this life or after death, as when, in Russian law-courts in Siberia, the curious spectacle may be seen of bringing in a bear's head that an Ostyak may bite at it, thereby calling on a bear to bite him if he is forsworn. The legal oaths in our own country bear in their gestures the trace of high antiquity.   In Scotland the witness holds up his hand toward heaven, the gesture by which Greek and Jew took the supreme Deity to witness, and called down divine vengeance on the perjurer.   In England the kissing of the book comes from the practice of touching a halidome, or sacred object, as an ancient Roman touched the altar, or Harold the casket of relics. The form " So help me God," is inherited from ancient Teutonic-Scandinavian law, under which the old Northman, touching the blood-daubed ring on the altar, swore " So help me Frey, and Niordh, and the almighty god " (that is, Thor).   The first and last of these are the two old English gods whose names we keep up in *Friday* and *Thursday*.

To come now to the last subject of this volume, the history of government.   Complicated as are the political arrangements of civilized nations, their study is made easier by their simple forms being already found in savage and barbaric life.   The foundation of society, as has been already seen, is the self-government of each family.   Its authority is apt to be vested in the head of the household; thus among low barbaric tribes in the Brazilian forests, the father may do as he pleases with his own wives and children, even selling them for slaves, and the neighbours have no right or wish to interfere.   Even what civilized nations now take as a matter of course, that every human being coming into the world has a right to live, is scarcely recognized by the lower races. In such a life of hardship as the Australians and many savages lead, new-born children are often put out of the way from sheer need, because the parents have already as many mouths as they can feed.   That among such tribes this comes of hardness of life, rather than hardness of

heart, is often seen when the parents will go through fire
and water to save the very child they were doubting
about, a few weeks before, whether it should live or die.
Even where the struggle for existence is not so severe, the
wretched custom of infanticide remains still common in
the world. Nothing more clearly shows that European
nations came up from a barbaric stage than the law
which the ancient Romans had in common with our
Teutonic ancestors, that it was for the father of the
family to say whether the new-born child should be
brought up or exposed. Once become a member of the
household, the child has a firmer assurance of life; and
when the young barbarian grows up to be a warrior, and
becomes himself the head of a new household, he is
usually a free man. But the oldest Roman law shows
the head of the family ruling with a strictness hardly
imaginable to our modern minds, for the father might
chastise or put to death his grown-up sons, give them in
marriage or divorce them, and even sell them. With the
advance of civilization, in Rome as elsewhere, the sons
gradually gained their rights of persons and property;
and in comparing old-world life with our own, it is plainly
seen how Christianity, looking not to family rights but to
individual souls, tended toward personal freedom. With
all the growth of individual freedom in modern life, the
best features of family despotism remain in force; it is
under parental authority that children are trained for
their future duties, and the law is careful how it gives the
child personal rights against the parent, lest it should
weaken the very cement which binds society together.
As, however, the family ceased to be so perfect a little
kingdom within itself, the individual became responsible
for his own doings. We have seen how, in rude society,
when a crime is committed, the family of the aggrieved
take vengeance on the culprit's family. Modern ideas of
justice may teach us that this is wrong, that it is punishing the innocent for the guilty. But in the lower barbaric life it is practically the best way to keep order, and,
to those who live under it, it seems right and natural, as
where, among the Australians, when one of a family has
done a murder the others take it as a matter of course
that they are guilty too. Far from this idea being confined to savages, the student becomes familiar with it in
the law of ancient nations, such as Greece and Rome.
Here it will be enough to quote the remarkable passage
from the Hebrew law which at once records what the old

principle was, and reforms it by bringing in the ideas of
higher jurisprudence :—" The fathers shall not be put to
death for the children, neither shall the children be put to
death for the fathers : every man shall be put to death for
his own sin." (Deut. xxiv. 16.)

Wherever the traveller in wild regions meets a few
families roaming together over the desert, or comes upon
a cluster of huts by a stream in the tropical forest, he
may find, if he looks closely enough, some rudiments of
government; for there is business which concerns the
whole little community, such as a camping-ground to be
chosen, or a fishery quarrel to be settled with the next
tribe down the river. Even among the Greenlanders, as
little governed a people as almost any in the world, it was
noticed that, when several families lived together all the
winter, one weather-wise old fisherman would have the
north end of the snow-house for his place and be
appointed to look after the inmates, taking care about
their keeping the snow walls in repair, and going out
and coming in together so as not to waste heat; also when
they went out in hunting parties an experienced path-
finder would be chosen as leader. It is common to find
among rude tribes such a headman or chief, chosen as the
most important or shrewdest; but he has little or no
actual authority over the families, and gets his way by
persuasion and public opinion. Naturally such a head-
man's family is of consequence already, or, if not, he
makes them so, and thus there is a tendency for his office
to become hereditary. In tribes formed under the rule
of female kinship, where the chief's own son may be out
of the succession, the new chosen chief will probably be
a younger brother or a nephew on the mother's side.
Under the rule of succession on the father's side, which
is so much more familiar to us, the very growth of the
family brings on a patriarchal government. Suppose a
single household to move out into the wilds and found a
new settlement, it begins under the rule of the father,
who, as new huts are built round the first home, remains
head of the growing clan; but as old age comes on, his
eldest son more and more acts in his name, and at his
death will be recognized as succeeding him in the head-
ship of the community. Here then is seen the rise of the
hereditary chief or patriarch of the tribe, first in rank as
representing the ancestor, and with more or less of real
authority. But here also there is a practical power of
setting the successor aside if he is too timid or wilful or

dull, when perhaps his uncle or brother will be put in his
place, though the line of succession is not set aside by
this. The patriarchal system extends far on in civilization. It is not confined to one particular race or nation,
but may at this day be studied alike among the brown
hill-men of India and the negroes of West Africa. To us
it is especially well known from the Old Testament,
which shows it in the form it takes in a pastoral nation,
and which still may be seen with little change among the
Arabs of the desert, whose clans and tribes are governed
by their patriarchs, the sheykhs or ,old men. Not less
does it lie at the foundation of the politics of the Aryan
race, where its remains may still be traced in the village
communities of India and Russia, the village elder
presiding in the council of " white-heads " being the
modern representative of the earlier patriarch with the
chiefs of younger branches of the clan around him.
Under such mild rule, people of few wants may prosper
in time of peace, in the kindly communism which is possible where there are no rich and no poor. The weak
point of such a society is that it can hardly advance, for
civilization is at a standstill where it is regulated by
ancestral custom administered by great-grandfathers.
Everywhere in the world, in war some stronger and
more intelligent rule than this is needed and found.
The changes which have shaped the descendants of wild
hordes into civilized nations have been in great measure
the work of the war-chief.

When among such uncultured tribes war breaks out,
the peace-chief is pushed aside and a leader chosen, or in
war-like tribes the war-chief may be the acting head at all
times. Of course he is a tried warrior, and his endurance
may even be put to a special examination, as when the
Caribs would test a candidate for war-chief by merci-
lessly flogging and scratching him, smoking him in a
hammock over a fire of green leaves, or burying him up
to the middle in a nest of stinging-ants. We even find in
America the principle of competitive examination for
king, when Chilian tribes would choose as their chief the
man who could lift the biggest tree on his shoulder and
carry it longest. In these rude countries the change is
wonderful when war turns the loose crowd into an army
under a leader, with powers of life and death to enforce
discipline. When Martius the naturalist was travelling
through a Brazilian forest with a Miranha chief, they
came to a fig-tree where the skeleton of a man was bound

to the trunk with cords of creepers, and the chief grimly explained that this was one of his men who had disobeyed orders by not summoning a neighbouring tribe to help against the invading Umauas, and he had him tied up there and shot to death with arrows. In barbarous countries the tribe-chief and the war-chief may be found side by side; but when the power of the bow and spear once asserts itself, it is apt to grow further. Throughout history, war gives the bold and able leader a supremacy which may nominally end with the campaign, but which tends to pass into dictatorship for life. Military government in civil affairs is, in fact, despotism; and if the military leader can thus become the tyrant of his own land, still more can he rule with a rod of iron a conquered country. The negro kingdom of Dahome, the result of two centuries of barbaric military rule, is an astounding specimen of what a people will submit to from a despot whom they regard as a kind of deity; they approach him grovelling on all-fours, and throwing dust over their heads; the whole nation are his slaves, whose lives he takes at will; the women are all his, to give or sell; the land is all his, and none owns anything but at his pleasure. The kings of Asiatic nations have been theoretically as absolute as this, but practically in advancing civilization the king makes or sanctions laws which bind himself and his successors, making society more fixed and life more tolerable. Also, as soon as religion becomes a power in the state, it becomes joined or mixed with civil and military government. Thus among negroes the high-priest and war-chief may be the two heads of the government, while the Incas of Peru, as descendants and representatives of the divine sun, ruled their nation with paternal despotism which settled for the people what they should do and eat and wear, and whom they should marry. In such a kingdom royalty must be hereditary in the divine ruling family. Indeed, monarchy, however gained, tends to become hereditary, and especially the military usurper will found a dynasty on the model of a patriarchal chief. Thus sovereignty may be elective, hereditary, military, ecclesiastical, and, difficult as is the history of kingdoms, some combination of these causes can always be traced in them.

The effects of war in consolidating a loosely formed society are described by travellers who have seen a barbaric tribe prepare to invade an enemy or defend their own borders. Provisions and property are brought into the common stock; the warriors submit their unruly wills to a leader, and private quarrels are sunk in a larger patriotism. Distant clans of kinsfolk come together against the common enemy, and neighbouring tribes with no such natural union make an alliance, their chiefs serving under the orders of a leader chosen by them all. Here are seen in their simplest forms two of the greatest facts in history—the organized army, where the several forces are led by their own captains under a general, and the confederation of tribes, such as in higher civilization brings on political federations of states like those in Greece and Switzerland. Out of such alliances of tribes, when they last beyond the campaign, there arise nations, where often, as in old Mexico, the head of the strongest tribe will become king. Tribes which thus unite are apt to be of common race, speaking kindred dialects, for this is everywhere a natural bond of union; and when they have allied themselves into one people, and come to bear a common name, such as Dorians or Hellenes, they willingly take up the old patriarchal idea, and imagine themselves more closely of one *nation* or " birth " than they really are, even setting up, as we have seen (p. 237), a fictitious as a national ancestor. Events take a different course, but with a somewhat like effect, when some Kafir leader conquers other tribes around, and, setting himself above them all, forces the conquered chiefs to bring him tribute and warriors to fight his battles. This is empire on a small scale and with rude surroundings, but on the same principles as that of a Cæsar or a Napoleon. Thus one understands why in the early history of nations it is so inextricably difficult to make out how far any people have grown up from a single unmixed tribe, or have been built up by alliance and conquest. What shows how this piecing together of nations must have gone on is the number and variety of their gods. While a tribe grows of itself, the names and worship of the same tribe-gods will be a bond of union in all the clans, and even when they move far off they will sometimes go on pilgrimage to the shrines of their old home. But when peoples amalgamate, their different gods are kept up, as when the Peruvians gave places to the gods of conquered tribes under their own great deities. Every district in ancient Egypt shows by its varied combination of gods how many little states and local religions went to make up the great despotism and hierarchy. It was plainly through this growth of nations, which had been going on we know not how long before history began, that the higher civilization of mankind arose. Scattered families of barbarians in a land where there is still elbow room may thrive without strong government; but when men live in populous nations and crowded cities, there has to be public order. That this political order came out of military order cannot be doubted. War not only put into the hands of the sovereign the power over a whole nation, but his army served as his model on which to organize his nation. It is one of the plainest lessons of history that through military discipline mankind were taught to submit to authority and act in masses under command. Egypt and Babylon, with military system pervading not only the standing army, but the orders of priests and civilians, developed industry and wealth highest in the ancient world, and were the very founders of literature and science. They built up for future ages the framework of government, which we freer moderns of our own will submit ourselves to for our own benefit. A constitutional government, whether called republic or kingdom, is an arrangement by which the nation governs itself by means of the machinery of a military despotism.

As society in tribes and nations became a more complex system, it early began to divide into classes or ranks. If we look for an example of the famous first principle of the United States, " that all men are created equal," we shall in fact scarcely find such equality except among savage hunters and foresters, and by no means always then. The greatest of all divisions, that between freeman and slave, appears as soon as the barbaric warrior spares the life of his enemy when he has him down, and brings him home to drudge for him and till the soil. How low in civilization this begins appears by a slave caste forbidden to bear arms forming part of several of the lower American tribes. How thoroughly slavery was recognized as belonging to old-world society may be seen by the way it formed part of the Hebrew patriarchal system, where the man-servant and maid-servant are reckoned as a man's wealth just before his ox and his ass. It was no less so under Roman law, as is evident from the very word *family*, which at first meant not the children but the slaves (*famulus*). We live in days when the last remains of slavery are disappearing from the higher nations; but though the civilized world has outgrown the ancient institution, the benefits which early society gained from it still remain. It was through slave labour that agri-

culture and industry increased, that wealth accumu-
lated, and leisure was given to priests, scribes, poets,
philosophers, to raise the level of men's minds. Out of
slavery probably arose the later custom of hired *service*,
the very name of which, as derived from *servus*, a slave,
tells the story of a great social change. The master at
first let out his slaves to work for his profit, and then free
men found it to their advantage to work for their own
profit, so that there grew up the great wage-earning class
whose numbers and influence make so marked a difference
between ancient and modern society. In all communities, except the smallest and simplest, the freemen
divide themselves into ranks. The old Northmen divided
men into three classes, " earls, churls, and thralls," which
roughly match what we should now call nobles, freemen,
and slaves. Nobles again fall into different orders,
especially those who can claim royal blood forming a
princely order, and looking down on the chieftains and
officers of the army, state, and church who fill the lower
ranks of nobility.

As nations become more populous, rich, and intelligent, the machinery of government has to be improved.
The old rough-and-ready methods no longer answer, and
the division of labour has to be applied to politics. Thus,
one of the chief's early duties was to be judge. A Kafir
chieftain will make it his business to hear suits between
his people; each side brings him a gift of oxen. At
higher levels of civilization the Eastern monarch sits in
the gate of justice; and it was so among the ancient
Germans, where the king sat crowned and gave judgment
in his own court. It is still the king's court, but the
actual administration has long passed into the hands
of professional judges. So with other departments of
government. By the time civilization had come to the
level of ancient Egypt and Babylon public affairs were
administered by officials in grades like an army, who
collected the taxes, attended to public works, punished
offences, and did justice between man and man. It has
just been noticed how far a modern nation is worked by
an official system similar to that of the ancients, and how
we, really among the freest of peoples, preserve the forms
of an absolute monarchy, where sovereign power is
administered through servants of the Crown down to the
exciseman and constable. In the politics of savages
and barbarians, the outlines of the civilized system of
government already come into view. We have seen how

among such rude tribes the chief or king appears, who
holds his place in some form through higher nations.
Even the consul or president of a republic is a kind of
temporary elective king. Of not less antiquity is the
senate. The old men squatting round the council fire of
an Indian tribe on the prairies have in their way a
greater influence than a civilized senate, for where there
are no written records and books the old men are the
very sources and treasures of wisdom. In the nations
of the world, seats at such councils are given to wise old
men, priests and officers of high rank, and heads of great
families, so that the two terms *senate* and *house of lords*
both have their proper meaning, and the two claims of
wisdom and rank are more or less combined. With the
very beginning of political life appears also the popular
assembly. In small tribes the whole community, or at
least the freemen, come together. It may be only a
forest tribe in Brazil called together by the chief to
decide some question of an expedition to net wildfowl or
attack a neighbouring tribe, yet solemn form will be
observed. There is silence for the orators, and if the
assembly approve they will at last cry " good ! " or " be
it so ! " More civilized forms of the assembly of the
people may be studied in Freeman's comparison of the
Achaian *agora* described in the second book of the Iliad,
with the " great meeting " held outside London in
Edward the Confessor's time. Even in our own day the
great meeting of the people has not disappeared from
Europe. The wonderful sight is still to be seen of the
people of a Swiss canton gathered together in a wide
meadow or market-place to vote Yes or No on the great
questions which their supreme authority decides. With
the growth of nations the folk-moot or assembly of the
whole people, never a good deliberative body, soon
becomes unmanageable by mere numbers; but there is
a way by which its authority may be kept in a less un-
wieldy form when the people, no longer able to go themselves, send chosen representatives to act for them.
This seems a simple device enough, and indeed the first
savage tribe that ever sent a discreet orator to negotiate
peace or war on its behalf had seized the idea of a political
representative. But in fact it is one of the most remarkable points in political history, how the principle of
popular representation has been worked out in England
from the time of Simon de Montfort's famous parliament
in the 13th century. It is for historians to discuss how

the knights and burgesses who came up to grant the king's supplies passed into the lower house of parliament as it is now; what has to be noticed here is the change which, while the huge promiscuous assembly of the people shrank into an aristocratic upper house, gave us a new elective popular body, the *house of commons*. It is not too much to say that no event in English history has had so great an effect in shaping the course of modern civilization. On the whole, looking at what government is coming to among the most enlightened nations, it will be seen that it attains its ends, not so much by casting off the methods of our remote barbaric ancestors, as by improving and regulating them. The administration of the state under the system of sovereign authority, the control of the senate, and the source of political power in the will of the nation itself, are made to work together and restrain one another so as fairly to keep the benefits and neutralize the excesses of all, while the constitution has within it the power of continual reform, so that the machine of government may be ever shaping itself into more perfect fitness to its work.

Here this sketch of Anthropology may close. The examination of man's age on the earth, his bodily structure and varieties of race and language, has led us on to enquire into his intellectual and social history. In his many-sided life there may be clearly traced a development, which, notwithstanding long periods of stoppage and frequent falling back, has on the whole adapted modern civilized man for a far higher and happier career than his ruder ancestors. In this development, the preceding chapters have shown a difference between low and high nations, which it only remains to put before the reader as a practical moral to the tale of civilization. It is true that both among savage and civilized peoples progress in culture takes place, but not under the same conditions. The savage by no means goes through life with the intention of gathering more knowledge and framing better laws than his fathers. On the contrary, his tendency is to consider his ancestors as having handed down to him the perfection of wisdom, which it would be impiety to make the least alteration in. Hence among the lower races there is obstinate resistance to the most desirable reforms, and progress can only force its way with a slowness and difficulty which we of this century can hardly imagine. Looking at the condition of the rude man, it may be seen that his aversion to change was not always unreasonable, and indeed may often have arisen from a true instinct. With his ignorance of any life but his own, he would be rash to break loose from the old tried machinery of society, to plunge into revolutionary change, which might destroy the present good without putting better in its place. Had the experience of ancient men been larger, they would have seen their way to faster steps in culture. But we civilized moderns have just that wider knowledge which the rude ancients wanted. Acquainted with events and their consequences far and wide over the world, we are able to direct our own course with more confidence toward improvement. In a word, mankind is passing from the age of unconscious to that of conscious progress. Readers who have come thus far need not be told in many words of what the facts must have already brought to their minds—that the study of man and civilization is not only a matter of scientific interest, but at once passes into the practical business of life. We have in it the means of understanding our own lives and our place in the world, vaguely and imperfectly it is true, but at any rate more clearly than any former generation. The knowledge of man's course of life, from the remote past to the present, will not only help us to forecast the future, but may guide us in our duty of leaving the world better than we found it.

Selected Ann Arbor Paperbacks
Works of enduring merit

For a complete list of Ann Arbor Paperback titles write:
THE UNIVERSITY OF MICHIGAN PRESS ANN ARBOR